THE
CATHOLIC
HERITAGE

THE CATHOLIC HERITAGE

Martyrs, Ascetics, Pilgrims, Warriors, Mystics, Theologians, Artists, Humanists, Activists, Outsiders, and Saints

Lawrence S. Cunningham

CROSSROAD · NEW YORK

Grateful acknowledgment is made to the following:

Oxford University Press, for excerpts from *The Acts of the Christian Martyrs*, ed. H. Musurillo. Copyright 1972.

Darton, Longman, and Todd, Ltd. and Doubleday and Co., Inc., for excerpts from *The Jerusalem Bible*.

America Press, Inc. 106 West 56th St. New York, NY 10019, for excerpts from *The Documents of Vatican II*, ed. Abbott and Gallagher. Copyright, 1966.

Farrar, Straus, and Giroux, Inc., for excerpts from the following works of Flannery O'Connor: *Mystery and Manners*. Copyright, 1962 by Flannery O'Connor. *Everything That Rises Must Converge*. Copyright, 1965 by the estate of Mary Flannery O'Connor. *The Habit of Being: The Letters of Flannery O'Connor*. Copyright, 1979 by Regina O'Connor.

1983

The Crossroad Publishing Company
575 Lexington Avenue, New York, N.Y. 10022

Copyright © 1983 by Lawrence S. Cunningham

Printed in the United States of America

Library of Congress Cataloging in Publication Data

Cunningham, Lawrence.
  The Catholic heritage.

  Bibliography: p.
  Includes index.
  1. Catholic Church–History. 2. Catholic Church–Doctrinal and contoversial works. 3. Catholics.
I. Title.
BX945.2.C86   1983   282'.09   83-10108
ISBN 0-8245-0592-1

Contents

Introduction

This book emerges from a number of personal concerns, convictions, and intellectual encounters.

As a professor in a large state university I have been called upon regularly to lecture on the general topic of Roman Catholicism. A single semester course on something as global as "Catholicism" presents problems of structure, emphases, and readings about which I have already addressed myself in print and feel no need to repeat here.[1] The basic problem I have encountered, however, is that time and again students lack any sense of the historical perspective of Western culture in general and the part Catholicism played in the formation of that culture in particular. They not only have scant memory of the Latin liturgy (hardly their fault), but have no sense of the kind of church which existed before the Second Vatican Council. Students have this strong conviction that what is important happens now and the "now" has little or no link with the past. They tend to see the life of the church rather as they see the surface of a video game screen: active, immediate, and graspable as a whole. I would argue that the Catholic tradition, or heritage, is more like a van Eyck painting or a poem by Yeats (perhaps these elitist examples are a proper giveaway!): dense, allusive, polyvalent—rendering full meaning only by close attention, reflection, and a second look. There is no second look in a video game.

This lack of feeling for historical texture in the church will not be easily assuaged for the many by an appeal to traditional

1

church history, no matter how engagingly taught. History, like Scotch whiskey, is an acquired taste. There is, however, a *via media*. This book attempts to tread it.

A basic conviction of this work is that one can detect, however imperfectly, certain emphases in the living out of the Gospel tradition which characterized or gave color to certain past ages of the church's life. Fully aware of the arbitrary nature of the periodizations of history and suspicious of the "great person" approach to historical narrative, one can argue, I believe, that the character of the pre-Constantinian church—to cite an obvious example—focused on martyrs in a manner that the Baroque church did not, even though that latter period also claims many who died for the faith. In time the period of the martyrs gave way to "white" forms of martyrdom in the person of the desert ascetic. There were later ascetics, but they harkened back to this tradition just as the later generations looked to the ancient martyrs for an understanding of martyrdom in their own day. Today, again, there are martyrs and ascetics who stand in a tradition and also give currency to the present life of the church. That dialectic of past and present is something I wish to pursue in these pages.

What I have attempted, then, is to sketch out some (obviously, not all) ideal types which have characterized certain eras of the church's life in order to make the following points: (a) These types tell us something about the culture in which they live; (b) the ways these people lived out their fidelity to the Gospel is very much tied to that culture but not entirely bound to it; and (c) these types, though rooted in a particular time and place, also find a permanent place in the tradition of the church. They serve, if in a changed or abridged way, as models for subsequent generations.

Why make these points?

First, I would invite the sympathetic reader to grasp that the Catholic tradition is not a set of free-floating ideas locked in an ahistorical repository even if one wants to name that repository with venerable titles like *Magisterium*. The Catholic tradition is a history of people extended in time in all their particularities. They have encountered Jesus who is the Christ and, in that encounter, have attempted with faltering steps to imitate him and encapsulate the meaning of his life into their own.

Secondly, this following of Christ is open to all races, classes, genders, and types of people. If I may be so bold as to announce in advance a merit of this book, it would be to note that this text focuses on styles of life in which hierarchy and laity, male and female, aristocrat and peasant all have their place. The ways of which I speak are open without respect to rank or condition. The church is a hierarchical one in fact; I do not dispute that. For my purposes strata, rank, and social standing have less significance since I am concerned with the following of Christ and, in the imitation of St. Paul, "I owe a duty to the Greeks just as much to the barbarians, to the educated just as much as to the uneducated" (Rom. 1:14).

Finally, an understanding of the Catholic tradition allows us to see more clearly certain threads of continuity in the tradition. Our intention is to show the heroes and saints of the past as models for the present. The ascetics of the Egyptian desert appear today as strange and fanatical phantasms, but they seem less strange when we study the contemporary ascetics who have had to wrestle with the demonic in the artificial deserts of culture which have names like Bergen Belsen and Gulag Archipelago or locations like secret police stations in Latin America.

This work developed from my long-standing interest in saints as paradigmatic figures in the history of Catholicism.[2] My interest in these figures seems all the more justified now that David Tracy has encouraged theologians to reflect on the classics of the theological tradition. In his excellent theoretical study *The Analogical Imagination*, Tracy argues that the classics include not only texts but also artifacts and *persons.* By that reckoning, if I take his meaning correctly, St. Francis of Assisi is as much a classic as the *Pensées* of Pascal. Both demand the reflective concern of the theological hermeneute. David Tracy, then, provides one strategy for understanding the Catholic tradition. William Clebsch's *Christianity in European History* provides a model for doing what I have attempted. Though our purposes are somewhat different, I have profited enormously from his book.

This book is very much a first step, written for the beginner. I simply want to make a case for the continuity of the Catholic experience. I would like to communicate to sympathetic readers my own profound respect for the tradition which is behind, under, and, in a real sense, "in front of" our current Catholic experience. I would like that hypothetical reader to understand, for example, that the Franciscan spirit is not a relic of a past age but a very real way of being for those who, like the Catholic Workers, daily serve the most battered and afflicted of our society, just as I would like them to understand that theologians today wrestle with intellectual problems as dense and intractable as those encountered by Aquinas in the thirteenth century or Pascal in the seventeenth.

My use of the term "Catholic" throughout this book almost always means "Roman Catholic," just as my frequent use of the word "Christian" almost always means a Christian who is in the Roman Catholic tradition. I apologize to those who have a wider notion of Catholicism by simply noting that I am aware of that broader notion of Catholicism and am not unsympathetic with it. My more narrow focus on Roman Catholicism derives from my obedience to the wisdom of those who insist that one writes about what one knows. I do not use the term "Roman Catholic" in any invidious way; I use it according to the canons of common usage. Much of what I say, as will be clear, has equal applicability, *mutatis mutandis*, to both the Reformed and Orthodox traditions (to say nothing of the Anglican), but I am simply not equipped to make those applications with any authority.

This work is very brief for what it wants to do. The single most vexatious problem in its planning stage was to decide what not to discuss. In that sense the work is idiosyncratic. Every critic can chide me with justice for this or that omission. My only defense is to say—as the Zen masters would have it— that I serve here only as a finger pointing the way. One must attend, not to the finger, but to the direction in which it points. At the close of each chapter there is a brief excursus (called "Readings and Trajectories") on a few of the books and articles which have shaped my thinking. In the text itself I have tried

to quote with some liberality in order to allow the more in-
dustrious reader to follow up on the questions at hand.

If this book is used in a class setting, the instructor will be
able to enlarge where I have passed over in haste; expand what
I have only mentioned; develop where I have been silent. My
conviction is that the text opens out a whole range of possibilities for further study and/or discussion. Without presuming
on the class style of the instructor, let me set out, for purely
pedagogical purposes, some other possibilities which occur to
me that might be of use to the teacher:

(a) First, and foremost, the paradigms I use could be expanded and studied. For example, I speak *en passant* about
missionaries but do not devote a chapter to their consideration.
Other categories come easily to mind.

(b) Every attempt to follow Christ in actual life is, in one
sense, to "make over" Christ according to the cultural and
personal pressures brought to bear on the acting out of the
Gospel. That fact leads us naturally to explore who the Christ
of the martyrs, ascetics, mystics,[3] activists, etc., might be.

(c) Following on (b) one might speculate (or actually com-
pose) prayers which reflect the concerns of the various types
discussed in the text or research the prayers actually written
and used in various eras. The field of iconography is another
fertile field for research. We are all familiar with the traditional
iconography of the martyr (the crown, the palm, etc.), but what
would an iconography of the activist look like? Where would
we get the hints from which such an iconography could be
constructed?

(d) There are certain characteristics of the Catholic tradition
which shape it as a peculiar tradition distinguishable from, say,
the Reformed tradition. Those characteristics might be traced
as they develop in the lives of certain types. What is the relationship between mysticism and sacramentality? Between
community and theological work? Between authority and the
outsider? The permutations are numerous.

(e) Are there "new" types in the contemporary church who
do not model—or who radically modify—the traditional ty-
pologies discussed in this book? We have discussed one trans-

valuation in the changing appreciation of the "Christian warrior." The emergence of liberation theologies (third world, feminist, etc.) suggest that new kinds of understanding are now aborning. How these "postmodern" theologies will enflesh themselves is not yet clear. It may be that the now hotly debated question of women priests will not be resolved either by contestation or by fiat but by persons who will (or who may now) live out a new vision of what sacramental ministry means.

(f) As a follow-up to (e) we need to focus on the emergence of global spiritualities in which theologies use insights from thinkers like Teilhard de Chardin or ascetical theologians in transreligious dialogue (e.g., Thomas Merton, Bede Griffiths, William Johnston, etc.) who articulate a theology which moves beyond (but in touch with) the traditional assumptions of Western understanding. Strategies on how these visions are to be lived out are far from clear even if strong statements of transtraditional life already exist.

Trajectories like those suggested above can be multiplied as far as the theological imagination will stretch. I hope that this book will suggest many such possibilities since this work is not meant to be exhaustive but suggestive.

I have been thinking about these ideas for over a decade. I still grope for clarity. The book appears at this moment as a spur for others either in creating informal dialogue or formally in further research. At this juncture let me thank my colleagues at the Department of Religion at Florida State University, especially its chairman, John Priest, who makes it easy for one to do research. Avery Dulles, S.J., Richard McBrien, and Keith Egan encouraged me to pursue this idea, but, of course, are not responsible for the end product. The Academic Study of Religion seminar of the American Academy of Religion (San Francisco, 1981) under the leadership of John and Denise Carmody provided me with a forum for my ideas. To the participants in that seminar and those who later wrote me, I would like to express my thanks. Finally, I would like to thank Werner Mark Linz, Richard Payne, and Frank Oveis at Crossroad, Dianne Weinstein, who typed the manuscript, and John Carey, who read an early draft of this book.

While this book was in an early draft, our first child, Sarah

Mary, was born. I could not have imagined a more welcome or more beautiful distraction. This book is for her.

Notes

1. See Lawrence S. Cunningham, "On Teaching Catholicism to Undergraduates," *Bulletin of the Council on the Study of Religion*, April 1979, pp. 43–54, and "Recent Books on Catholicism," *Horizons*, Fall 1981, pp. 340–46.
2. Lawrence S. Cunningham, *The Meaning of Saints* (San Francisco, 1980).
3. George Tavard's "The Christology of the Mystics," *Theological Studies*, December 1981, pp. 561–79, is a model for what I have in mind.

1

MARTYRS

The Roman Persecutions

The very mention of "early Christianity" brings to mind, almost instinctively, visions of Roman persecution and Christian martyrdom. Fed by a tradition of nineteenth-century novels (e.g., *Ben Hur, Quo Vadis, Fabiola,* etc.), many turned into movie spectaculars, and popular religious art based on erroneous history, we are inclined to think of that period as peopled by maniacal emperors, sighing maidens, cruelly indifferent crowds turning thumbs down, and very hungry lions. These popular images are often spiced up by having the sighing maiden the object of intense devotion by a bewildered yet loving pagan centurion who promises her the world if she will only put a pinch of incense on the altar of the Roman gods. She, of course, will not. Against this background of doomed love the other Christians hide out in underground catacombs, identify each other with cryptic signs (in the movies it is usually a fish drawn into the dust), and call each other "brother" and "sister" a good deal. The Christians in these movies tend to be overly good and, if the truth must be known, not as interesting as their pagan tormentors. Screen Caligulas always fascinate; who can resist a politician who makes his favorite horse a senator?

It is very difficult to shake off this haze of half truth, misinformation, and sheer fiction. Tourists visiting Rome are still told by guides that the early Christians lived in the catacombs (they did not) and that the graves of the catacombs contain the bodies of martyrs (almost none did originally and none do today).

We must cut through the romantic and the legendary to really understand the early martyrs. In many ways they stand as a link to the experience of some of the bravest of contemporary Christians. To understand the early martyrs is to understand one of the oldest and most persistent forms of religious witness.

One basic fact must be understood about Christian life in the Roman empire: Christians did suffer and die for their faith. That is our starting point. Writing about fifty years after the event, the Roman historian Tacitus (A.D. 54–119) wrote this about the emperor Nero who had attempted to burn down the city of Rome in July of 64:

> To squash the rumor Nero charged, and viciously punished, people called Christians who were despised on account of their wicked practices. The founder of the sect, Christus, was executed by the procurator Pontius Pilate during the reign of Tiberius. The evil superstition was suppressed for a time but soon broke out afresh not only in Judea where it started but also in Rome where every filthy outrage arrives and prospers. First, those who confessed were seized and then, on their word, a huge number were convicted, less for arson than for their hatred of the human race.

> In their death they were mocked. Some were sewn in animal skins and worried to death by dogs; others were crucified or burned so that, when the daylight was over, they could serve as evening light. Nero provided his own gardens for this show and made it into a circus. He mingled with the commoners dressed as a charioteer or posed in his chariot. As a result the sufferers, guilty and deserving of punishment though they were, did arouse the pity of the crowd who saw their suffering was not for the public good, but because of the savagery of one man.[1]

There are a number of things to note about that famous passage. One is that within thirty years of the time of Jesus there was already a Christian community at Rome large enough to be identified and singled out by the authorities. Secondly, Tacitus, despite his open contempt for the emperor, had no love or respect for the Christians. He is expressing personal sentiments nearly fifty years after the persecution of Nero, but his sympathies are hardly with the Christians. Finally, and most importantly, Tacitus does not provide any explanation as to why the Christians were singled out for persecution in the first place. He talks about their "wicked practices," their "hatred for the human race," and their "deserving punishment," but provides no specific charges upon which the emperor acted.

Two generations after the burning of Rome in about A.D. 112 Pliny the Younger wrote to the emperor Trajan about the Christians he punished in the distant province of Bithynia. The emperor wrote him back, commended him for his labors, and told him not to seek out Christians but to punish those who were brought before him. The emperor also warned him to be skeptical about anonymous denunciations which did not reflect well on the "spirit of the age." The question, of course, was why were the Christians to be punished. Trajan did not say in his response to Pliny. It was simply assumed that Christians could be punished.

The legal basis for the Roman persecutions has been the subject of a heated, and, as yet, unsolved debate among legal scholars. That debate need not detain us here. Whether the Roman persecution of the Christians was rooted in a law (passed during the time of Nero?) or sprung from the *ad hoc* use of police powers is a vexatious issue. What we can do is to indicate some of the more obvious reasons why particular persecutions broke out.

In general, Christianity was looked on as a threat to the common good of the state. Roman *pietas* was the virtue by which citizens showed their love and respect for the state. *Pietas* was the same virtue which children were expected to cultivate in their relationship with their parents. *Pietas* toward the state was expressed externally through the rites and usages by which the gods of Rome were honored. The Roman pantheon expressed the values of Roman culture; to honor these values was to insure the *pax deorum*—the peace of the gods—upon which the prosperity and health of the empire depended. Not to participate in that common expression of *pietas* struck the Roman citizen as both blasphemous and disloyal; it was, in short, an act of treason. The common charge of the Romans that the Christians were atheists must be seen in that light. The Christians, in fact, did deny the existence of the Roman gods. From the vantage point of Roman culture a group like the Christians were nothing more than an obscure and secretive alien religious sect which had sprung up on the edges of the empire. With its fantastic beliefs (a god who had been executed for sedition!) and its drawing power among the slaves and malcontents of the lower orders, Christianity was viewed as an antisocial and potentially dangerous society. The "decent" Romans looked on Christianity much the same way many of us today look on the more bizarre religious sects and cults: ridiculous but vaguely menacing.

Christianity today is an established part of our culture and has been for well over a millennium. It is extremely difficult for us to appreciate how Christianity looked to Roman pagans in the second and third centuries. Because Christians were relatively few in numbers and, by and large, not well represented among the influential classes, they could serve as a handy scapegoat. The acerbic Christian writer Tertullian (c. 120–c. 222) wrote that if the Tiber flooded its banks or the Nile failed to flood, or if the stars stood still or the earth trembled, the cry in the streets was always the same: "Christians to the lions!"

Tertullian was not exaggerating. In 177 in the Roman province of Southern Gaul (present-day France) the Christian population of Lyons, for reasons which are not clear but which may have had something to do with the large number of Christians who were of Asian origin, began to feel the weight of social and legal discrimination. Christians were excluded from the public baths. Then they were forbidden to frequent the public markets and, finally, they were forbidden access to any public place under the protection of the Roman gods. After these more or less official acts an urban mob attacked the Christian quarter one day, assaulted Christians, and drove those that they could round up to the public forum where they demanded the condemnation of the Christians. The public authorities, fearful of the mob, gave in to their wishes. Those who would not recant their Christianity were put to the torture in prison.

Those that survived the prison experience were sent to the amphitheater as bait for the wild animals. A letter from the church of Lyons, later preserved in the *Ecclesiastical History* of Eusebius (d. c. 340), tells of the wretched suffering of the martyrs among whom stood out a heroic slave girl named Blandina:

> ... The Blessed Blandina was last of all: like a noble mother encouraging her children ... she hastened to rejoin them, rejoicing and glorying in her death as though she had been invited to a bridal banquet instead of being the victim of the beasts. After the scourges, the animals, and the hot griddle, she was at last tossed into a net and exposed to a bull. After being tossed a good deal by the animal, she no longer perceived what was happening because of the hope and possession of all she believed in and because of her intimacy with Christ.[2]

Many episodes of persecution broke out in the Roman empire because of such prejudice or as the result of the zeal of a particular government official in this or that province. Well into the third century the persecution of the Christians was episodic, localized, and somewhat capricious. We must not think of a consistent and total reign of terror from Nero to Constantine. In the third century, however, Roman political fortunes began to take a turn for the worse. With political reversals the Christian unwillingness to observe the rites of Roman *pietas* began to be looked at in a more ominously threatening manner. The story is an old one. Any time a country feels itself threatened by political forces it (a) begins to wave the flag of patriotism and (b) reacts strongly against the hostile and alien forces in the society who are perceived—rightly or wrongly—as contributing to the threat or sapping the national strength to deal with it.

In the year 250 the emperor Decius had good reason to worry about the future of his empire. The Visigoths harried the Mediterranean while the barbarian tribes pressured the Roman borders of Gaul, Spain, and Asia Minor. Internally the empire seemed incapable of checking its inflation or stopping the constant devaluation of its currency. Decius was determined to unite the energies of the empire under the traditional protection of the Roman gods. As part of this strategy Decius ordered that in a certain short period every citizen in the empire was to sacrifice in honor of the Roman gods. As contemporary inscriptions indicate, these religious sacrifices were meant to symbolize Roman solidarity before the gods.

The decrees of Decius put the then rather numerous Christians in an extremely delicate position: to comply with the imperial decree was to deny the uniqueness of Jesus and the single reality of God, while resistance was an invitation to the charge of treason and the attendant penalty of execution. The Christian response to the imperial edict was not all that original when one reflects how any group would act when faced with such alternatives: (a) Many—including prominent clerics—complied with the imperial edicts and made the required sacrifices; (b) some evaded the decrees either by getting forged certificates saying they had sacrificed or by keeping away from official attention by subterfuge or bribe; and (c) a tiny minority resisted the decrees openly even to death. It has been estimated that in the entire Roman empire less than a thousand died, but it was the constancy and bravery of that singular minority which has been remembered for centuries by the Christian church. The compliance or evasion of the many has been all but forgotten except by historians of the period.

The persecution of Decius was empirewide and systematic, but it lasted only a year. After his death there were other attempts at suppressing the Christian religion, but the efforts were in vain. The last large persecution—often called "the Great Persecution"—was managed by the emperor Diocletian and it lasted from roughly 303 to 312. Diocletian used a number of tactics against the strength of the Christian church: He destroyed Christian buildings. Diocletian further ordered the destruction of all official Christian books, the imprisonment of the clergy, the torture of those who would not recant their faith; in a decree of 304, he revived the Decian decree of ritual acts before the Roman gods. The persistence of Diocletian was a last gesture. Christianity was too rooted in the empire to be eradicated. In A.D. 313 Constantine issued a decree at Milan giving the Christians toleration. Except for a brief period in the later part of the century under the emperor Julian the Apostate the period of persecution was over. The age of the martyrs could now become the stuff both of history and of legend.

The Character of Martyrdom

We know that under the Roman emperors slaves and free persons died as well as the high-born and the poor, the civilian and the soldier. We also know that some of the martyrs wished the Roman Empire well, while others saw it as an evil manifestation of the antichrist. Some of the martyrs eagerly sought out persecution, while others were handed over to their tormentors. The very complexity of the events and their later glorification (and, to be sure, mystification) make it very difficult to characterize the "typical" martyr. Nonetheless, it is possible to make some generalizations about the period which are pertinent for understanding both the martyrs of that time and martyrdom as a religious category.

The Christian church used the term *martyr* (the word means "a witness" in Greek) only for those who died for their faith in the imitation of Christ during persecution. There was a distinction made between those who openly professed their faith before a hostile public or in front of a judicial hearing—these persons were called *confessores* or confessors—and those who made the ultimate sacrifice. The letter from the church of Lyons to which we have already alluded makes the distinction quite clear:

> . . . After being brought back from their encounter with the beasts covered with burns, bruises, and wounds, they would not proclaim that they were martyrs nor would they allow us to call them by that name. Rather, if anyone of us would speak of them as martyrs either by word or letter, they would give a sharp rebuke. For it was their joy to yield the title of martyr to Christ alone who was the true and faithful witness (*martyr*), the first born of the dead [cf. Col. 1:18], and the prince of God's life. And they would recall the martyrs that had already passed away saying: "They were indeed martyrs, whom Christ had deigned to take up in their hour of confession, putting his seal on their witness by death; but we are simple, humble confessors."[3]

Lest we think that all Christians were that noble and sacrificial, listen to the testimony of Dionysius, the bishop of Alexandria (who himself barely escaped death), describing Christian behavior when the decrees against the Christians became known in his area during the Decian persecution of A.D. 250:

> . . . The defection was widespread. A large number of high ranking persons and officials on their own account approached the Roman authorities. Called by name and invited to make sacrifice, they stepped forward livid and trembling as if they themselves were about to be sacrificed. Those with greater assurance ran towards the pagan altars, protesting out loud that they had never been Christians. . . .[4]

Secondly, martyrs die because they lived in a culture hostile to their beliefs. At first glance that seems so obvious as to require no notice, but, in fact, it does bear some reflection. A close reading of the *Acta* of the martyrs and other sources which have come down to us depicts public officials who were stupefied and frustrated by the tenacity of the Christians. The famous Stoic emperor Marcus Aurelius (reigned from 161 to 180) expressed (in his *Meditations*) a disgust with the Christians for what he considered their obstinacy in choosing death. The emperor, and many others, one suspects, regarded the Christians as fanatics with whom it was impossible to deal rationally. The frustrations of the enlightened public of Rome were also tinged with a certain fear about the potential of such fanaticism turning into a subversive or revolutionary movement. One noted scholar of this period has shown rather convincingly that the distaste for Christianity in the Roman Empire expressed by both the aristocracy and the urban masses dovetailed rather nicely.[5] The upper classes feared the revolutionary potential of a semisecret religious sect which resolutely resisted their patriotic duties, while the mobs feared the "atheists" whose strange ways could unleash the ire of the gods in the form of famine or plague. In either case, as Tertullian noted, it was easy to say, "Christians to the lions!"

It was precisely this animosity that impelled certain Christian writers in the second century (called "apologists") to write in defense of Christianity. Their aim was twofold: to refute the charges of immorality and crime brought against the Christians and to convince the Roman authorities (some of the apologies were addressed directly to the reigning emperors) that the Christians were not unpatriotic or subversive. The apologists made the argument—an argument familiar to anyone who has listened to a contemporary tax or draft resister—that the Christians could be—indeed, were—exemplary citizens despite their inability to comply with certain legal demands of the government. The apologists appealed to a higher law, that of God, to justify their position. The case of the apologists were eloquently put but ultimately fruitless as the increased persecutions of the third century so clearly demonstrate.

We should try and recapture some sense of how lonely and brave a decision it was to endure even to death for the sake of belief in Christ. While the martyrs enjoyed the adulation of the Christian community, that adulation came either from a safe distance or posthumously as the believing community commemorated the brave deeds of the martyrs. The actual decision to confess Christ in the face of certain death was seen as more than heroic; it was considered a special grace. The extant records of these early martyrdoms state over and over that the martyrs endured their fate despite the pleas of friends and family. In the beautiful account of the martyrdom of Perpetua and Felicity, an early third-century testimony from North Africa which was partly written by Perpetua herself and quite possibly edited by the famous Tertullian, we see the situation of a woman who gave up her infant child whom she had even nursed while in prison. The account makes it very clear that she got neither comprehension nor support from her own family:

> . . . Then, when it came to my turn, my father appeared with my son, dragged me from the step and said, "Perform the sacrifice—have pity on your baby!"
>
> Hilarianus the governor, who had received his judicial powers as successor of the late proconsul Minucius Timinianus, said to me: "Have pity on your father's grey head; have pity on your infant son. Offer the sacrifice for the welfare of the emperor!"
>
> "I will not." I retorted.
>
> "Are you a Christian?" said Hilarianus.

And I said: "Yes, I am."

When my father persisted in trying to dissuade me, Hilarianus ordered him to be thrown to the ground and beaten with a rod. I felt sorry for my father, just as if I myself had been beaten. I felt sorry for his pathetic old age.

Then Hilarianus passed sentence on all of us. We were condemned to the beasts, and we returned to prison in high spirits. But my baby had got used to being nursed at the breast and to staying with me in prison. So I sent the deacon Pomponius straight away to my father to ask for the baby. But father refused to give him over. . . .[6]

The solitary splendor of their witness as well as their steadfast faith made the martyrs more than heroes for the early church. They were venerated and exalted; those awaiting execution had unparalleled authority among the believers. Even before the end of the persecution era their "birthdays" (natalicia), that is, the date of their death, were liturgically commemorated and their tombs became the goal of pious pilgrims.

What motivated the Christian community to so honor the martyrs is not difficult to understand. There is something deep in the human consciousness that wishes to recognize those who die for an issue, especially if that issue is dear to the hearts of many. Tertullian wrote that the blood of the martyrs was the seed of the church. He was stating a truth for Christianity which we all understand more generically. One need only visit the tomb of the unknown soldier at the national cemetery at Arlington to see the symbolic power of sacrificial death and its ritual remembrance as an instrument of social cohesion. At times, that ritual can take on a prophetic or revolutionary edge. In the main square in Prague one can still see a spot, usually adorned with flowers from anonymous hands, where Jan Palach burned himself to death in 1968 to protest the suppression of the "Prague Spring" by the Soviet authorities. The death of that individual gives specific reference to an otherwise objective and somewhat abstract idea. The Czechs today are completely subservient to the political and military power of the Soviet Union, but the individual can still specify what he or she thinks by a little, and in some way, trivial, gesture of setting flowers on the cobblestones of a city square.

The contemporary martyr, whether religious or political, differs from the ancient martyrs of the Roman Empire in one extremely important manner. In the ancient world, it was widely, if not universally, held that the martyrs were the source of sacred power. Their tombs, housing their relics, were places where intercessory prayer could provoke divine intervention by the showing forth of divine power. The cult of the saints developed rapidly after the Constantinian peace of the church in the early fourth century. Devotion to the martyrs (and, by the sixty century, to saints who were not martyrs) became one of the hallmarks of early medieval Christianity. Along with the places hallowed by the life of Jesus in the Holy Land, the great cities of the martyrs like Antioch, Constantinople, and, particularly, Rome became magnets for pilgrims who journeyed to pray at the tombs of the martyrs. It was at these tombs, as the noted scholar Peter Brown has written, that the "geyserlike force" of miracles and prodigies erupted.

As the era of the Roman persecution receded into the past, it was inevitable that the stories of the martyrs would become shaped by the powers of imagination and the haze of romanticism. The martyrs became more bold (and numerous), their answers more polished and theological, the persecutors more demonic, and, in general, the stories of the saints became wrapped into a great web of imagination. One need only read the rather chaste *Acta* that are nearly contemporary with the events of persecution with something like Jacobus de Voragine's *Golden Legend*, written in the Middle Ages, to see the difference. In the course of time it inevitably happened that the flesh and blood sufferers of the Roman arenas had now become stereotyped figures enshrined in the artistic and churchly tradition of Western culture: St. Lawrence with his symbolic grill; Catherine with her wheel—both of them holding the palm branch symbolic of their death for Christ.

Martyrdom: The Later Tradition

By the end of the fourth century Christianity had gone from a state of toleration to becoming the state religion of the Roman Empire. For the next millennium those who died for

the faith did so either as missionaries on the edges of the civ-
ilized world, at the hands of the Moslems after the latter's
foundation in the seventh century, or in encounters with dissident bodies of Christians (i.e., heretics). It should be noted
that in the latter two cases the Catholic Christians were quite
capable of creating martyrs for both the Moslems and the Dissidents in the Christian West.

It was only in those eras when the church engaged in wholesale missionary activity in parts of the world hitherto unex-
plored or unknown in the West that we begin to see martyrs
dying in circumstances similar to the early martyrs of Roman
times, namely, as a minority whose religious beliefs were seen
as totally inimical to the good of society and culture.

In the great period of Renaissance exploration, the period
which saw the exploration of the New World and its coloni-
zations by Europeans, there was an intense interest in closer
relationships with the Far East. Christian missions had pene-
trated China in the later patristic period and again in the Middle
Ages. It was in the sixteenth century, however, that missionaries, energized by the reform movements after the Protestant
Reformation, began to penetrate China, Japan, and other parts
of the East.

In the mid-sixteenth century, largely due to the zealous work
of the Jesuit missionary St. Francis Xavier (1506–1552), Catholic missions began to make their mark on the hitherto closed
society of Japan. By the 1580's Catholic Christians were in the
hundreds of thousands. It was in 1587 that the first outbreak
of anti-Catholic sentiment happened. This short official persecution was to be followed by intermittent persecutions and
periods of relative peace until the last missionary priest in Japan
died of starvation in a prison cell in Tokyo.

The period between 1587 and the end of the seventeenth
century is studded with the names of Catholic martyrs. In 1597,
for example, twenty-six persons, seventeen of them Japanese
laypersons, were crucified in Nagasaki. In 1614 there was an
attempt, accompanied by some executions, to expel all Christians from the country. From then on there were sporadic persecutions of Catholics in Japan.

What triggered these fierce persecutions? The reasons are

easy to guess: There was a yawning cultural gap between the Europeanized version of Catholicism brought to Japan by the Jesuit missionaries and the cultural life of the country; there was the religious clash with both Shinto (which strongly identified religion and state) and Buddhism; there was the worry that the Christianization of the country could undermine the authority of the Shoguns. There was, finally, the real fear that Christianity represented, more than anything else, the economic and political aspirations of the Portuguese and the Spanish.

Apart from these complex social factors one thing is very clear: Japanese Catholicism in the late sixteenth century and throughout the seventeenth is a story of immense courage and of fierce religious tenacity. During that period immense numbers of native believers died. To this day one can view in museums "tread pictures," that is, small plaques depicting the crucified Christ which were employed to ferret out believers. Those who would not tread on the pictures were considered believers. The "tread pictures" remind us of Pliny's test to discover true Christians in second-century Bithynia: He would ask them to curse Christ and venerate the image of the emperor. True Christians, he wrote to the emperor Trajan, would not do that. The fortitude and persistence of the Japanese Christians was such that when missionaries went back to Japan in the last century, they found small groups of "hidden Christians" who, without priests or other external support, had handed down a somewhat truncated version of the Catholic faith. Evidently family member taught family member throughout the generations when there were no missionaries or native clerics in the country. As a sectarian movement in Japan the "hidden Christians" still remain as a reminder of that past.

The plight of the Japanese martyrs might profitably be compared to the nineteenth-century experience of the Catholics of Uganda. In 1877 Anglican missionaries began to evangelize in Uganda, followed, two years later, by Roman Catholic missionaries. In the years 1885–87 King Mwanga of Uganda executed a large number of Christians including some who served in the royal household. It is thought that many were executed because they resisted the irregular sexual advances of the king. In that period of persecution there were both Anglican and Roman Catholic Christians executed, although, in a rather sad lapse in ecumenism, the late Pope Paul VI canonized only the Roman Catholic martyrs in 1964.

When looking at these instances of persecution and martyrdom,[7] one can raise an objection. Did all of these people die because their persecutors hated Christ and his teaching or did they persecute out of reasons which were sociological and/or political? In the case of the brave martyrs during the reign of Elizabeth I in England, is it not true that the priests who entered England were sworn enemies of the Crown and hence from England's perspective dangerous traitors? From the perspective of the Japanese were not the Christians alien to all the traditional values of the society of Japan? From the perspective of the Africans in the last century were not the Christian missionaries mere extensions of the colonial powers (who not so long before raided the coast for slaves) who were not only destroying native culture but exploiting native resources, land, and wealth? Were not the horrible massacres of the European missionaries in the Congo in the 1960's merely the last eruption of hatred which many Africans nourished in their bosoms for over a century?

These questions are very difficult ones; they have been asked (and answered variously) by groups as diverse as Marxist political historians and liberation theologians. For our purposes we should state this one fact that derives from such questions: There is something socially subversive about tenaciously held religious belief. The corollary of that for Christians is a fact that is not always clearly recognized: Deep Christian belief should result in some kind of tension with whatever established order it encounters. When persons hold a religious conviction so tenaciously that they are willing to risk life for it, that witness is not only a puzzle to many, it is a source of scandal and division. That is what St. Paul meant about the cross being a stumbling block.

On August 9, 1943, Franz Jägerstatter was executed in Berlin for refusing to serve in the German army. Jägerstatter's admittedly minimal religious understanding (he was an Austrian peasant with little schooling) had brought him to the conviction that Hitler's rule was idolatrous and that simple Christian fidelity demanded noncompliance with the armed forces. Today, we honor him as a martyr to pacifism and to Nazi resistance, but in his own day the villagers of his home town thought him a madman who thought nothing of the grief he was bringing on his wife and three small children. Even after the war the Catholic bishop of the area preferred that not too much be made of Jägerstatter's sacrifice for fear that it would demoralize those who had served in the army or cause disrespect to those who had died in the war. A martyr, freed from the pious constraints of the holy card or the stained glass window, was just too awkward to deal with.[8]

Lest we become too righteously judgmental about that Austrian bishop and Jägerstatter's village contemporaries (we, after all, have the benefit of hindsight), we might well remember that every day people pick martyrs to fit their political prejudices. Those who are persons of the right love to recount the horrors of religious persecution behind the Iron Curtain and the Christian witness of the Gulag. There are plenty of horror stories to relate. Those on the left, by contrast, point to the clergy and laity in Latin America who have been tortured, kidnapped, and murdered by various and sundry military juntas. This tendency to selective canonization points up clearly how close genuine martyrdom cuts into the understanding we have of life in society. It is only through a close and sympathetic understanding of the sufferings of the martyrs today that we can begin to get some sense of the suffering of the martyrs of the past.

Martyrdom: A Reflection

It should be clear that the great model for the martyr is Jesus himself. The ultimate test of love is the willingness to give oneself for others. That is the final lesson of the life of Jesus as the New Testament clearly shows. It was the self-giving of Jesus on the cross which made Jesus the model witness—martyr. The *Acta* and the *Passiones* of the early martyrs repeat the constant theme of the invocation of the name of Christ by those who were to suffer the ultimate penalty:

> ... We could never abandon Christ, for it was he who suffered for the redemption of those who are saved in the entire world, the innocent one dying on behalf of sinners. Nor could we worship anyone else. For him we reverence as the Son of God, whereas we love the martyrs as the disciples and imitators of the Lord, and rightly so because of their unsurpassed loyalty towards their king and master. May we too share with them as fellow disciples.[9]

The willingness to die for one's faith is the ultimate test of faith commitment. The threat of death is so powerful that it becomes the touchstone by which we measure what we hold as ultimate and nonnegotiable in life. What is it we would die for? Honor? Country? Family? Possessions? Love? When we read of the religious martyrs, they remind us—they test us— about the degree to which we have or have not accepted the discipleship of Jesus. They force us to ask: Would we go *that far*? Even in the days of the Roman persecutions there were those who worried about that issue. Clement of Alexandria (c. 150–215), who lived through a series of persecutions, saw martyrdom as the culminating act of a life given over to the search for God and his love. As such, he wrote in the *Stromata*, it was a grace not given to all. It was a gesture available only to those who had prepared for it throughout their life.

Precisely because martyrdom is so ultimate an affirmation, we have historically honored the great martyrs both for their strength and for the example they have provided for the rest of us. In the long history of Christianity certain martyrs—often those who have been killed by other "Christians"—have become folk heroes because of the drama, panache, or fortitude with which they died. We remember Joan of Arc calling on the name of Jesus as the flames licked at her body. We recall St. Thomas More asking for help up the steps of the scaffold, saying that he would come down without problem. Others, like Joan and Thomas More, have been celebrated in literature, film, and drama. Thomas à Becket is so much a part of English history that he seems beyond history. Certainly the spiritual tug of his relics in the Middle Ages was phenomenal. In T. S. Eliot's *Murder in the Cathedral* the prospect of future martyrdom is depicted as a positive temptation to pride. In the course of the play the voice of temptation puts before the eyes of Thomas à Becket the glory of martyrdom as a way of getting revenge on those who would slay him. For a moment's pain, Thomas would get heaven and his killers, damnation: "Seek the way of martyrdom, make yourself the lowest/On earth, to be high in heaven./ And see far off below you, where the gulf is fixed,/Your persecutors, in timeless torment,/Parched passions, beyond expiation."[10]

It is precisely because we can romanticize the martyr's end in some heroic fashion that we need to keep the very gritty reality of martyrdom close to the texture of present experience and contemporary history. The stuff of contemporary *Acta* and *Passiones* are coming to us on a huge scale in the memoirs of those who have escaped the gulags and through the reports of organizations such as Amnesty International.

The heroics of martyrdom are possible to the degree that we can distance the experience of the martyr from our reality. The martyrs of ancient Rome speak to us only across the chasm of history. Martyrs, in that sense, filter down to us through the haze of legends, medieval and renaissance art, the hieratic stories of the liturgy, and so on. It is the world of St. Sebastian pincushioned with arrows or Agnes demurely waiting for death. That is a far cry from the lives of those who are being turned into vegetables with drugs in Soviet mental hospitals or shocked with electrodes in the basements of Latin American jails. That, however, happens every day in our world. Martyrs are the subject of headlines in today's newspaper.

How would one convey the reality of contemporary martyrdom? What would we think of seeing a mosaic depicting a person being shocked by electrodes in the genital area? Would that be a scandal or a distraction? If so, it is because we have so distanced ourselves from present reality that martyrdom now belongs to the world of "once upon a time." If we were to create an iconography of martyrdom for today's world, we would have to dispense with wheels, gridirons, lions, and swords to replace them with hypodermic needles, electrodes, bright lights, and jackboots. We would have to learn how to depict a new kind of death—the death of a mind. How would our Christian art depict the metamorphosis of a sentient human being into an abject mindless vegetable?

Which brings us to another point. Many of the accounts of martyrdom began to identify the persecutors with the world of the demonic. Theologians loved to contrast the purity of the martyrs with the satanic persecutors of the Roman Empire. The death of the martyr became seen as an apocalyptic struggle between the forces of Christ and the forces of Satan. Medieval art even depicted the torturers of the martyrs as demons. We tend to look upon such depictions as quaint folk art since our allegiance to the idea of a devil or the demonic is minimal at best. But when we look beyond the cultural stereotypes of the past, we might ask whether or not the medieval hagiographer may not have given us an important insight.

When we read of the concentration camps, the gulags, the police states, and the death squads, we see forces which attack the very nature of human dignity and truth. Books as diverse as Arthur Koestler's novel *Darkness at Noon* and Hannah Arendt's *Eichmann in Jerusalem* have discussed the nature, not of bad acts of wrongdoing, but of evil itself. Works like this make us realize that evil is not an abstraction; it is a powerful reality which can seize people in such a way that they, in turn, can degrade others even to the point of death.

Martyrs, then, are as ancient as those figures we see frozen in stained glass and as contemporary as those whose stories get leaked to the most recent issue of the *New York Times*. When we hear the stories of the ancient martyrs as they are commemorated in the liturgy, we need to remember not only those who died centuries ago but those who, in the name of Christ, die today.

Notes

1. Tacitus, *Annales*, XV, 44; my translation. Nero's gardens are just to the south of Saint Peter's Square. The obelisk in the square once stood in the gardens. Tradition has it that Saint Peter died in those same gardens during this persecution.

2. "The Letter of the Church of Lyons and Vienne," in *The Acts of the Christian Martyrs*, trans. and introduced by H. Musurillo (Oxford, 1972), pp. 79–81. The letter is preserved in Eusebius's *Ecclesiastical History*, book V.

3. Musurillo, p. 83.

4. Eusebius, *Ecclesiastical History*, book VI, 40.

5. W. H. C. Frend, *Martyrdom and Persecution in the Early Church* (Oxford, 1965).

6. "The Martyrdom of Perpetua and Felicity," in Musurillo, pp. 113–15.

7. We are being very selective; we could have used the English martyrs under Elizabeth or the North American martyrs to make the same point.

8. See Donald J. Moore," The Contemporary Witness of Franz Jägerstatter," *America*, 30 October 1982, pp. 247–50.

9. "The Martyrdom of Saint Polycarp," in Musurillo, pp. 15–17.

10. T. S. Eliot, *Collected Poems* (New York, 1964), pp. 192–93.

Readings and Trajectories

The best study of the Roman persecutions is still W. H. C. Frend's *Martyrdom and Persecution in the Early Church* (Oxford, 1965). M. I. Finley's *Studies in Ancient Society* (London, 1974) has excellent essays on the legal basis for the persecution of the Christians. As is evident from the text, there is much useful primary material in H. Musurillo's edition of *The Acts of the Christian Martyrs* (Oxford, 1972).

The relationship of the martyrs to the rise of the cult of the saints in Catholicism is a fascinating subject. More detail on that topic may be gained from Lawrence S. Cunningham's *The Meaning of Saints* (San Francisco, 1980) and Peter Brown's *The Cult of Saints* (Chicago, 1981). Both books have bibliographies.

The heroism of the martyrs has fascinated literary artists for centuries. The list of works which deal with martyrdom is endless. One might begin with some of the more familiar works such as George Bernard Shaw's *Saint Joan* (1923) on St. Joan of Arc or T. S. Eliot's *Murder in the Cathedral* (1935) on the martyrdom of Saint Thomas à Becket. For those with a musical inclination one might study Poulenc's opera *Dialogue of the Carmelites*, which is based on the George Bernanos adaptation of Gertrud von LeFort's novel *The Song of the Scaffold* (1938), which described the death of nuns during the French Revolution.

Modern novelists have shown some concern with the less romantic aspects of martyrdom. For the picture of the martyr as "antihero" one should read the now classic novel of Graham Greene *The Power and the Glory* (New York, 1940). Shusaku Endo's novel *Silence* (English translation by William Johnston—New York, 1980) is set in the period of the Japanese persecutions and treats of a missionary who apostasizes under torture.

Catholics can forget that in their long history they have been seen as persecutors of other Christians. One might look at the Protestant classic *The Book of Martyrs* (first published in 1950) by John Foxe which chronicles the persecution of the "saints" by the papists. Foxe mentions his work as a parallel to the popular medieval compilation of saints called *The Golden Legend.*

To acquire some sense of the religious persecutions of the present day it would be helpful to become acquainted with the *Matchbox*—the regular publication of Amnesty International which monitors religious, social, and political repression around the world. The *Bulletin of Religion in Communist Dominated Areas* is published in New York and monitors the persecution of Christians behind the Iron Curtain. *Maryknoll Magazine* regularly features articles about the repression of Christians in the noncommunist third world.

An understanding of the iconography of the martyrs can be obtained from a study of the many helpful articles in *The New Catholic Encyclopedia* or the more common surveys of art history. Such a study might lead one to speculate on how a contemporary iconography of martyrdom might look. While pursuing this line of thought, one might well do some research on some recent martyrs like those who died at the hands of the Nazis during the last world war: Maximilian Kolbe, Alfred Delp, Franz Jägerstatter, Edith Stein, or the Protestant theologian Dietrich Bonhoeffer, whose *Letters and Papers from Prison* (English version: 1953) might be read. For a more contemporary assessment of Christian repression one can consult *Witnesses of Hope: The Persecution of Christians in Latin America*, ed. Martin Lange and Reinhold Iblacker (Maryknoll, N.Y., 1981).

2

ASCETICS

Beginning in the middle of the third century we begin to read that Christians in certain parts of the Roman empire—most notably in the Roman province of Egypt, other parts of Roman North Africa, and the countries in and around the Holy Land—began to flee the cities and the company of society to begin to live in a rather strange new fashion. These "dropouts" began to form an alternative culture in desert wastelands based on a firm rejection of material goods, a simple life of manual labor and isolation from city life, a radical simplification of dress, diet, and behavior. Most of them lived alone (the word "monk" comes from the Greek *monos*, meaning alone), but some lived in small clustered communities in the company of a senior person who was experienced in that sort of life. These desert solitaries passed their days in harsh penance, silence, prayer, manual labor, and solitude. They were often called "ascetics." The Greek word *askesis* means literally exercise in the physical or athletic sense of that term. And indeed some writers called the desert dwellers "athletes for Christ." Who were they? Why did they flee society? What was their life trying to say? What were they trying to accomplish?

Many Christians fled to the desert (especially after 250, the year of the Decian persecution) for a simple reason: They wanted to get away from the corruption of the Roman Empire. They fled to avoid both the persecutor and the injustices of the tax collector. Others fled for the same reasons which impel people to go to rural areas today: They were disgusted with the crime,

28

decadence, and immorality of Roman urban culture. They firmly believed that the deserts were the places where—like Moses, Elijah, and Jesus—they could hear the voice of God.

One constant theme among these early ascetics was that their life was a new form of martyrdom. With the martyrs so admired it should not be a surprise that zealous Christians thought out ways to emulate the bravery, fidelity, and heroism of those who would die for their faith. The life of asceticism was to be a form of slow martyrdom. Long after the persecutions were over, ascetics would still appeal to the martyrs as examples to explain their life. A seventh-century Irish monastic sermon makes the point quite openly:

> . . . There are three kinds of martyrdom which are accounted as a cross to a man, to wit, white martyrdom, green martyrdom, and red martyrdom. White martyrdom consists in a man's abandoning everything he loves for God's sake, though he suffer fasting and labor threat. Green martyrdom consists in this, that by means of fasting and labour he free himself from evil desire; or suffers toil in penance and repentance. Red martyrdom consists in the endurance of a cross or death for Christ's sake, as happened to the apostles in the persecutions of the wicked and in teaching the law of God.[1]

Besides citing the model of the martyrs, the early ascetics in the desert often described the goal of their life as attaining an *angelic* existence; they wanted to live *bodilessly* as angels. They wished to become as pure spirits standing and praising God like the angels in heaven. This was not merely a literary turn of phrase. There was an element of bodily hatred or bodily suspicion in their thinking. They wished to subdue the body in order for the soul to rise to God. They did this by a two-step procedure of ascetic discipline: (*a*) the total renunciation (*apotaxis*) of the world and (*b*) the subduing (*enkrateia*) of one's being through poverty, chastity, and obedience. When ascetics overcame the lure of the world and subdued the body, they lived in a state of inner peace and discipline which they called *apatheia* (the word "apathy" does not do the term justice). The maintenance of this spiritual equilibrium was a constant battle as the great female ascetic Theodora once noted:

. . . You should realize that as soon as you intend to live in peace, at once evil comes and weighs down your soul through *accidie*, faintheartedness, and evil thoughts. It also attacks your body through sickness, debility, weakness of the knees, and all the members. It dissipates the strength of soul and body so that one believes that one is ill and no longer able to pray. But if we are vigilant, all these temptations fall away.[2]

Where did these rather rigid ideas come from? For well over a century scholars have debated that question, but no single source of ideas proposed has gained scholarly assent. Some students of early asceticism attempted to link the desert ascetics with the Qumran community of Judaism or even to Buddhist monasticism entering the West through the trade routes of Persia (modern Iran). It is relatively clear that certain pagan philosophical systems—notably Neoplatonism and Neopythagorianism—held bodily discipline in high esteem and praised a life of silence, bodily indifference, lack of greed, and other ascetic practices as ways of gaining self-knowledge and ultimate wisdom. These ideas were very much in the air in late Roman culture as a reading of Augustine's *Confessions* makes clear. It is safe to say that such pagan philosophical preoccupations contributed to the rise of asceticism.

For all the cultural influences of the time one cannot discount the particular contribution of Christianity itself to the ascetic ideal. There was, as we have noted, the powerful image of the martyr and the equally powerful notion that the world would not last; that society was "in the last days." To this one could add a selective reading of the New Testament with a bias toward the ascetical life. Did not the Gospel demand that those who wished to be perfect should give up everything and follow Christ with a cross on one's shoulders? Did not Paul and John sharply contrast the "world" with all of its demonic overtones and the Christian? Did not Jesus himself go out into the desert and wrestle with the temptations of the evil? Did not Jesus praise Mary who sat at his feet rather than Martha who was busy about many things? Did not the Gospel put forward the images of the hidden life of Mary in her obedience and the simple lovers of God like Anna and Simeon? There was, in short, ready material for those who wished to read the Gospel as the pattern for the ascetic life. In a certain sense the ascetics were fundamentalists about certain texts that recommended that we "pray always" or "give up everything" or "deny ourselves and take up our crosses" or "die with Christ."

The most celebrated of these early desert dwellers was St. Anthony of the desert. Born circa 251 in Middle Egypt, Anthony was about twenty when he heard the Gospel words "If you will be perfect, go and sell what you have, and come follow me." Anthony, an orphan, distributed his patrimony to the poor, provided an income for his sister, moved to the edge of his native town, and put himself under the tutelage of an old recluse. Around 285 Anthony went further into the desert where he found an old abandoned Roman fort into which he shut himself for about twenty years of solitude and prayerful privation. In 305 he emerged from his solitude to organize other ascetics. From then until his death in 355 Anthony spent his period of retirement with active work either in comforting Christians during persecution (especially under Maximian in A.D. 311) or combatting Arian heretics. He set a familiar pattern of the ascetic who shuts himself up in solitude to reach *apatheia* and then emerges as a teacher and model for others.

We would know nothing of Anthony or his long life had not the famous theologian and bishop St. Athanasius (297–373) written his *Life of Anthony* about the same year that the old monk had died. It was less a biography and more an *aretology*, that is, a book designed to praise the heroic virtues of someone and offer them as models to be emulated. Athanasius's book is filled with stories of Anthony stuggling with demons in battles so loud that terrified pilgrims to his ancient fort would stand outside the walls quaking with fear; he recounted heroic fasts, incessant prayer, rivers of penitent tears, hardships of great intensity, and steadfastness so regular as seem inhuman. By the end of his life, Athanasius wrote, Anthony's life was so angelic that he calmed all of the powers of the demonic both in nature and in humanity. For Anthony and his companions the harsh deserts had become like a peaceful utopia—perhaps an anticipation of heaven itself:

> And truly one could see a land set apart, a land of piety and justice. For neither wrongdoer or wronged was there, nor complaint of the tax collector, but of a great number of ascetics, all of one mind towards virtue. As one looked again on the cells and the regularity of the monks, one cried aloud saying, "How beautiful are thy tabernacles, O Jacob, thy tents, O Israel: As wooded valleys, as watered gardens near the rivers: as tabernacles which the Lord has pitched: as cedars by the waterside." (Num. 24:5–6)[3]

Based on our contemporary experience, we find it difficult to see how the *Life of Anthony* could have been so popular in its own day. It was, in fact, an immense success and, as happens, led to the production of other such "lives" by writers like St. Jerome. St. Augustine in the *Confessions* testifies to the power of the book and the hold that it had on the philosophical seekers who were his own friends in Milan. The very vividness of the book has also inspired artists from the Middle Ages through Hieronymous Bosch down to Salvador Dali to try to capture on canvas the fierce vigor of Anthony's temptations.

Although Anthony was the ascetic model for the later church, his was not the only name associated with the rise of early asceticism. Pachomius (286–348) organized ascetics into a communal life (called "cenobitic" life). At its height his *cenobium* or monastery at Tabennisi in Egypt numbered several thousands of men and women in separate monasteries living a disciplined life of prayer and penance. Melania the Elder (fl. 370) took Egyptian ascetic ideas to the Holy Land where she and other Roman noble women founded monasteries in Jerusalem and other cities. In Bethlehem, for example, Paula ruled a large monastery, while the redoubtable St. Jerome headed the male monastery which was its companion. Basil the Great (329–379) wrote a rule of life for monks which became the model for all monastic life in the Eastern church. To this day the Orthodox church observes the Basilian style of life in its monastic institutions.

One unwholesome characteristic of asceticism was the tendency toward fanaticism. The desire to subdue the body could easily turn into hatred for the body. The emulation of the ascetics (and they were passionately admired by many) could lead to bizarre and extreme acts of penance. In fact, there is a strain in the history of this asceticism which did emphasize with some approval starvation, mutilation, and grotesque penances—practices which belong more to the history of psychological pathology than to ascetical theology. Yet many encouraged such practices of the ascetics and found power in them. Simeon Stylites (c. 390–459) lived on a succession of increasingly high pillars in the area of Antioch. He began this kind of life and, indifferent to sun, cold, wind, or rain, remained on pillars from 423 until his death over thirty-five years later. He depended on people to send food and water up to him via a basket. He was considered a wonder worker (he probably would get lots of attention even today) and an oracle. Thousands flocked to see him and consult him on matters of importance. Prelates and emperors stood at the foot of his pillar and shouted up their problems.

The asceticism of the East slowly filtered into the West in the fourth and fifth centuries. A definitive break with the Eastern style of ascetic monasticism was made by Benedict of Nursia (c. 480–c. 547) whose *Rule* would in time become the basis for monasticism in the West in the same way that Basilian monasticism became the norm for the Eastern church.

St. Benedict and the Benedictine Tradition

We know nothing of Benedict's life beyond what we read in the second book of Pope Gregory's *Dialogues*, an account more pious than reliable. As a young man of twenty Benedict embraced the monastic life after having been a student in Rome. He attracted some followers because of the severity of his life and founded a monastic community at Subiaco outside of Rome. In about 525 he settled at Monte Cassino near Naples where he built a monastery. It was there that he wrote the *Rule* which was to be forever linked with his name and which was to become, in time, the monastic rule of the Western church.

Two preliminary points need to be made about Benedict's *Rule*. First, the rule can make no claim to originality; it is largely a compilation from earlier monastic sources and most likely existed in another form from the pen of an unknown writer who is simply called the "master of the Rule" (*magister reguli*). Secondly, not every Western monastery followed Benedict's rule from the beginning. Although the Benedictine ideals spread to various parts of Europe through such missionaries as Pope Gregory the Great (c. 540–604), it was not until the end of the eighth century when Charlemagne imposed the rule on the monasteries of the Frankish kingdom that Benedictine monasticism triumphed in the Western church.

The genius of St. Benedict rested in his wise sense of balance and moderation. When seen against the ascetical practices of the monasticism of Egypt or Palestine or Syria, Benedict's rule of life seems almost lax. He insisted on adequate sleep, two meals a day, usable clothing, and a harmonious balance of work, prayer, and study. Benedict did not see the monastery simply as a battleground where monks wrestled with their unruly passions to achieve *apatheia*; he saw the monastery as a "school of God's service, in which we hope nothing harsh or oppressive will be directed."[4]

It was in this school that the monks and nuns (Benedict's twin sister Scholastica had founded a convent using the rule) were to lead a life balanced between public prayer at set times throughout the day (this crucial task of the monks was called the "work of God"—*opus Dei*), the constant reading and meditation on the Bible (the "divine reading"—*lectio divina*), and manual work for the physical and economical support of the whole monastery. This life was designed to perfect the monk as an individual, but it also had at least two social values: Monastic life was to be *exemplary* (i.e., here is how Christians might live together in harmony) and it was to be *eschatological* (i.e., monastic life "waited" for the coming of the Lord without attachment to the things of this world).

Benedict did not neglect the long ascetical tradition which had come before him. Indeed, he was nurtured on it. In his *Rule* he legislated in very precise language the life of obedience under an abbot, a life of celibate chastity, and a life of poverty. While Benedict recognized the dignity of the eremetical life and its place in the ascetical tradition, he legislated for those who would live in community under the authority of a spiritual father or mother. It was in this setting that Benedict hoped that the committed religious would convert *from* the world *to* Christ.

That conversion process requires discipline and maturity. When the process is complete, the religious has undergone a transformation:

> When a monk has climbed all twelve steps (i.e., of humility), he will find that perfect love of God which casts out fear, by means of which everything he had observed anxiously before will now appear natural and simple. He will no longer act out of fear of hell, but for the love of Christ, out of good habits, and with a pleasure derived of virtue. The Lord, through the Holy Spirit, will show this to his servant, cleansed of sin and vice.[5]

Between the death of St. Benedict and the reemergence of urban life in the high Middle Ages around 1200 the Benedictine ideal slowly grew and finally predominated European religious life. Indeed, some historians have called the early Middle Ages the Benedictine Centuries. Benedictine influence was strong in the great English monasteries of the seventh century, while missionaries like St. Boniface (680–754) carried the Benedictine ideals to Germany and further north. We have already noted that it was during the reign of Charlemagne that the Benedictine Rule was imposed on the monasteries of the Frankish kingdom. After the Carolingian period, when monasticism needed cleansing, it was the vigorous Benedictine reforms emanating from Cluny (founded 905) that provided the impetus for church reform at all levels during the eleventh and twelfth centuries.

Many of the movements in the Middle Ages which set out to reform monastic life did so by appealing to the original spirit of the Benedictine rule. Reform in the here and now almost always worked on that sense of return to the sources. Cluny began as a reform at Carolingian monasticism and the Cistercians began as conscious reformers of what they considered to be the excesses of Cluny. St. Bernard of Clairvaux (1090–1153) reacted against the wealth, pomp, and splendor of the life at Cluny. His appeal was to those aspects of Benedictine life which emphasized simplicity, solitude, hard work, poverty, and austerity of life. It should come as no surprise that after initial success the Cistercians themselves became lax and other reformers attempted to call them back to their original ideals.

Every student of history knows that monasticism was fundamental for the survival of culture during the harsh centuries of the early Middle Ages. Both the *Opus Dei* and the Benedictine emphasis on the study of scripture made basic literacy obligatory in the monastery. The result was a book culture which put an emphasis on the production of books (a prodigious task before printing) and schooling of some kind to provide future generations of copyists, readers, and students. The liturgy also fostered an interest in both music and drama. The fact that there was little town life in the early Middle Ages made the monasteries (and the feudal castles) the social centers of what was preserved of communal life. It was the monasteries which provided granaries for the famine times, hostels, courts to settle disputes, rudimentary hospitals, places of refuge, and schools for both layfolk and monastic novices. Sketches for ideal monasteries like that found in the ninth-century St. Gall manuscript (a beautiful facsimile of which was published by the University of California in 1980) show how monasteries in the early Middle Ages became almost the equivalent of a highly organized village.

Beyond the Benedictine Ideal

Monasticism from its beginning had been largely rural and isolated from the commerce of people. From the days of the desert solitaries there had been an ascetic and theological tradition of *fuga mundi*—"flight from the world": "The monastery should be planned, if possible, with all the necessities—water, mill, garden, shops—within the walls. Thus the monk will not need to wander about outside, for this is not good for their souls."[6] Even to this day many monastic establishments seek the rural life as a way of being far from the busy commerce of city life, or like the enclosed Carmelite nuns they seek to create a hidden oasis in the midst of the city. The monastery as retreat serves a powerful need in an urban culture as the streams of people who visit the monasteries of today attest.

Despite this continuity there was an obvious need for new kinds of organized ascetic life as the social character of Europe changed. It would require many volumes to chart those new experiments in religious life. In this section four kinds of different religious movements will be mentioned that represent in some rough historical order ways in which the Catholic tradition attempted to adapt the ascetic and monastic life to the complex changes in the culture of the West.

(1) The Franciscan Friars

St. Francis of Assisi (1182–1226) knew the traditional life of asceticism well after his conversion. For a period he lived as a hermit formally adapting the traditional hermit's garb (a belted habit with heavy shoes) and staff. When in 1209 he "heard" the Gospel in a new way, he decided to live an entirely different manner of life. He and his brethren were to live in the total poverty of the urban poor, that is, he would risk everything out of faith by not owning anything. The early Franciscans were to work at menial tasks like the poor and when there was no work they were to do what the poor always did: They begged. Francis envisioned his friars as moving about the cities and towns preaching in the open air in the market squares. He did not want his friars isolated from the people (even though he counselled periods of withdrawal for prayer). His ideas were in sharp contrast to the hidden life of the Benedictines (to whom, however, he was deeply in debt) who were behind the monastic enclosure dedicated to solitude and the round of prayer. The Franciscans were to be contemplative also, but contemplatives on the move. Gilbert Keith Chesterton caught it perfectly when he said that what St. Benedict stored, Saint Francis scattered.

The early Franciscans maintained certain elements from the earlier monastic tradition. They said the Office in common and lived in community. Eventually, as the original impulse to roam and preach was modified, the Franciscans accepted more of the traditional restraints and disciplines of monastic life.

(2) The Jesuits

St. Ignatius of Loyola and his companions took religious vows in 1534, just a few years after the outbreak of the Protestant Reformation. Six years later Pope Paul III approved Ignatius of Loyola's religious order. When Ignatius died in 1556, a scant sixteen years later, there were nearly a thousand Jesuits. It was the peculiar genius of Ignatius to start a religious society perfectly adapted to the needs of the church in the Reformation period. The Society of Jesus was highly centralized with its headquarters in Rome, militant in its obedience to the papacy, rigorous in its prayer life, free from the demands of a common liturgical life, and adaptable enough in its various milieus. The Jesuits put a tremendous effort into missionary work both in Europe and in the newer parts of the world opening up to the Renaissance explorers and to the apostolate of education and learning. The Jesuits thrived because their emphasis dovetailed nicely with the post-Renaissance developments of education with its accompanying interest in science and scholarship.

In the sixteenth century the Jesuits represented the modern thrust of Catholicism. They were considered radical and avant garde. For that reason it is easy to forget how firmly Ignatius's life and vision rooted itself in the ascetical tradition of historical Christianity. The formative elements in the conversion of Ignatius Loyola after his convalescence from battle wounds in 1521 included vigils, spiritual direction under a Benedictine monk, and—shades of the desert anchorites!—days spent in prayer and solitude in the caves about Manresa in Spain. It was there at Manresa where he began to write *The Spiritual Exercises,* which was to be the charter of Jesuit life. The Jesuits wished to put the fruits of contemplation in action, but contemplation itself was done according to the ancient tradition of withdrawal. We should leave the normal world to make the exercises, Ignatius wrote, because "the more the soul is in solitude and seclusion, the more fit it renders itself to approach and be united with its creator and Lord; and the more closely it is united with him, the more it disposes itself to receive graces and gifts from the infinite goodness of God."[7]

(3) The Daughters of Charity

Founded by Sts. Vincent de Paul (1580–1660) and Louise de Marillac (1591–1660), the group first consisted of some devout women who joined the widowed Louise in aiding the poor of Paris. It was only in 1642 that these women took any formal religious vows and then only on a yearly basis. What Vincent and Louise did was to free religious women from the restrictions of the cloister. They envisioned groups of religious women who would be totally active performing corporal works of mercy but within the framework of a religious society. To these women Vincent offered an entirely new vision of religious life: "Your convent will be the house of the sick, your cell a hired room, your chapel the parish church, your cloister the city streets or the hospital wards, your grill the fear of God, your veil modesty."[8]

While the idea of religious women actively working among the needy of the world is today a commonplace, it was a revolutionary idea in the seventeenth century. Indeed, Louise de Marillac had to recruit her candidates from the lower classes for a long time since the idea of women working so actively was simply unheard of among the upper classes. If women were called to the religious life, it was expected that they would be in cloistered convents performing seemly works such as teaching young girls. Vincent and Louise so changed that idea that by the end of the seventeenth century there were Daughters of Charity working with the aged, galley slaves, orphans, mentally and physically handicapped, as well as the sick and the poor. They were the first women to care for the wounded on battlefields. By 1660—the year that both Vincent and Louise died— France had over forty houses of these sisters. One would be tempted to think that they are the remote ancestor of many of the caring professions in which women predominate: social work, nursing, counseling, child care, etc.

The Daughters of Charity, like the Jesuits before them, broke with the old ascetic ideal of contemplation and prayer as an end in itself. Their more modern idea was to see the contemplative life as the energizing force for a life of action. This was not a negative judgment on the older ideal; it was, however, a radical variation from some of its basic suppositions.

(4) The Little Brothers and Sisters of Jesus

Inspired by the life and teachings of the French mystic and solitary Charles de Foucauld (1858–1916), this modern religious order was founded in the 1930's in order to combine a life of austere contemplation with labor in the world. The Little Brothers and Sisters might live in an urban ghetto while working to support themselves in a factory. Their basic thrust is to provide a presence of prayer and adoration in the most alienated areas of our culture. One little sister has even lived with female prisoners for extended periods of time.

The new insight of the Little Brothers and Sisters is to recognize that the desert might be quite different from places of natural desolation and aridity. Deserts can be created by human beings. The new deserts, the followers of Charles de Foucauld remind us, are the desolate urban areas of our postindustrial cities. One need not go out to the Sahara to wrestle with the forces of the demonic; they are available to the new ascetic in the South Bronx. Instead of weaving mats and living in caves the new ascetics live in poor apartments and do piece work in sweat shops. It is a new setting but a very old vocation.

Asceticism: A Reflection

Under the general rubric of asceticism we have discussed a number of related topics which are reducible down to two items. One is that asceticism generally considered can be seen as a spiritual discipline used on an occasional basis (e.g., fasting) or as a life commitment (e.g., a life of voluntary poverty or virginity). Secondly, we spoke of how this ascetic life became institutionalized into what is called in the Catholic tradition the "religious life." Obviously one can include ascetical practices into the spiritual life without joining a religious order. Indeed, every Christian is called to some form of the ascetic life. We emphasize in this chapter the formal religious life (especially monasticism and its derivatives) because it has been such a notable feature of the Catholic tradition. It is, in fact, one of the hallmarks of that tradition.[9]

Neither individual asceticism nor asceticism organized into formal religious life seems much in vogue today. Even the mild ascetic legislation of the Roman Catholic Church (e.g., Friday abstinence from flesh meats and Lenten fasts) has been radically mitigated. Current discussions on spirituality seem more focused on positive experiences than on the self-denying demands of the older asceticism. Furthermore, there have been many outspoken reservations about the older forms of asceticism as antihuman or self-hating or more rooted in Plato, Pythagoras, or the Stoics than in the Gospels. One of the great ironies of our time is that people will fast for their waistlines and deny themselves for cardiovascular fitness (think of the asceticism of the runner), but regard ascetic practices in the search for God suspiciously.

A good deal of formal religious life falls under the same suspicion. It would be otiose and time-consuming to document the wholesale flight from religious life in our time and the mountains of explanatory or condemnatory literature accompanying that flight. Today there is a certain residual romanticism about the formal religious life that often falls into trivialization as the TV ads featuring monks and nuns so amply attest.

As quickly as we note the apparent erosion of interest in asceticism and the flight from religious life, we should also mark some equally apparent countersigns. The first—and most blatant—countersign is the fascination that Westerners have shown in the disciples of Eastern religion. This interest is very complex, ranging from a use of some disciples for health (e.g., yoga) through an adaptation of Eastern spiritual techniques for Christian prayer (e.g., the interest in Zen) or the adoption of Eastern religion as a total way of life. Furthermore, beyond the interest in the esoterica of the East there is a persistent hunger for genuine spiritual experience within the Church and a desire to experiment with new forms of religious life.

The interest in spirituality, both Eastern and Western, and the vitality of the monastic tradition can be seen clearly by considering the impact of Thomas Merton (1915–1968), the most famous apologist for the ascetic life in the modern world. What is interesting about Merton is not only the incisive way in which he was able to communicate the contemporary worth of asceticism and monasticism, but the phenomenal response his ideas generated. His books sell in the hundreds of thousands, are translated in most major languages, and continue, long after his death, to provoke discussion and comment.

Merton published his autobiography *The Seven Storey Mountain* some seven years after he entered a Trappist monastery in

Kentucky. An instant critical success when it appeared in 1948, *The Seven Storey Mountain* recounted the restless life of a young alienated intellectual who had been raised in France and England before coming to America for his university studies. His collegiate career in New York City in the late thirties was framed in the best bohemian fashion by restless reading, a flirtation with Marxism, smoky nights at jazz clubs, women, wine, song, and a genuine puzzlement about what his life was adding up to. His conversion to Catholicism seems to have resulted from his own reading in literature and philosophy, his disgust with the moral emptiness of his life, and a genuine thirst for some transcendent experience in life. One enthusiastic reviewer at the time of publication called *The Seven Storey Mountain* the modern version of The *Confessions* of Saint Augustine.

From the publication of *The Seven Storey Mountain* until his tragically bizarre death in 1968 (he was accidentally electrocuted while in Thailand) Merton wrote dozens of books and hundreds of articles on topics ranging from nuclear disarmament to Latin American poets. What is most significant about this great and amorphous body of work was his singular point of view as a contemplative monk and, in the last years of his life, as a hermit. Thomas Merton never did write a systematic work on spirituality or monasticism, but it was a subject to which he always returned. It is possible to see in his scattered writings a broad framework of ideas which were central to his vision. For our purposes there are two claims which Merton makes which are useful as a summary of this chapter on ascetics in the Catholic tradition.

(1) The experience of the desert ascetics is neither an irrelevancy nor a historical aberration. Merton realized that there were eccentricities and excesses in the lives of the old ascetics, but, as he has written, their eccentricities may have been grossly exaggerated by their devoted biographers and partisans.

What do those early ascetics have to say to us today?

Merton described the early ascetics as searchers and explorers—people who were willing to risk everything in order to ask ultimate questions about the nature of the self and the human relationship to the Ultimate. The desert solitaries were not people who ruminated about ideas; they were people who sought experience. They were willing to strike out for the unknown and uncharted ends of human experience. Merton writes:

> What the Fathers sought most of all was their own true self in Christ. And in order to do this, they had to reject completely the false, formal, self, fabricated under social compulsion in "the world." They sought a way to God that was uncharted and freely chosen, not inherited from others who had mapped it out beforehand. They sought a God whom they alone could find, not one who was "given" in a set stereotyped form by somebody else. Not that they rejected any of the dogmatic formulas of the Christian faith: they accepted and clung to them in their simplest and most elementary shape. But they were slow (at least in the beginning, in the time of their primitive wisdom) to get involved in theological controversy. Their flight to the arid horizons of the desert meant also a refusal to be content with arguments, concepts, and technical verbiage.[10]

The search for the authentic sense of the self has a certain contemporary ring to it. Merton sees spiritual discipline as a way, not of killing or abusing the self, to seek out the very frontiers of human experience. This insight, then, brings us to another important proposition of Merton's which pertains to the organized life of asceticism, that is, monasticism.

(2) Monasticism is not to be identified with any romantic or nostalgic style of life based on the appearances of what monasticism once was. An old spiritual aphorism says that "the habit does not make the monk." That saying speaks in moral terms. But there is another sense in which that is true. Monasticism does not depend on its hoods, cloisters, spires, chants, or scriptoria to create monastic life. Monasticism is not a manner of doing things; monasticism is a way of being. How should a monk "be" in our time? Merton claims, paradoxically enough, that the monastic life is, by its nature, a life of irrelevancy. Those who choose the monastic life should move to the edge of human endeavors so that in freedom and silence they can ask the ultimate questions of human existence. Here is Thomas Merton's mature thinking on the role of the monastic life for our time:

... Monasticism aims at the cultivation of a certain quality of life, a level of awareness, a depth of consciousness, an area of transcendence, and of adoration which are not usually possible in an actively secular existence. This does not imply that the secular world is entirely godless or reprobate, or that there can be no real awareness of God in secular life. Nor does it mean that worldly life is to be considered wicked or inferior. But it does mean that more immersion and total absorption in worldly business end by robbing one of a certain necessary perspective. The monk seeks to be free from what William Faulkner calls "The same frantic steeplechase towards nothing" which is the essence of worldliness everywhere."[11]

In that paragraph Merton insists that the monastic charism speaks to the world. It does that in a variety of ways. First of all, monasticism offers to the world a vision of peace, a haven of silence in a busy world, stable community, harmony with nature, seasons, and time, integrated work and worship. Beyond that, the monastic life is an act of faith in the reality of God and the life with God beyond the present. Monastic life says that this life is not all; one can give up things for Someone better. The monastic life is an act of faith in the satisfying reality of God. In that sense the monastic life is eschatological, which is to say, it is a life that points to final things (the *eschaton*) beyond immediate experience. It is for this reason that the tradition has always called the monastic life a risk. If the monk is wrong in making his act of faith, he has lived a very foolish life indeed, not from circumstance, but by choice.

Our modern world manifests a deep spiritual hunger. We have seen in the United States over the past generation a keen interest in Eastern spirituality, meditation techniques, and ascetic discipline. What many do not realize is that the Catholic tradition has a rich vein of asceticism and spiritual discipline that goes back to its very origins. Writers like Thomas Merton and other contemporary spiritual masters reflect on ancient tradition. They see that tradition as pertinent for today. The very loneliness and seriousness of the ascetic calling may be just what makes it pertinent and timely for our time:

... experience of the contemplative life in the modern world shows that the most crucial focus for contemplative and meditative discipline, and for the life of prayer, for many moderns, is precisely this so-called sense of absence, desolation, and even apparent "inability to believe." I stress the word "apparent" because though this experience may to some be extremely painful and confusing and to raise all kinds of crucial "religious problems," it can be very well a sign of authentic Christian growth and a point of decisive development in faith, if they are able to cope with it. . . . One must, on a new level of meditation and prayer, live through this crisis of belief and grow to a more complete personal and Christian integration of experience.[12]

Notes

1. As quoted in John Ryan, *Irish Monasticism: Origins and Early Development* (Ithaca, N.Y., 1972), pp. 197–98. This book is a reprint of the original 1931 work.

2. Benedicta Ward, ed. and trans., *The Sayings of the Desert Fathers* (Kalamazoo, Mich., 1975), p. 71.

3. "Life of St. Anthony," trans. Mary Keenan, in *Early Christian Biographies,* ed. Roy DeFerrarri (Washington, D.C., 1952), p. 175.

4. Prologue to the *Rule of Saint Benedict.* I cite the translation of Anthony Meisel and M. L. del Mastro (Garden City, N.Y., 1975), p. 45.

5. *Rule of Saint Benedict,* chap. 8. The metaphor of climbing would become a central idea in spiritual literature with spiritual writers interpreting Jacob's Ladder as an allegorical text referring to the desire for spiritual perfection. The books using the climbing imagery range from Benedict's *Rule* to Thomas Merton's *The Seven Storey Mountain.*

6. *Rule of Saint Benedict,* chap. 66.

7. Prologue to *The Spiritual Exercises of St. Ignatius of Loyola,* trans. Louis J. Pohl, S.J. (Chicago, 1951), p. 10.

8. Quoted in *The Oxford Dictionary of Saints,* ed. D. H. Farmer (New York and Oxford, 1980), p. 263.

9. There are experiments in the formal religious life in the Reformed tradition like the Community of Taizé. They remain exceptions to the general rule that the Reformation almost thoroughly rejected the monastic and religious life. After Luther, Max Weber once wrote, every Christian was called to be a monk.

10. Thomas Merton, *The Wisdom of the Desert,* (New York, 1970), pp. 5–6. This volume includes Merton's selected translations from the sayings of the desert solitaries.

11. Thomas Merton, *Contemplation in a World of Action,* (Garden City, N.Y., 1973), p. 27. This entire book is a splendid meditation on the contemporary significance of asceticism and monasticism.

12. Ibid., pp. 177–78.

Readings and Trajectories

Besides the works cited in the notes of this chapter the following have been helpful on the early desert ascetics: Derwas Chitty, *The Desert a City* (Oxford, 1966); Margaret

Smith, *The Way of the Mystics* (Oxford, 1978; reprint of 1931 study); Jacques La-Carriere, *Men Possessed by God* (Garden City, N.Y., 1964).

For a literary approach to the desert experience one should read Gustave Flaubert's *The Temptation of Saint Antony*. The new translation by Kitty Mrosovsky (Ithaca, N.Y., 1981) is quite valuable because the introduction gives a splendid cultural survey of the figure of St. Antony in the history of Western culture.

The theme of the "desert" in Christian spirituality is crucial and persistent. It has been studied by Thomas Gannon and George Traub's *The Desert and The City* (New York, 1969) and in chapter 4 of my own *The Meaning of Saints* (San Francisco, 1980).

Books on monasticism are without end. For helpful surveys one can consult David Knowles' *Christian Monasticism* (New York, 1969) and Christopher Brooke's lavishly illustrated *The Monastic World* (New York, 1971). The reprinting of the classic study of John Ryan, *Irish Monasticism* (Ithaca, N.Y., 1972), has an exhaustive bibliography.

One of the best sources for monastic history and monastic spirituality are the books and monographs published by Cistercian Publications (WMU Station, Kalamazoo, Mich. 49008). Titles range from translations of original monastic sources to studies on the problems and prospects of monasticism today.

Monastic life is today in a great state of change and ferment. Some of the more adventuresome experiments in monastic life have been chronicled in Charles Fracchia's *Living Together Alone: The New American Monasticism* (San Francisco, 1979).

Two books, both edited by Brother Patrick Hart, deal with Merton from the purely monastic perspective: *Thomas Merton: The Monastic Journey* (Garden City, N.Y., 1978) and *Thomas Merton, Monk: A Monastic Tribute* (Garden City, N.Y., 1976). For a sympathetic study of Merton's thought with excellent bibliographies of his writings and the secondary literature, see Elena Malits' *The Solitary Explorer: Merton's Transforming Journey* (San Francisco, 1980).

The ascetic life and the monastic life are not identical realities. One can undertake the spiritual discipline of prayer without being a member of a religious community. For a sensitive approach to contemporary spirituality one should note the works of William Johnston, S.J. Johnston is an Irish Jesuit who has lived in Japan for most of his adult life. He is extremely knowledgeable about Zen Buddhism, is a passionately devoted Catholic Christian, and a spiritual master who has blended together the insights of Eastern spiritual discipline with the Catholic tradition. His major books are: *Silent Music* (San Francisco, 1974); *The Inner Eye of Love* (San Francisco, 1978); and *The Mirror Mind* (San Francisco, 1981).

There has been an intense interest in recent years in the social role of women ascetics. A preliminary approach to this topic can be gleaned from a consideration of the essays by Elizabeth Clark in *Jerome, Chrysostom, and Friends* (New York, 1979) and the opposite articles in the anthology *Women in Religion*, edited by Herbert Richardson and Elizabeth Clark (San Francisco, 1977). For background the standard biography of J. N. D. Kelly, *Jerome* (San Francisco, 1975), is helpful.

For a better social understanding of the whole movement of the ascetics in the early church one should read John Gager's *Kingdom and Community* (Englewood Cliffs, N.J., 1975) and the seminal article of Peter Brown: "The Rise and Function of the Holy Man in Late Antiquity," *Journal of Roman Studies*, 1971, pp. 80–101. Philip Rousseau's *Ascetics, Authority, and the Church in the Age of Jerome and Cassian* (Oxford, 1978) is an important study for linking the Eastern ascetical tradition to Western monasticism.

Margaret Miles's *Fullness of Life: Historical Foundations for a New Asceticism* (Philadelphia, 1981) is an engaging historical study of asceticism in the patristic and medieval period focusing on the respect (or lack thereof) for the body. It can be profitably read in tandem with the author's earlier *Augustine on the Body* (Missoula, Mont., 1979).

3

PILGRIMS

Pilgrimage is a religious exercise found in all of the world's religions. In Islam, to cite the most conspicuous example, the pilgrimage to Mecca (the so-called *Haj*) is regarded as one of the five basic pillars of the Islamic faith. Both the Old Testament and the New reflects the religious journeys of pious Jews up to Jerusalem and to other sacred sites connected with their faith. The Book of Deuteronomy (16:16) prescribes visits to the place God chooses for the feasts of Passover, Pentecost, and Tabernacles. The pilgrimage motif echoes in the Book of Psalms in the songs of those who "go up" to the Temple:

> Happy those who live in your house
>   and can praise you all day long;
> and happy the pilgrims inspired by you
>   with courage to make the ascents.
>
> As they go through the Valley of the Weeper,
>   they make it a place of springs,
> clothed in blessings by early rains,
>   thence they make their way from height to height,
> soon to be seen before God on Zion.
>   (Ps 84:4–7)

A pilgrimage may be defined as a journey taken to visit a sacred place or person of such a kind that the journey as well as the visit takes on a sacred aura and constitutes an act of piety. According to that definition the journey as well as the destination is part of the religious act. People leave the rhythms of their ordinary life to focus on a journey to a goal and for a purpose. We see many secular counterparts of pilgrimage on television news with some regularity. People leave their jobs, homes, or schooling in order to "go up" to Washington to act out their concern about solar energy, atomic weapons, or some other great issue. For the time of their pilgrimage they find a new community of friends who are bound together by their common concerns, their common ritual acts (chants, carrying placards, etc.), and their common ideological consensus.

Christian pilgrimage is an appropriate topic to address at this particular juncture of our study because it ties in so closely with the martyrs and the ascetics we have discussed before. We have already noted in passing, for example, that the aristocratic women who were the leading ascetics in Jerome's circle first made a pilgrimage to the great ascetic circles of Egypt before they settled in the Holy Land. After the peace of Constantine we also note a large number of people who begin to travel for religious reasons with one of three goals (or a combination of all three): to the tombs of the martyrs; to the places in the Holy Land associated with the great events of the Bible; or to visit the great ascetics for spiritual advice or edification. This early pilgrimage impulse energized many Christians in the fourth century including two extraordinary women who, in a very real way, sum up the leading ideas of the pilgrimage in the early church: Helena, the mother of the emperor Constantine, and the indefatigable traveller and writer, the nun Egeria (also spelled Etheria).

The empress Helena (c. 250–330) became a Christian in 312. She had an apparently deserved reputation for great piety and goodness, with stories told of her generosity to the sick, poor, and imprisoned. At about the time her son moved the capitol from Rome to the city he named for himself (Constantinople) she made an extended pilgrimage to the Holy Land. It was there she was able to watch the extended building program being accomplished under the patronage of her son. After her own death, Helena's name became associated with a story about the rediscovery of the cross on which Jesus had been executed.

While the historical veracity of the story is slight, the legend of the True Cross, in its various forms, is a good case study in the growth and embellishment of the Christian imagination—the tradition reminds us of the deep folk roots of Christianity.

According to several legends (or variations on the same legend) Helena decided to find the True Cross. After consulting wise Jews and Christians she eventually found three crosses while the excavations were being done for the church on the site of Golgotha. The power of one of these crosses to raise a dead man indicated which one was the cross of Christ. In one version of the story a Jew named Judas (a descendant of the traitorous apostle) helps in the founding of the cross, becomes a convert, and eventually the bishop of Jerusalem.

The story of Helena and the True Cross is very hard to accept as a historical fact. We do know that at the end of the fourth century the pilgrim Egeria talks about the veneration of relics of the cross, but makes no mention of Helena in connection with those relics. We also know that by the end of the fourth century fragments of the cross had been sent to other cities in the empire. In the later course of Christian history the story of the founding of the True Cross was told and retold in various forms. It entered the cultural heritage of the Christian tradition. It inspired one of the earliest and most beautiful poems in Anglo-Saxon, "The Dream of the Rood." Later variations of the legend were recorded in the influential medieval *Golden Legend* and immortalized in such painting cycles as the frescoes depicting the founding of the cross done in Arezzo (Italy) by Piero della Francesca in the fifteenth century. Until 1960 there was a feast celebrating the founding of the True Cross in the liturgical calendar. The entire tradition of the True Cross has had an immense impact on the devotional life of the church.

There is no such continuity that one can speak of when discussing the *Travels* of Egeria. The book had been lost for over seven hundred years. It was mentioned by a medieval monk but not studied again until the last century when an Italian scholar found a copy of it which lacked both its opening pages and which breaks off in the middle of the narrative. What we do have is the wonderful travel story of the extended pilgrimage of a nun named Egeria who came—we think—from either the coast of Gaul or Spain.

Egeria toured the Holy Land, Egypt, and Constantinople during the years 381–384 and wrote her sisters about her experiences. By the time Egeria visited the Holy Land Constantine had been long dead (he died in 337) and the ambitious building program he had initiated was complete. St. Jerome had also made his first visit to the East and a year after Egeria's visit would establish himself in a monastery in the Holy Land. We know from her writings that Jerusalem and its environs were heavily populated with nuns, monks, solitaries, ascetics, and Christian clergy of every rank. Her own interests were purely religious. She never alludes to the Roman civilization of the area or its monuments. She singlemindedly visits *holy* persons, *holy* places, and *holy* buildings. She is interested in places mentioned in the Bible, the burial place of biblical figures, the dwellings of the famous ascetics, and the sites associated with the life of Christ.

Egeria's *Travels* are particularly important for their detailed descriptions of Christian worship in Jerusalem in the fourth century. She described the daily prayer services and liturgy of the church of the Holy Sepulchre, how Lent was celebrated, the order of services for Holy Week, and most importantly, the rather formal rites, ceremonies, and duties of those who were preparing for baptism into the church as adults. Of particular interest is her discussion of the instruction of prospective converts during the Lenten period. Egeria says that every day during Lent the bishop would gather the catechumens (the name used for the converts) in the church in a circle around his bishop's chair in order to instruct them for three hours. This would take place every day of the seven weeks of Lent. The course of instruction was centered on the great story of salvation recounted in the Bible:

> ... During the forty days he goes through the whole Bible, beginning with Genesis, and first relating the literal meaning of each passage, then interpreting the spiritual meaning. He also teaches them at this time all about the resurrection and the faith. And this is called *catechesis*. After five weeks teaching they receive the creed, whose content he explains article by

article the same way he explains the scriptures, first literally and then spiritually. Thus all the people in these parts are able to follow the scriptures when they are read in church, since there has been teaching on all the scriptures from six to nine in the morning all through Lent, three hours of catechesis a day. At ordinary services when the bishop sits and preaches, ladies and sisters, the faithful utter exclamations, but when they come and hear him explaining the catechesis, their exclamations are far louder, God is my witness; and when it is related and interpreted like this they ask questions on each point.[1]

While scholars treasure Egeria's *Travels* for its mine of information about the life and worship of the early church, others love the book because of its straightforward love for the church in all its particularities. Egeria is a pious woman of great stamina, unbounded curiosity, and a high spirit of adventure. She sees her life, not as an idle tour, but as a spiritual journey in which she is learning to deepen her faith, and by extension, the faith of her sisters. In the middle of one of her descriptions she pauses to talk about her future. Its adventuresomeness and its faith are typical of the tone of Egeria; she is writing from Constantinople:

... My present plan is to travel to Asia, since I want to make a pilgrimage to Ephesus, and the martyrium of the holy and blessed Apostle John. If after that I am still alive, and able to visit further places, I will either tell you about them face to face (if God so wills), or at any rate write to you about them if my plans change. In any case, ladies, light of my heart, whether I am "in the body" or "out of the body" please do not forget me.[2]

What possessed these people—and thousands others like them—to go on pilgrimage? There is, to be sure, a human reason, one that motivates us to travel today: curiosity. *Ut sum satis curiosa:* "I am very curious," admitted Etheria in her book. It is clear, however, that travel and its satisfactions were not the sole motivating impulses to understand the religious motivations of pilgrimage. The major aim was to understand some of the basic notions of Catholic spirituality and theology.

Christianity is a religion founded on a person who existed at a particular place in a particular time. Christianity did not begin its story "once upon a time" but "in the fifteenth year of the reign of Tiberius Caesar." As a consequence the events and places surrounding Jesus are palpable. For that reason Christians could visit the places where the central events of their religion took place: It was here that the Eucharist was instituted; there that Jesus died; over yonder is where he was buried. The going to places made the stories of the Gospels, heard in the liturgy, take on a peculiar reality. "We understand sacred scripture better," Jerome once wrote, "when we have seen Judea with our own eyes."

The places where Jesus worked miracles, preached, or underwent his passion were not only important because they were the geographical evidence of the truth of the Gospels. For the people of the fourth century the places associated with Jesus were sources of sacred power. One prayed at the church of the Holy Sepulchre more piously because it had a sacred aura; it was there, at that spot, that the work of salvation was effected.

The Holy Land was the arena where Jesus lived; its focal point was Jerusalem. We need to remember that even in the Bible itself Jerusalem had a significance far beyond its role as the city of the Jewish people. It had a symbolic purpose and it served as a figure for any number of institutions which were central to the faith: Jerusalem was a *figura* of the messianic period (the New Jerusalem) or of heaven itself (the Jerusalem on High). It was also a symbol of the church and the city of God as opposed to the city of man. The earthly Jerusalem was a reflection of the Jerusalem on high. The possession of Jerusalem—as we shall see later in this book—was the cherished goal of the Crusaders. Their desire for the city must be seen not only as a nationalistic and military goal but against the rich, biblical, theological understanding of the meaning of the city itself. It is not a rhetorical exaggeration to say that contemporary disputes about the "status" of the Holy Places in Jerusalem and of the city itself reflect not only the vexatious questions which swirl around the policies of the state of Israel but of the symbolic nature of Jerusalem itself. Jerusalem has a deep and mystical significance for Jews, Moslems, and Christians—the three great religions of the Book.

In that sense the places associated with Jesus and other figures of the Bible had a certain resemblance to the shrines of the martyrs. As we have already noted in a previous chapter, it was assumed without question that the tombs of the martyrs were places which exuded sacred power. That is why Egeria, as a pilgrim, could show such an intense interest both in the sacred places of the Holy Land and the *martyria*; not because they were of equal stature, but because they both were places where the connection with the divine was special in its potency.

Finally, people went on pilgrimages in this period to see the holy ascetics. As recent scholars have noted, the ascetics served many functions for the faithful of the fourth and fifth centuries: they gave spiritual advice, they settled quarrels, they gave direction in the way of religious perfection, they consoled people in their need. However bizarre we may find the pillar-dwelling ascetics (to name the most extreme of the ascetics), the fact is that people of every class and race went to them for advice or to beg their intercession. The pilgrim hungered to come in contact with the holy athletes of God.

Medieval Pilgrimage

One of the most unforgettable characters in English literature is Geoffrey Chaucer's Wife of Bath. She is also the most experienced of pilgrims as the prologue to *The Canterbury Tales* makes clear:

> Three times she travelled to Jerusalem;
> And many a foreign stream she had to stem;
> At Rome she'd been, and she'd been in Boulogne,
> In Spain at Santiago, and at Cologne.
> She could tell much of wandering by the way.[3]

The shrines visited by the Wife of Bath is a catalogue of the most important places in medieval Europe which drew the greatest number of pilgrims. Rome and Jerusalem, of course, had been the goal of pilgrims since the earliest centuries as we have already noted. Jerusalem was all the more important and impressive as a pilgrimage goal because it was in an area controlled by the "infidel" Muslims; as such it was the object of much concern for the medieval Christian and the energizing symbol for the medieval crusades as we shall presently see. To go to Jerusalem in the Middle Ages was not only a penitential act, but an act of some daring. Rome attracted pilgrims not only because of the tombs of the Apostles Sts. Peter and Paul, but because of the presence of such relics as the veil of Veronica with the imprint of the face of Christ and the spear of Longinus—both preserved in the basilica of St. Peter. The other places mentioned by Chaucer were extremely popular shrines with established pilgrimage routes leading to them: Santiago in Campostella (Spain) was the burial place of James the Apostle. The Cathedral of Cologne was thought to contain the bodies of the Three Kings who worshipped Christ at his birth. Boulogne-sur-mer was a famous Marian shrine in the Middle Ages. In the story, of course, the Wife of Bath was on her way to the shrine of St. Thomas à Becket at Canterbury, the most famous shrine site in all of England.

Pilgrimage in the Middle Ages was a highly complex part of the social fabric. Tourists today love to visit the town of Chartres to see its magnificent Gothic cathedral and its incomparable stained glass. The new cathedral was built in the twelfth century to house the relic of the Blessed Virgin Mary which the town had possessed since the time of Charlemagne: the tunic of the Virgin—*la saint chemise.* Pilgrims were encouraged to come to Chartres on four feasts of the Virgin when great trade fairs were held in the shadow of the cathedral. Piety and commerce were thus combined for the glory of God, the good of the town, and the general betterment of the populace. Pilgrimage was thus tightly intertwined with the social life of the town.

Pilgrimage in the Middle Ages was highly formalized. There were regular pilgrimage routes, seasons, and customs. From the early Middle Ages pilgrimage was a favorite penance imposed on public sinners as well as a form of self-imposed asceticism. Irish monasticism even knew of a form of lifelong pilgrimage as an extreme form of self-denial and ascetic renunciation, namely, the giving up of home and place for the love of God. In the high Middle Ages the decision to go on pilgrimage was considered to be a quasi-public act of religion. The pilgrims would receive a formal liturgical blessing from the church after which they could don an identifiable kind of clothing (a large hat, a staff, pouch, and heavy shoes) and carry a set of official documents (*testimoniales*) which attested their serious intentions and their goodness of life. There is a wonderfully crisp description of the pilgrim in the fourteenth-century classic English poem *Piers Plowman*:

> He bore a staff with a broad fillet,
> That like a winding weed wound about it.
> At his belt he bore a bowl and wallet.
> A hundred ampules hung at his hatband,
> Signs from Sinai and shells from Campostela,
> Many a cross on his cloak, and keys from Rome,
> And the vernicle in front, that friends might find it,
> And see by his signs what shrines he had been to.[4]

The church not only encouraged and supported the pilgrimage idea, but, on occasion, promoted new forms of pilgrimage to foster devotion or to display fidelity to the church. In 1300 Pope Boniface VIII declared a jubilee year—the first of the "Holy Years" which are now celebrated every quarter of a century in Rome—in which pilgrims were invited to Rome to visit the tombs of the Apostles Sts. Peter and Paul and the Roman basilicas. The response to this invitation was enormous. Dante, who must have visited Rome during the celebrations that year despite his intense dislike for the pope, uses the images of the pilgrim hordes to describe a crowd of damned souls in one of the *malebolge* of the *Inferno*:

> The sinners at the bottom were naked. On this side of the middle they faced us while the others walked in our direction though more quickly. It was like the great crowds in the Jubilee year when the Romans took steps so that people crossing the bridge walked either toward the castle on their way to St. Peter's or with their back to the castle toward the mount.[5]

Fifty years after this event Petrarch (1304–1374), the greatest poet in Italy in the generation after Dante, visited Rome in 1350 during the Jubilee celebrations. Despite the hazards of travel and the lamentable social conditions of Italy (the Plague of two years before wiped out nearly half the population of Italy) Petrarch was piously enthusiastic about his visit to the city as one of his familiar letters makes clear:

> How well it is for a Christian soul to behold the city which is like a heaven on earth, full of the precious bones and relics of the martyrs, and bedewed with the precious blood of those witnesses for the truth; to look upon the image of the saviour, venerable to all the world, to mark the footprints in the solid stone forever worthy of the worship of the nations . . . to roam from tomb to tomb rich with memories of the saints, to wander at will through the Basilicas of the apostles, with no other company than good thoughts.[6]

In the opening lines of Chaucer's *Canterbury Tales* the poet says emphatically that when the fair weather of spring comes, "folks *long* to go on pilgrimage." Pilgrimages were as common to certain medieval classes as vacations are to the middle classes today. It was part of the texture of life. People had innumerable shrines close to home to visit for a special religious need, for fulfillment of a vow, for a penance, or for an outing—a change of scenery.

For all of the going on pilgrimage we should also note that the idea of pilgrimage was a widely used concept and widely employed metaphor for the Christian life itself. It was one of the common motifs of Christian preaching that life itself was a pilgrimage.

Pilgrimage as a metaphor for the Christian life has a long history in Western Christianity. The Vulgate Bible, for example, gives warrant for such a usage by describing Christians (in Hebrews 11:13) as *"peregrini et hospites super terram"*—"pilgrims and sojourners on the earth." Both St. Augustine in *The City of God* and Pope Gregory the Great in the *Moralia*—books widely read and most influential in the Middle Ages—speak of the Christian life as a journey or pilgrimage leading to a heavenly goal. St. Thomas Aquinas, the great medieval theologian, calls the Holy Eucharist *esca viatorum* ("food for travellers"). Every student of medieval literature knows how important the pilgrimage motif was in medieval English prose and poetry. Even medieval plays which used the theme of the disciples on the road to Emmaus after the resurrection of Christ depicted the disciples as pilgrims; they even called the plays "Pilgrim Plays." The persistence of that tradition can be best noted by recalling that one of the most influential English Christian classics is the Puritan John Bunyan's *Pilgrim's Progress* (1677–1784), an allegorical work written at a time when actual pilgrimages had long disappeared in England as papist superstitions.

Of all the medieval writers it was Dante Aligheri (1265–1321) who most deeply explored the pilgrimage motif. It would be impossible to cite all of the structural and verbal usages which pertain to pilgrimage in *The Divine Comedy*. For our more modest purposes let us simply note the main thrust of the *Comedy*: the journey of an individual through the world of hell, up the mount of purgatory, and through the spheres of the heavens until the vision of God is attained. Even though this journey is described as being Dante's own, it is clear from the poem that Dante thought of it as an example for every person. To emphasize that journey Dante drew on a complex series of images, metaphors, figures, and symbols related to other journeys: the Exodus of the People of Israel from Egypt to the Holy Land; the actual pilgrimages of those who went from Europe to the Holy Land; the journey of the soul to God as described by the medieval theologian St. Bonaventure; the Augustinian notion of life as a journey toward the City of God. When Dante finally nears the end of his own poetic journey, as he sees the great crystal rose in which sit enthroned all of the saved around God, he instinctively reaches again for the imagery of the pilgrimage:

> And like a pilgrim refreshed
> by looking around the church of his vow,
> with hopes of telling of it again;
> So, taking my way through the living light
> I carried my eyes up and down, through the ranks,
> looking around again and again.[7]

It should be apparent that pilgrimage as an activity was open to abuse. At the most obvious level pilgrimage could be a convenient excuse for evasion of responsibility, flight from the

reach of the law, or as an opportunity for mischief or crimi-
nality. The *testimoniales* we alluded to earlier in this chapter
were, in effect, an official response to just such abuses. The
letters, issued by legal authorities of the church, were meant
to be letters of character for deserving pilgrims. In England,
after the twelfth century, one could be arrested as a vagabond
if one acted the pilgrim role without such letters.

More serious than this kind of abuse was the very real problem of theological or religious degradation of the pilgrimage
idea. Catholicism historically has been a religion of signs; one
of its salient characteristics has been its emphasis on the sacramental nature of religion. It understands Christ as an external
sign of God's love for the world and the church with its sacraments as signs of God's activity in Christ in the world. Because of this emphasis on the palpable realities of religion there
has always been a danger in Catholicism of a mechanical form
of religious manipulation replacing a sense of personal conversion and commitment. Catholic piety always ran the risk of
turning into magic, namely, the use of things to get desired
effects. Thus it was with something as innocuous as pilgrimages. There was always a danger that people could make the
pilgrimage act without thinking about the interior dispositions
necessary to make that act a religious one. The great Catholic
humanist Erasmus of Rotterdam (1466–1536), a bitter critic of
abuses and superstition in the church, put the matter succinctly
in a passage in one of the first books he wrote: "You could run
off to Rome or Compostela and buy up a million indulgences,
but in the last analysis there is no better way of reconciling
yourself with God than reconciling yourself with your brother."[8]

At the end of the Middle Ages there was a good deal of this
kind of criticism of pilgrimage. Much of it clustered around
those things which were also associated with pilgrimage: the
veneration of saints and their relics; the system of indulgences;
the mechanization of religious acts. *The Imitation of Christ*, a
fifteenth-century religious classic which came from the same
spiritual milieu that had nurtured the early Erasmus, chastised
those who wished always to go out and travel abroad but who
had little stomach for solitude, quiet, meditation, and stability
of life. This *devotio moderna*, as it was called, put a high pre-

mium on interior conversion, moral living, and a following of Christ in quiet and simplicity. This spirit surely contributed to the success of the Reformation. Martin Luther, the most medieval of the Protestant reformers, thought that pilgrimage was unnecessary and superfluous for Christian life, but when he wrote out his objections to it, one detects a grudging acceptance of the popularity of the idea and its deep place in the mores of European Christianity:

> If any man today wants to go on pilgrimages or esteems them highly, let him first go to his pastor or liege lord and tell him. If it turns out that his purpose is to do a good work, then let the pastor or the liege boldly trample the vow and the work underfoot as a satanic delusion, and tell the man to apply the money and effort required for the pilgrimage to fulfilling God's commandments, and to doing works a thousand times better than a pilgrimage, namely, meeting the needs of his family and his poor neighbors. But if his object is only to satisfy his curiosity and go sightseeing in city and country, let him have his way. If, however, he vowed a pilgrimage during an illness, the vow must be annulled and set aside.[9]

With the success of the Protestant Reformation pilgrimage became an almost exclusively Catholic (or Orthodox) spiritual activity, although varieties of pilgrimage—such as trips to the Holy Land—are very much a part of the contemporary Protestant experience. What has also happened is that the idea of pilgrimage has subtly changed under Protestant influence even in Catholic circles. Pilgrimages are seen more and more as acts of piety and devotion, but less and less as the fulfillment of vows or as acts of penance. The idea of pilgrimage as a way of life was still strong in the Orthodox church well into this century,[10] but as a Roman Catholic practice it has few devotees. The contemporary experience of pilgrimage has both continuities and sharp differences with the past tradition.

What has happened, of course, is that the medieval pilgrim has given way to the modern tourist. When one reflects on the sociology of pilgrimage, it is striking how similar social factors influenced its popularity as does the popularity of tourism: the desire to get away, the belief that the trip is good for one both mentally and physically (the medieval would have said spiritually), and the sheer thrill of seeing new things in new settings. Modern tour companies offer "packages" to whisk pious tourist/pilgrims to the Holy Land, Lourdes, or wherever in a manner which makes the pilgrimage less than penitential (except, perhaps, that one must eat airline food). Such trips combine an ancient impulse with a modern sensibility to create the tourist-pilgrim.

Pilgrimage Today: A Reflection

Anyone who has stood in St. Peter's square in Rome on any given day of the year can testify that pilgrimages are still very much alive in our time. Apart from the hordes of tourists who come to do the sights in a half day of frenzied activity, there are those groups of faithful Catholics of every race, color, class, and nationality who come to pray at St. Peter's tomb, arrange for a public audience in order to see the pope, and visit the other sites made famous in the history of Christianity. Similarly, we see annually the television reports of the pilgrims who crowd the streets of Jerusalem during Holy Week to trace the steps of Christ on the *Via dolorosa* or celebrate the Easter liturgy at the basilica of the Holy Sepulchre just as the pilgrims did in the days of Egeria.

Pilgrimage of other sorts also attract some people with the same urgency and the same piety today as they did hundreds of years ago. To go to the shrine of Our Lady of Guadalupe in Mexico or Our Lady of Lourdes in France is to see acts of penitential devotion or acts of faith for health that are as old as Christianity itself. To go to either of those sites (or others like them) is to step back—as any visitor who has been there will tell you—into a milieu of piety and devotion which has little resonance with the secular world in which most of us live.

Pilgrimage sites can also be the focal point for the widest and deepest aspirations of a people. The shrine of Our Lady of Czestochowa in Poland has been a center of Polish national consciousness and identity since the fourteenth century. Since the city itself has undergone anti-Polish sieges since the seventeenth century (from the Swedes, Russians, and French), the shrine takes on a special significance for the nation. The millions who go there on pilgrimage today can express both their deep faith and their silent antagonism to a government which seems out of sympathy for their own people. Pilgrimage in Poland is a way of protesting against alien and alienating forces in a society.

Despite the continuing popularity of pilgrimage there is no doubt that the character of pilgrimage is changing radically. No longer are pilgrimages arduous and dangerous journeys requiring immense personal commitments. Only the rare English pilgrim, for example, would cross the Channel and then walk to Rome today,[11] but that is what the Wife of Bath had done on a number of occasions. Nor is pilgrimage much utilized as a penitential act or a lifetime vocation as it was in the past. Both the changing style of religious practice and the character of technological society have made the very act of pilgrimage different.

If pilgrimage as an act has diminished in its rigor, the idea of pilgrimage, or, better, pilgrimage as metaphor, has not only been widely used today, but has become one of the primary metaphors for the church itself in these post-Vatican II days.

It is generally recognized that one of the more notable accomplishments of the Second Vatican Council (1962–1965) was to reorient the thinking of Catholics away from a notion of the church as an institutional monarchy to an idea of the church as a community of believers in Christ who are bound together by common Baptism, common sharing of the Eucharist, and their common profession of faith. To enhance that conception of the church, the conciliar documents made use of a whole range of images, symbols, and metaphors to describe the church: the church as the people of God; the church as sign; the church as mystery; and, finally, the pilgrim church.

There are a number of things that make the idea of the church as being a pilgrim church (or to personalize it: to think of everyone in the church as pilgrims) a very attractive one. In this regard we can think back to some of the observations we have made in earlier parts of this chapter.

First, there is an admirable egalitarian spirit connected with the idea of pilgrimage. The Moslems have a wonderful practice connected with the *Haj* to Mecca. At the start of the pilgrimage journey everyone puts aside his or her ordinary clothes in order to dress in a seamless white garment which is peculiarly designed for the pilgrim. Everyone dresses in that exact same manner. The idea behind this is so that everyone arrives in Mecca to worship as an absolute equal; nobody looks richer or better clothed. Everyone is the same. While Chaucer's pilgrims came from various classes (Chaucer, after all, saw the pilgrimage as a metaphor for human society), they travelled together in harmony of life and purpose. Their unity as pilgrims did not erase their diversity as individuals. The pilgrims to Canterbury included a pious parson, a venal monk, an exemplary knight, the ribald wife of Bath, and the rather modest poet himself.

When the church is viewed as a pilgrim church, it is a church which is neither clerical nor lay, male nor female, rich nor poor, European nor Asian. It is all of those and more in its complexity. Furthermore, those who are on pilgrimage are not perfect (those who are perfect have no need of pilgrimage); they seek perfection. Hence the pilgrim church is a church of sinners.

Pilgrimage implies both a voyage and a goal which is at the end of the voyage. The pilgrim church is *in via*. To use the old formulation: The pilgrim church is a people on the way. The pilgrims have not arrived at the goal because we have not arrived at the end time (*eschaton*) in vicissitudes of history and all the limitations of time. Hence we must be patient with the imperfections of the church while always being aware of their likelihood.

Finally, when we speak of the pilgrim church, we are also speaking, in effect, as members of the church as pilgrims. We have not arrived, we are not perfect, we are *in via*, we look to the end time in Christ, we are part of the pilgrimage group equally; we are part of that group in which sex, rank, sanctity, position, wit, and so on differentiate us, but do not give us more right to be one of the pilgrim band. Like all pilgrims, the pilgrim Christians get tired, irritated, discouraged, and, at times, disoriented. But, like all pilgrims, they think of the goal and they persevere. What the Second Vatican Council said of the pilgrim church is equally true of each of its members:

The Church "like a pilgrim in a foreign land, presses forward amid the persecutions of the world and the consolations of God," [St. Augustine, *Civ. Dei*, XVIII, 51, 2] announcing the cross and death of the Lord until He comes (cf. 1 Cor. 11:26). By the power of the risen Lord, she is given strength to overcome patiently and lovingly the afflictions and hardships which assail her from within and without, and to show forth in the world the mystery of the Lord in faithful though shadowed way, until at last it will be revealed in total splendor.[12]

Notes

1. *Egeria's Travels*, trans. and introduced by John Wilkinson (London, 1971), pp. 144–45. All citations are from this excellent and helpful edition.
2. Ibid., pp. 122–23.
3. Prologue to *The Canterbury Tales*, lines 463–67.
4. *Piers Plowman*, cited from the translation of H. W. Wells (London, 1935). Not all pilgrims were so poor. A fifteenth-century Italian went to the Holy Land with a retinue which included a doctor, four waiters, a chaplain, a purser, a cook and an under cook, a tailor, a barber, two trumpeters, a page, and a secretary.
5. *Inferno*, XVIII, 25–33. I have paraphrased the Italian. The castle is the Castel Sant' Angelo; the mount is the bank of the Tiber opposite the castle.
6. Petrarch, as quoted in John Demaray, *The Invention of Dante's Commedia* (New Haven, Conn., 1974), p. 10. The reference to the "image of the saviour" is to the veil of Veronica. Petrarch saw it and was so moved that he wrote a sonnet on the subject.
7. *Paradiso*, XXXI, 44–48; my translation.
8. *Enchiridion Militis Christiani*, cited from *The Essential Erasmus*, trans. John Dolan (New York, 1964), p. 91.
9. "An Appeal to the Ruling Class," in *Martin Luther: Selections from His Writings*, ed. John Dillenberger (Garden City, N.Y., 1961), p. 444.
10. The great Russian Orthodox spiritual classic *The Way of a Pilgrim*, which teaches the usage of the "Jesus Prayer," was written by an unknown pilgrim who lived a full life of pilgrimage in nineteenth-century Russia.
11. One who did was Hilaire Belloc, whose *The Path to Rome* (1902) is a classic account of such a walking pilgrimage.
12. Dogmatic Constitution on the Church, art. 8, in *The Documents of Vatican II*, ed. Walter M. Abbott, and Joseph Gallagher (New York, 1969), p. 24.

Readings and Trajectories

For the connection between early Christian asceticism and pilgrimage I was aided by Hans von Campenhausen's essay "The Ascetic Idea of Exile in Ancient and Early Medieval Monasticism," in *Tradition and Life in the Church* (Philadelphia, 1969), pp. 231–51.

Alan Kendall's *Medieval Pilgrims* (London, 1970) is a brief introduction to the whole subject of pilgrimage. A much fuller, if considerably older, work is Sidney Heath's *In the Steps of the Pilgrims* (New York, 1950). On the idea of pilgrimage the essential study is Jonathan Sumption's *Pilgrimage: An Image of Medieval Religion* (Totowa, N.J., 1975). Donald Howard's *Writers and Pilgrims: Medieval Pilgrimage Narratives and Their Posterity* (Berkeley, Calif., 1980), is a wonderfully readable work by an eminent Chaucer scholar.

On the use of pilgrimage in medieval literature there are two indispensable works: John Demaray, *The Invention of Dante's Commedia* (New Haven, Conn., 1974), and Donald Howard, *The Idea of the Canterbury Tales* (Berkeley, Calif., 1976). Both books are seminal studies and very suggestive for further directions and investigation. Both have exhaustive bibliographies. F. C. Gardiner's *The Pilgrimage of Desire: A Study of Theme and Genre in Medieval Literature* (Leiden, 1971) is a study of the intellectual and theological background of the so-called pilgrim plays. Its background chapters are useful for our purposes.

Pilgrimage was a favorite devotional exercise in the Orthodox church; from it came one of the great classics of Orthodox spirituality: the anonymous *The Way of a Pilgrim*, trans. by R. M. French (London, 1972).

For an anthropological and structural understanding of pilgrimage, see Victor Turner, *The Ritual Process* (Chicago, 1969); Victor and Edith Turner, *Image and Pilgrimage in Christian Culture* (Oxford, 1978).

There have been some recent attempts to understand pilgrimage in a spiritual way: pilgrimage of the self to God. As this concept pertains to literature and spirituality, see Mary Jo Weaver's "Quest for Self/Quest for God," in *The Bent World: Essays on Religion and Culture* (Chico, Calif., 1981), pp. 177–190. For a profound meditation on the contemporary significance of pilgrimage as a metaphor for the Christian life one should read the novels of Walker Percy, especially his *Love in the Ruins* (1971) with its bewildered hero, Doctor Thomas More, who desires no more than to be a pilgrim and, in Percy's words, "a sovereign wayfarer."

4

WARRIORS

When this work was still in outline, a friendly critic wrote to ask me to omit this chapter on the warrior. He wrote that a "Christian or Catholic warrior is a contradiction in terms." It is easy to understand the sentiment of my friend given the current intellectual climate and even easier to sympathize with it. The criticism, nonetheless, is misplaced. The fact is, as we shall see, the image of the Christian warrior has a long history going back to the earliest centuries of Christianity. However complex the Christian attitude toward war and fighting may have been (and it is very complex), military imagery is deeply rooted in the Christian consciousness. In the Middle Ages the image of the knight was not only praised, but held up as a model of sanctity as the immense popularity of the cult of the semilegendary St. George (of dragon fame) shows. Even in our own day we sing "Onward Christian Soldiers!", donate monies to the Salvation Army, have friends who join the Knights of Columbus or the Legion of Mary, and admire the military discipline of the Jesuits.

The New Testament is of little assistance with respect to the place of the military in the Christian scheme of things. St. John the Baptist demanded that soldiers act in righteousness (cf. Luke 3:14), but did not order them to leave the ranks of the military. Jesus did not deal with the question of the military directly, but had much to say on the avoidance of any violence. St. Paul used military language for rhetorical purposes in his letters. These texts would be, in the course of time, important spiritual texts for spiritual writers and theologians:

> Put God's armour on so as to be able to resist the devil's tactics. For it is not against human enemies that we have to struggle but against the Sovereignties and the Powers who originate in the darkness of the world, the spiritual army of evil in the heavens. That is why you must rely on God's armour, or you will not be able to put up any resistance when the worst happens or have enough resources to hold your ground. So stand your ground with truth buckled around your waist, and integrity for a breastplate, wearing for shoes on your feet the eagerness to spread the gospel of peace; and always carrying the shield of faith so that you can use it to put out the burning arrows of the evil one. And then you must accept salvation from God to be your helmet and receive the word of God from the Spirit to use as a sword. (Eph. 6:11–17)

That passage, a mosaic of texts from the Old Testament, does not reflect actual experience but imagery and ideas taken from the biblical tradition and the commonplaces of Paul's culture. The same could be said of the early writings of Christianity in the postbiblical period. Before the later part of the second century there is no evidence that Christians were in the military or that Christian writers had any concern about the problems of the military. It is only after A.D. 170 that we have any evidence that there were Christians serving in the Roman army.

What did the church think about Christians serving in the military services of the Roman Empire? That question has been studied a great deal by scholars and their conclusions are of both historical and ethical interest. In the first place, there is no evidence that any Christian writer called into question the right of the empire to have an army. Indeed, it was assumed that an army was necessary for civil life. Granted the legitimacy of the army for the needs of the society, it was, nonetheless, the opinion of the early Christian writers that Christians ought not to serve in that army. That was a standard opinion of almost all Christian writers until after the Peace of Constantine. The arguments for this position were not based on a reflexive antimilitarism nor was there any attempt to extend the arguments to non-Christians. We might look at the reasons against military service offered by Tertullian at the end of the second century since his reasoning was not atypical:

(a) The Gospel says that no person can serve two masters and Christians are called on to serve Christ alone.

(b) Christians are called upon to avoid any shedding of blood and any acts of violence.

(c) By choosing to be a Christian a person chooses not to participate in the larger pagan culture. If Christians should not frequent the law courts, then *a fortiori* they ought not serve in the military.

(d) Soldiers, in the course of their ordinary duties, are called upon to do things which for a Christian would be an act of idolatry such as serve as a temple guard or eat meats which were first offered in pagan sacrifice.[1]

In the century after Tertullian (especially after the Decian persecution of A.D. 250) there would be the added problem that even common soldiers would have to pledge fealty to the god-emperors or to demonstrate visibly their loyalty by acts connected with Roman religious practice. This was considered totally unacceptable by Christians who were more and more to be found in the ranks of the military. One witness to the gravity of this problem is the large number of soldier-martyrs who are venerated in the church who died in the late third and early fourth centuries. While many of their legends are historically unreliable, they did reflect a factual core which reflects the problem.

According to one legend, St. Maurice (who was an Egyptian and depicted in art as a Negro) and the Theban legion, all Christian, refused the emperor Maximian's order to assault the Gauls near Matigny on Lake Geneva. Maurice, the ranking officer, refused both to offer the customary sacrifices before the attack or to attack because he did not want to slay innocent people. For his disobedience Maurice and the entire legion were put to death. A good deal of the story is exaggerated (there is no evidence that an entire company of soldiers was executed), but behind it rests (a) a refusal to do pagan religious duties and (b) the unwillingness to shed innocent blood or to do violence. We might note that the cult of St. Maurice was widespread in certain parts of Europe (he is the patron of the papal Swiss Guard) and immortalized by the brilliant painting "Saint Maurice and the Theban Legion," done by El Greco in 1584 and now in the Escorial.

The legend of St. Maurice is not unlike that of other soldier-martyrs (Sts. Theodore, George, Demitius, Sebastian, and others) who refused to sacrifice to the pagan gods. Others were like Maximilian who was executed in A.D. 295 for refusing induction into the army of Rome: *"Non possum militare; Christianus sum"*—"I cannot serve in the army; I am a Christian." In the fourth century St. Martin of Tours (A.D. 316–397) became a Christian while serving in the military, but then asked for a release from service on grounds of what we would call today "conscientious objection." This plea went unanswered and Martin spent time in military imprisonment before he could be released to pursue the ascetic life of a Christian monk.

St. Martin lived after the Peace of Constantine. In general, however, the tension between the Christian vocation and the military life had lessened after the decline of official support for the pagan gods. In the early fifth century Augustine could write to a frontier commander comparing his lonely life as an outpost against the barbarians to that of the ascetic in his solitude. By the sixth century—as the San Vitale mosaics in Ravenna so amply testify—it was an honorable thing to put the Christian Chi/Rho on the shields of soldiers. For all of the amelioration of the tension between church and state there was still a certain lingering Christian ambivalence toward soldiery which has never been eradicated. Tertullian's problem of the "two masters" had been solved by the accession of Christian emperors; pagan rites and duties had been purged from the military roster of duties in time. There remained only the question of violence and the shedding of blood—a question to which ready answers seemed unconvincing as even current debates over pacifism and military strategy show. Between the end of the Roman Empire and the rise of the cities in the West there was a great span of time, a span marked by fierce warfare, bloody combat, and unchecked violence. It is against that background that a new understanding of the Christian soldier would emerge as both a reality and a powerful spiritual image.

Miles Christianus—The Christian Knight

We know from the history of literature that the early Middle Ages prized military valor and made heroes of the warrior. That is the clear message of *Beowulf* and the *Nibelungenlied*. We also know that the church, while accepting the legitimacy of self-defense and admitting, with St. Augustine, that there were conditions when a "just war" might be fought, had a tradition, rooted in the sayings of Jesus, which held out nonviolence as an ideal and the taking of life an immoral act. There has been—and continues to be—a tension between the ideal of Jesus's teaching on nonviolence and the practical needs of Christians who live in an imperfect world. One attempt to lessen that tension was the medieval idea of knights who would ply their martial skills in the service of the Gospel. Beginning in the eleventh century the church would hold out the ideal of those who would take up arms in defense of the widow, the orphan, and the proverbial damsel in distress.

By blending together the teutonic love for war with the Christian ethic of service and personal morality, the medieval church channeled the violence of society into the *beau idéal* of chivalry, courtesy, and knightly valor. The knight, in the words of Chaucer, "loved chivalry,/truth, honor, freedom, and all courtesy."[2] The church not only proposed this ideal, but developed a whole series of liturgical and legal strategies to legitimate it as a worthy sacred state in life.

One entered the ranks of the knights with the observation of the same solemnity when one married or took vows as a religious. The would-be knight was expected to maintain a night-long vigil alone in a chapel with only his new weapons to accompany him. In the morning there was a symbolic bath and a clothing with white raiment. In a solemn service the presiding church officer blessed the sword, lance, and other military accouterments before the young knight received them from the hands of an elder knight. The religious significance of these rites is not hard to spot. In the rite of passage from squire to knight there are significant parallels with the sacrament of Baptism and its attendant symbolism of rebirth. The young knight was, as it were, reborn into a new state of life.

The knight was expected to perform heroic deeds as models like Roland, Lancelot, Perceval, and other knightly paradigms from the period suggest. The highest deed of heroism that a knight could perform in the eyes of the church was to fight for the defense of the faith. For those who fought and died there was the added glory of being considered a martyr. The most perfect way to defend the faith was to go on Crusades to rescue the Holy Places of Jerusalem from the Moslems.

We have neither the space nor the aim to outline the history of the Crusades in this book. Their history is complex. For our purposes it is enough to note that from 1096 when Pope Urban II called the First Crusade there went forth a whole series of armies—some successful, some pathetically inept (the Peasant's Crusade), others bizarre (the Children's Crusade), and yet others which were simply semiorganized exercises in rapine, pillage, and murder. It is also clear that when the First Crusade was preached, there was a genuine outpouring of enthusiasm in the West. When the crusading knights finally set out for the Holy Land, they were motivated by a plethora of reasons: glory, power, love of war, curiosity, and real religious concern. There is no doubt that the Crusades triggered a deeply spiritual impulse among Latin Christians. Many saw the Crusade as a form of military pilgrimage; as a way of atoning for their sins and glorifying the name of God. The idea of going to the Holy Land in order to redeem the places sanctified by the life of Christ combined the idea of military campaign and penitential pilgrimage. Jehan de Joinville (1225–1317), the biographer of the crusader monarch St. Louis IX of France, described his own Crusade departure in these words:

> On the day I left Joinville I sent for the abbot of Cheminon, who was said to be the wisest and worthiest monk of the Cistercian Order. This same abbot of Cheminon gave me my pilgrim's staff and scrip. I left Joinville immediately after—never to enter my castle again until my return from overseas—on foot, with my legs bare and dressed in my shirt. Thus attired I went to Blécourt and Saint-Urbain, and to other places where there are holy relics. And all the way to Blécourt and Saint-Urbain I never once let my eyes turn back to Joinville for fear my heart might be filled with longing at the thought of my lovely castle and the two children I had left behind.[3]

The vow to go on a Crusade was a serious one. It afforded the taker the same indulgences as did the pilgrimage; it also brought stern obligations. Willful failure to "take up the cross" (i.e., to wear the Crusader's cross on one's cloak) merited excommunication. After the First Crusade the popes often cajoled reluctant sovereigns to go on Crusades with monotonous regularity, just as they reminded (or, at times, threatened) them with the excommunications reserved to those who promised to go on Crusades and then did not fulfill the promise.

The actual conduct of the Crusader knights was often at total variance with the ideal of chivalry and Christian knighthood so often associated with the idea of the Crusader. Indeed, after the first flush of enthusiasm there was intense criticism of the Crusades from every quarter of Europe. This was especially true in the thirteenth and fourteenth centuries. By the thirteenth century there was not only secular reluctance to take up the Crusader cross but increasing instances where the papacy used the crusading ideals for what were ignoble ends. The most infamous perversion was the corruption of the Crusader ideal into an excuse for revenge or self-aggrandizement. "The Prince of the new Pharisees," wrote Dante bitterly of Pope Boniface VIII just after the last Christian stronghold fell in the Holy Land, "Being at war near the Lateran, not with Saracen or Jew, since all his enemies were Christian. . . ."[4]

For all of the excesses in practice the ideal of the Christian knight exercised a strong hold on the imagination of Christian Europe both in the time of the Crusades and long after. The ideal of the Christian knight manifested itself two ways in Christian culture: in the military religious orders which tried to institutionalize the ideals and in spiritual imagery which took over the ideals of the Christian knight into Christian ascetical and spiritual literature.

After the capture of Jerusalem by the Christians in 1099 a group of knights began to take care of the sick and wounded in an informal manner in Jerusalem. From this collective act of informal charity the knights adopted a monastic rule with the profession of the three traditional monastic vows of poverty, chastity, and obedience. This order of "Knights Hospitaller" (more fully described as "Knights of the Order of the Hospital of St. John of Jerusalem") was the first of over a dozen different religious orders that combined military and monastic values. The most famous of the military orders was that of the Knights Templar (so named because their headquarters was at the putative site of Solomon's Temple in Jerusalem), who devoted themselves to the defense of Holy Land borders, the manning of fortifications, and as convoy guards for pilgrims coming from the West.

The Templars, Hospitallers,[5] and other military orders were a resounding success with growth of houses both in the Holy Land and in Europe. The military orders offered a way of living which combined the romantic lifestyle of the cavalier and knight with the otherworldly ideal of the monk; a life which combined chivalry, *cortesia*, bravery, and Christian moral and spiritual ideals. The military orders stood in sharp contrast to those undisciplined hordes who so often dishonored the name of the crusaders. St. Bernard of Clairvaux (1090–1153)—himself an indefatigable preacher of crusade—praised them in both writing and sermon:

> They live in a community, soberly and in joy, without wife and children. And to reach evangelical perfection, they live in the same house, in the same manner, without calling anything their own, solicitous to preserve the unity of spirit in the bonds of peace. . . . They despise mimes, jugglers, story tellers, dirty songs, performances of buffons—all these they regard as vanities and inane follies.[6]

The military monastic orders reflected very strongly the biases and tastes of the Crusader culture. History has shown them to be so much a part of that culture that they are today only a nostalgic (or not so nostalgic) memory. The Templars, in one of the most curious and savage episodes of late medieval history, were suppressed with violence; all their goods were confiscated; their leaders burned for heresy. One is almost tempted in that entire gruesome episode to see the justice of the remark of Jesus that those who live by the sword also die from it.

What of the knightly ideal itself? It would be impossible to deal with it in any detail. The idea of the Christian knight is so deeply imbued in the Catholic historical consciousness that it could be traced like a leitmotif from the Renaissance (cf. the immensely popular book by the pacifist Erasmus entitled *The Handbook of the Christian Knight*) through the Counter-Reformation (cf. the *esprit* of the Jesuits) down to modern times (cf. the language and symbolism of a fraternal group like the Knights of Columbus). For our purposes let us think about the theme of the Christian knight in two canonized saints; one a rather famous warrior and the other a most unlikely one: St. Joan of Arc and St. Francis of Assisi.

Francis of Assisi

It seems almost wilfully perverse to speak of St. Francis of Assisi (1182–1226) under the rubric of the warrior or the knight. Is not St. Francis the saint of flowers, birds, and mystical kindness to the humble creatures of the world? Did not St. Francis walk unarmed into the camp of the Sultan at Damietta crossing the Crusader lines in the process? Is not, in short, St. Francis the complete antithesis of everything that war, warriors, and the military spirit stand for? The answer to that question is yes. And no.

The first thing to remember about St. Francis is that before his adult religious conversion he had fought in a war. In 1202 Francis went into battle against the Perugians in the company of his fellow citizens of Assisi. He was a member of the *compania dei cavalieri*, the elite group of middle class citizens who were able to afford the expenses of procuring armor and maintaining a horse. Despite his elite status, Francis was captured in battle, held for ransom, and until that ransom was paid, lived in a Perugian prison. For Francis, as for many people, the crisis of defeat and the humiliation of capture were also moments of grace. All of his early biographers credit the Perugia skirmish as the impetus for his turn to a greater awareness of God in his life.

When Francis returned to Assisi, he still wished to live the life of a knight. On the eve of his departure for Apulia to enter the service of a famous fighting lord, however, he had a dream which turned out to be prophetic. Francis dreamed of a glorious hall filled with all of the trappings of war and knighthood. A voice told him that all of the fine equipment would be useful for him and his followers in the many victories they would win. Francis interpreted the dream as a favorable augury for his career in Apulia. He never got to Apulia. His early biographers saw the dream in quite a different light:

> ... It is indeed quite fitting that mention be made of arms in the beginning and it is quite opportune that arms should be offered to the soldier about to engage one strongly armed, that like another David he might free Israel from the long-standing reproach of its enemies in the name of the Lord God of Hosts.[7]

In the life of St. Francis we have the spiritualization of the knightly ideal and, in a different sense, its antitype. His espousal of Lady Poverty was in close imitation of the chivalric pledge of fidelity to a chosen lady. Francis on occasion would liken his brethren to the Knights of the Round Table. He used the chivalric language of courtesy; indeed he appropriated the word *cortesia* from chivalry in order to give it a meaning in purely spiritual terms. His visit to Sultan Malik al Kamil in 1219 was in startling contrast to the armed Crusaders who ringed Damietta. Francis had to pass through the Crusader lines in order to see the sultan.

This spiritualization of the knightly ideal should not surprise us. Not only did St. Francis live in a culture where the knightly and chivalric ideals have a prized value, but he knew those values at first hand and, for a time, sought to live his life according to the knightly code. Beyond that, Francis, from his youth, knew and loved the Provençal culture which so commonly, both in song and literature, praised the chivalric ideal. For a young man of Francis's class and station admiration for the knightly ideal was a commonplace. It was natural enough for Francis to borrow the language of the Christian knight and the motifs of chivalric literature. What is more interesting is the extent to which he could change and transcend those ideals in the peculiar vision he had of Christian service and love. By the end of his life the courtesy toward all of God's creation, the struggle with the world, and the ideals of spiritual combat had been replaced by a person who completely identified with

Christ. Francis of Assisi, at the end of his life, had passed beyond the model of the Christian knight to that of an *alter Christus*.

It should be noted in passing that this spiritualization of the military code was not peculiar to St. Francis of Assisi. Another great saint, often identified as a soldier, St. Ignatius of Loyola (1491–1556), transmuted his military background into both a vocabulary and a worldview after his religious conversion. This is not the place to consider the military imagery associated with the Jesuit Order which Ignatius founded and ruled as its first "Father General," but simply to point to one of the earliest biographical remembrances of the saint, Father Gonzalez de Camara's recollection of Ignatius based on the saint's oral description of his life. One example will suffice to show the transmutation of the military man into the dedicated religious. When he arrived in Montserrat as a young convert, determined to go to Jerusalem as a pilgrim, his mind was "filled with the adventures of Amadis of Gaul and other such books" so that he decided to keep watch over his arms all night in a chapel as the knights of old did except his new arms were the "armor of Christ," which in this case was his pilgrim's gown and staff, and small drinking gourd.[8] In one symbolic transformation Ignatius combined the calling of pilgrim, knight, and new zealot for Christ. Behind his symbolic act in Montserrat was a millennium of Christian symbolism.

Joan of Arc

The life of Joan of Arc (1412–1431) stands in sharp contrast to that of St. Francis of Assisi. He was converted from the life of warrior while her conversion made her—improbably, given her sex, social status, and the age in which she lived—not only a soldier and knight but a military commander. Joan of Arc's precise calling (as she understood it) was to embrace the military life in its fullest, while the calling of St. Francis, as his prophetic dream demonstrated, was to transform his early life into a highly spiritual one in which only the language of knighthood remained.

The basic facts of Joan's short life are well known. Born to a peasant family in Domremy, a village in the Champagne area of France, Joan, around the age of fourteen, began to hear the voices of saints speaking to her. They insisted that she was to help drive the English from France (the Hundred Years War was in progress at this time) and see that the Dauphin be crowned the king of France. Some correct prophecies got her an audience with the Dauphin, who, impressed enough with her powers and her sincerity, allowed her some troops to help raise the English siege of the city of Orleans, a task she undertook with success. In the same year (1429) she tasted victory once again and also saw the Dauphin crowned as King Charles VII in the ancient cathedral at Rheims.

The following year her military successes were nonexistent. She was captured by the Burgundians (who were in league with the English) and handed over to the English forces. Joan went on trial for her life at Rouen before a church court presided over by the bishop of Beauvais, Pierre Cauchon. Charged with witchcraft and heresy, Joan made a spirited defense in a court whose prejudices were open and whose verdict was already decided. After a short and ambiguous period of recantation Joan resumed her male clothing (the issue of her clothing was paramount in the mind of the judges) for which she was declared a lapsed heretic. Handed over to the secular powers, she was burned at the stake in the public square of Rouen on May 30, 1431. Witnesses say that she died a rather slow and agonizing death, crying out at the last for holy water and uttering the word "Jésu." Twenty-five years later Pope Callistus III reversed the church condemnation of Rouen and declared Joan of Arc innocent of the charges brought against her. In 1920 Pope Benedict XV declared her a saint.

Joan of Arc remains an enigma for the historian and an inspiration for the artist. Her life seems so improbable, her actions so puzzling, and her character so singular that she has been interpreted as everything from a lesbian protofeminist to *the* symbol of French civic pride and patriotism. Her life has been a rich source of inspiration for the literary artist (Paul Claudel, Vita Sackville-West, George Bernard Shaw), the composer (Honegger and Verdi), as well as the film director both before (De Mille) and after the advent of sound (Bresson, Rossellini).

What is ultimately fascinating about Joan of Arc is how later generations interpreted her and her life to fit certain ideological needs. French social *arrivistes* tried to claim kinship with her to establish their ancestry, suffragettes saw her as the worthy symbol of their own modern crusade, while Catholic conservatives regarded her as a fountainhead of patriotism and a staunch defender of the monarchy.

Whatever be the enigmatic character of Joan's *persona*, one thing is very clear: She saw her own life as a warrior in terms of a direct call from God. To be a soldier was not a career for her; it was a vocation. She felt called by God, she thought her battles just and her actions correct. They were in conformity to the voices of the saints which spoke to her. But the very fact that she felt a divine call to fight in war creates an ambiguity. Nobody could ever claim that the undivided attention to the acquisition of wealth could be done in the imitation of St. Francis, but it is possible to follow Joan's example of warring in the name of patriotism under the aegis of divine protection in very ambivalent ways. It is pertinent here to remember that during the Second World War both the Nazi-backed Vichy government and the Gaullist government in exile called upon the example of Joan of Arc to justify their struggle and give symbolic weight to it.

There is, at the very heart of the notion of a Christian warrior, a paradox and an ambiguity. No matter how noble the cause or justified the end, the means of "battle," "military action," etc., seems somehow at variance with what the Gospel ultimately means. One may have to go to war, but to add the adjective "Christian" war seems discordant. It has been truly said that the church tolerates war and canonizes peace. It is for that reason that in the Christian tradition the metaphorical use of military imagery (e.g., among the Jesuits) seems so much more acceptable than the actual exercise of arms even for a Christian ideal (as, for example, in the Crusades).

The ambiguity at the heart of the notion of a "Christian warrior" can be noted in the life of Joan herself. When she went into battle, Joan carried a large white standard of her own design. It was white, with fleur-de-lys sewn on it, and bearing the words "Jhesu-Maria." At her trial Joan said that she carried the standard both to rally her troops and *to avoid using a weapon* since she did not want to kill. Despite her armor, her sword, and her willingness to lead troops into the thick of battle (she was wounded in her first engagement at Orleans) Joan was proudly insistent that she had never killed. Theoretically the tension between Christian peace and warmaking was eased in the person of the Crusader; in practice, as the case of Joan of Arc makes clear, that was never totally true.

Christ as Peacemaker—Christ as Revolutionary

Our age has been just as ready to embrace the *Gott mit Uns* ("God with us") philosophy as any other. An examination of old magazines, dated newsreels, or old movies will turn up countless examples of the clergy blessing weapons, presiding over ceremonies on the eve of battle, or participating in those rites by which we hallow our "Fallen Ones" and keep the military spirit alive for future needs. Until the Lord comes again, one presumes, every national group will succumb on occasion to the temptation of identifying one's foreign policy with the will of God. It is a clear, if lamentable, lesson of history that it should be so. The issue is all the more complicated by the fact that in specific instances it seems cruelly indifferent not to do battle. In the face of something of the magnitude of the Jewish Holocaust, for instance, it is hard to articulate a total pacifist stance.

The century in which we live has been one of unparalleled violence; one wonders whether future historians may not refer to it, for all its technical accomplishments, as a Dark Age. Our two world wars slaughtered millions of people. We have developed an array of sophisticated systems of weaponry which are capable of annihilating the entire planet. Government-sponsored terrorism in eras like Stalin's Russia, Hitler's Germany, and Pol Pot's Cambodia have all contributed a horrible new lexicon to modern social discourse: death camps, genocide, holocaust, gulags, etc. It may be that the sheer magnitude of the killing done in our century explains the general reserve with which military imagery gets used in contemporary spirituality and theology.

In the last generation the church has been acutely aware of

the problems of war and peace. The church's official pronouncements and unofficial movements have all turned to a better understanding of peace and a greater resistance to military usage. The "Christian Warrior" is not a phrase which one encounters with any frequency today. Apart from a militaristic fringe on both the right and the left there is very little attraction to the traditional military imagery of spirituality. The single significant exception to this generalization, as we shall see, is the current fascination with revolutionary violence and its relationship to theologies of revolution.

The general principles that underpin the official Catholic attitude toward war can best be seen by a consideration of the teachings of the Second Vatican Council. The Pastoral Constitution on the Church and the Modern World (*Gaudium et Spes*)[9] recognized that there would always be war in this sin-filled world. But, that being true, the church still had the obligation to work against war and to see that, in the tragic event of war, the basic canons of the natural laws are not broken. The council insisted that governments make "humane provisions" for those who were conscientious objectors to war. It also insisted that armies were for the defense of a country and not for the acquisition of advantage or territory. Those who were in the armed forces of a country should "regard themselves as agents of security and freedom on behalf of their people. As long as they fulfill this role properly they are making a genuine contribution to the establishment of peace" (art. 79).

In that limited sense the Second Vatican Council accepted the legitimacy of defensive war. Beyond that need the council had some very definite principles which it enunciated about war in a modern setting:

Total War
Any act of war aimed indiscriminately at the destruction of entire cities or extensive areas along with their populations is a crime against God and man himself. It merits unequivocal and unhesitating condemnation.

The unique hazard of modern warfare consists in this: It provides those who possess modern scientific weapons with a kind of occasion for perpetrating such abominations. Moreover, through a certain inexorable chain of events, it can urge men to the most atrocious decisions (art. 80).

The Arms Race

... The arms race is an utterly treacherous trap for humanity, and one which injures the poor to an intolerable degree. It is much to be feared that if this race persists, it will eventually spawn all the lethal ruin whose path it is now making ready. (art. 81)

Commitment to Peace

It is our clear duty, then, to strain every muscle as we work for the time when all war can be completely outlawed by international consent. This goal undoubtedly requires the establishment of some universal public authority acknowledged as such by all, and endowed with effective power to safeguard, for the sake of all, security, regard for justice, and respect for rights. (art. 82)

Causes of War

Wars thrive on these [causes of dissension], especially on injustice. Many of these causes stem from excessive economic inequalities and from excessive slowness in applying the needed remedies. Other causes spring from a quest for power and from a contempt for personal rights. If we look for deeper explanations, we can find them in human jealousy, distrust, pride, and other egoistic passions. (art. 83)

A good deal of the discussion about peace and war orbits around wars fought between the superpowers (e.g., the United States vs. the USSR) with all of the implications of atomic weaponry or those wars which have pitted developed nations or their surrogates against the indigenous population (the United States vs. Vietnam; the Soviet Union vs. Afghanistan). In the theological circles of most major Christian communities there is a rapidly growing consensus that large-scale wars between developed nations are becoming morally unthinkable precisely because of the globally lethal character of modern weaponry. Nor has war between developed nations and insurgent forces captured the patriotic imagination of people. Indeed, the involvement of the United States in southeast Asia may be one of the single most important factors in the shift away from any sympathetic use of military imagery in religious discourse. Indeed, it seems that the contemporary theological scene is more hostile to any sympathetic discussion of war or violence than at any other time in recent memory. Conscientious objection, once a lonely choice for the very few, is now discussed and—more importantly—more openly admired as an option for a committed Christian. It is also relatively new to see the explosion of serious religious and theological reflection on issues of peace.

Ironically enough, as this serious discussion of peace grows in importance in contemporary Catholicism, there is another Catholic voice which wishes to reexamine the whole question of the relationship of violence to Christian life. Some liberation theologians, especially those who come from Latin America and other parts of the third world, put this question: When does the sociopolitical situation of a country become so oppressive and inimical to human values that armed resistance or armed revolution becomes not only an option, but a duty? Understand that this question is asked not within the framework of a natural right but from the perspective of the *Christian* imperative. To put the question another way: Does not the Gospel premise of human liberation, freedom as a child of God, and the right to hope in the future carry with it a right to resist the inhuman, the demonic, and the enslaving? Should not the Gospel applied to a concrete situation permit or demand resistance if all other avenues are closed?

We must not be too quick to dismiss these questions as attempts to rationalize violence in the name of Christian theology. The medieval theologians, after all, permitted the overthrow of absolute despots in certain circumstances. The questions that arise when theologians propose or accede to violent answers to societal questions include these:

(a) Can violence even in a just cause be squared with the fundamental claims of Jesus in the Gospel?

(b) Does not the theological advocacy of violence reflect more a fascination with the Marxist call for revolution than the traditional Christian claim that there is power in suffering and the cross?

(c) Is there a real danger that violence will beget more violence, thus starting a never-ending spiral of death and destruction? Desperate solutions to desperate problems often provide less than satisfactory solutions in the long run.

These are very vexatious questions. From the relatively snug material position of North America we might also want to be a bit cautious in our answers. Furthermore—and to be fair—many of the most prominent liberation theologians believe that armed struggle may be necessary in certain extreme situations but in general, and certainly as the ideal, the force of nonviolence is what they preach. Such theologians are aware that violence can be a powerfully addictive drug. It is also easy to romanticize those who do violence. We have all seen those posters depicting Christ as a guerilla fighter with a bandelero of cartridges across his chest. Others will recall the pictures of the revolutionary Ernesto "Che" Guevera (1928–1967) who was made into a saint by some on the left. Guevera came from a middle class family and had a degree in medicine. He gave that up for revolutionary activity only to be shot down in Bolivia while operating with a dedicated, but inept, guerrila band. His life was made to sound like that of the saints of old: dedicated, abstemious, scornful of comforts or wealth, ready to follow his destiny of serving the poor, martyred.

But the church is giving genuine witness for the poor in Latin America, a witness, as we have seen, which has produced its share of martyrs. One of the most prominent of the liberation theologians has profiled the witnesses—the saints—which the contemporary church needs. He reaches for the ancient language of the Christian warrior, but it is clear that both the weapons and the strategies are to be spiritual. While his vocabulary is contemporary, his ideas are as old as the words of St. Paul with which we began this chapter:

> ... There are hardly any political and militant saints. In the process of liberation, the conditions are created for another type of sanctity: in addition to struggling against one's passions (a

permanent task), one struggles against the mechanisms of exploitation and the forces that destroy the community. Here, more real and difficult virtues emerge: solidarity with one's class, participation in community decisions, loyalty to the solutions which are defined, the overcoming of hatred against those who are agents of the mechanisms of impoverishment, the capacity to see beyond the immediate present and to work for the society which is not yet visible and will perhaps never be enjoyed. This new type of asceticism, if it is to keep the hearts pure and be led by the spirit of the beatitudes, has demands and renunciations of its own.[10]

Notes

1. I am indebted here to Stephen Gero's *"Miles Gloriosus:* The Christian and Military Service According to Tertullian," *Church History* 39 (1970): 285–98, where the appropriate texts of Tertullian are cited and studied.
2. Prologue to *The Canterbury Tales*, lines 45–46. At Chaucer's time the ideal knight was only a nostalgic memory. Chaucer's portrait has an air of elegy about it.
3. Jehan de Joinville, cited in Joshua Prawer, *The World of the Crusaders* (New York and London, 1972), pp. 111–12. Note the blending of the pilgrim and crusader motifs.
4. *Inferno* XXVII, 85–88. Dante is referring to Boniface's war with the Colonna family of Rome who were trying to depose the pope.
5. The Hospitallers now exist as the Knights of Malta with headquarters in Rome.
6. St. Bernard of Clairvaux, as quoted in Prawer, p. 116.
7. The *Vita Prima* of Thomas of Celano, in *Omnibus of Sources: Saint Francis of Assisi*, ed. M. Habig (Chicago, 1973), p. 233.
8. *St. Ignatius' Own Story As Told to Luis Gonzales de Camara*, trans. William Young, S.J. (Chicago, 1980; reprint ed. of 1956 publication).
9. To be found in *The Documents of Vatican II*, ed. Walter M. Abbott, pp. 199–308.
10. Leonardo Boff, "The Need for Political Saints," *Cross Currents*, Winter 1980/81, pp. 375–76.

Readings and Trajectories

The literature on Christians and military service in the Roman Empire is very large. There is a fine survey of it in J. Fontaine, "Christians and Military Service in the Early Church," *Concilium*, 1965, pp. 107–19. I also found the following very helpful: R. H. Bainton, "The Early Church and War," *Harvard Theological Review*, 1946, pp. 189–211. Adolf Harnack's *Militia Christi: The Christian Religion and the Military in the First Three Centuries* (Philadelphia, 1980) is a reprint of a classic with a very informative introduction. Hans von Campenhausen's essay "Christians and Military Service in the Early Church," in *Tradition and Life in the Church* (London and Philadelphia, 1968), pp. 160–71, is a very succinct and helpful survey. C. John Cadoux's *The Early Christian Attitude towards War* (New York, 1982) is a reprint of the 1919 classic.

R. W. Southern's *The Making of the Middle Ages* (London and New York, 1953) is essential for the background of the Crusades. The standard history in English is Sir

Steven Runciman's three-volume *A History of the Crusades* (Cambridge, 1968). I also found much helpful material and bibliography in: Joshua Prawer's *The World of the Crusaders* (New York, 1972); Anthony Bridges's *The Crusades* (London and New York, 1980); Martin Erbstösser's richly illustrated *The Crusades* (New York, 1979). For background on the medieval idea of the military one can consult A. V. B. Norman's *The Medieval Soldier* (New York, 1971). Stephen Howarth's *The Knights Templar: Christian Chivalry and the Crusades 1095–1314* (New York, 1982) is an important contribution.

Edward Lucie-Smith's *Joan of Arc* (New York, 1976) is a usable biography of the saint. Marina Werner's *Joan of Arc: The Image of Female Heroism* (New York, 1981) is a wonderful study of Joan both in her time and as an object of cultural interest. It is very well documented and immensely readable; it is to be lamented that there is no similar work for St. Francis of Assisi. Arnaldo Fortini's *Saint Francis of Assisi* (New York, 1981) gives valuable background for an understanding of Francis.

Perhaps the most persuasive voice for peace orientations in contemporary Catholic theology is James Douglas's *The Non-Violent Cross* (London and New York, 1969). For a survey of attitudes, see James Hanigan, "Militant Non-Violence: A Spirituality for the Pursuit of Social Justice," *Horizons*, Spring, 1982, pp. 7–22.

The contemporary debate on nuclear disarmament has produced a plethora of works; some recent titles: *Rumors of War: A Moral and Theological Perspective on the Arms Race*, edited by C. A. Cesaretti and J. Vitale (New York, 1982); Dale Aukerman, *Darkening Valley: A Biblical Perspective on Nuclear War* (New York, 1982); *The Risk of the Cross: Christian Discipleship in the Nuclear Age*, edited by J. Christopher Grannis et al. (New York, 1982). The number of journal articles devoted to this topic increases by the week. Among the more recent: in *Theological Studies*, September, 1982, two articles deal with the episcopacy and the questions of atomic weapons: Francis X. Winters, S.J., "Nuclear Deterrence Morality: Atlantic Community Bishops in Tension," pp. 428–46; and John Langan, "The American Hierarchy and Nuclear Weapons," pp. 447–67. These articles and many others have been prompted by the various drafts of the pastoral letter of the U.S. Catholic bishops on war and peace, *The Challenge of Peace: God's Promise and Our Response* (Washington, D.C., 1983). For an assessment of the pastoral, see Philip Murnion, ed., *Catholics and Nuclear War: A Commentary on the U.S. Catholic Bishops' Pastoral Letter on War and Peace* (New York, 1983). For a valuable anthology of previous church documents on peace, see Joseph Gremillion, *The Gospel of Peace and Justice* (Maryknoll, N.Y., 1975).

5

MYSTICS

Mysticism is one of the most abused words in modern religious discourse. Some identify mysticism with the occult or astrology; others use the word to mean a lack of intellectual precision (e.g., "that's a lot of mystical moonshine"), while still others regard it as some kind of exotic practice at the edges of true religion. It is shameful that the term "mysticism" should be so badly understood since it is a rather precise concept as well as a phenomenon found in all of the world's major religions. Furthermore, it is a strikingly persistent part of the Catholic tradition, found in every age and era of the church's history.

What is mysticism? It is hard to define because of the broad way in which the term is used by the various religions. Buddhist mystics strive for the experience of Nirvana; Christians thirst for the presence of God; nature mystics wish to identify with the mysterious reality which is nature itself. The very diversity of mysticism has led scholars to distinguish various kinds of mysticism (theist/nontheistic; introspective/extroverted, etc.), while its similarity has led others to argue that mysticism is of a piece with only accidental differences based on culture. All of this discussion is part of a larger and more crucial discussion of specifying a phenomenon which is a part of all major religions.

For the purposes of this chapter we will adapt a definition of mysticism borrowed from St. Thomas Aquinas: *Mysticism is the knowledge of God through experience.* Mysticism is something we experience and what we experience, however imperfectly, is God.[1] There are a number of things which derive from our definition which we need to note.

Mysticism is *experience of* rather than *knowledge about* God. The theologian may report on philosophical attempts to prove the existence of God, but the mystic communicates the sense of knowing God directly. It is the difference between writing about love and writing about the experience of being in love.

The object of the mystic's search is God. God, of course, is the ultimate source of the world and, as the Bible testifies, is incomprehensible. The mystic's experience of God is imperfect, far from exhaustive, and fleeting. How does one speak of that experience? For mystics the language appropriate for talking about the experience of God was a language also appropriate for talking about love: poetic, metaphorical, paradoxical, and, at times, at the very edge of comprehension. Thus St. John of the Cross (1542–1591) might refer to God's presence to the mystic in prayer as *todo y nada* ("everything and nothing") or a Hindu mystic might speak of Brahman as *neti neti* ("neither this nor that"); what both are driving at is the absolute uniqueness of the mystical experience. The point was beautifully made by the Apostle Paul who said of his own mystical experiences that he "heard things which must not and cannot be put into human language" (2 Cor. 12:4).

The mystical experience, which is always a transitory one, is not simply an illumination of the mind. Mystical prayer grips the person and exercises a profound influence on the way a person is. Mystical prayer, in short, often triggers new conversions and orientations in a person. It is for that reason that the greatest of the mystics in the church are often people who were able to accomplish much good for the church or exercise a profound personal influence on others after they had embarked on a life of mystical prayer. While some mystics have withdrawn from the world (as did many of the early ascetics we discussed in Chapter 2), others were active in the world and saw no incompatibility between their deepened sense of the presence of God and their life of activity.

What does the mystic do for the church? To paraphrase Thomas Merton's comment on monks, one answers that the vocation of mystics is not *to do* but *to be*. The very existence of mystics in the church (they are not a rare breed; mystics have lived in every age of the church) is a constant testimony to the reality of God. Mystics strengthen the faith of the church by providing opportunities for people to be reminded of the mystery of God. Secondly, mystics purify their lives in order to be worthy of the grace of mystical prayer. In that purification they get a rather keen sense of the vanity and sinfulness of an age. For that reason mystics often serve a prophetic function in the church either because the purity of their lives is a judgment in its own right or because they inspire others to a life of prayer or because they feel moved—as St. Teresa of Avila (1515–1582) did—to reform religious mores in an active manner.

Like prophets, mystics have often incurred the suspicion of the church. It is surprising how many of these deeply spiritual people have never been canonized. The reasons for this suspicion are not hard to identify. Their language at times seems so extreme that there are suspicions about their orthodoxy. When Meister Eckhart (1260–1328), one of the greatest of all the medieval mystics, spoke of a "Godhead beyond God," theological eyebrows were raised. At times, paradox sounded like heresy. The other reason why mystics have been viewed with suspicion is because their claim to have a direct experience of God seems to short-circuit the established mediation of the church's sacramental and liturgical life.[2] The mystic enjoys intimacy with God without the instrumentality of the church ministrations. The church—rightly at times—feared that the mystic's claim to direct access to God could create a sort of spiritual elitism or spiritual anarchy. Thus "fidelity to the church" is much praised in the lives of the great mystics.

Finally, the mystics expand our vocabulary for talking about God. Their insights into the experience of God has enriched both our theology and our devotional literature. One specific example might help to make that point concretely. The noted Protestant theologian Paul Tillich (1886–1965) sought a way to describe God which would be meaningful for modern people. He wanted a description which did not describe God as "up there" or "out there," that is, he did not want people to think of God as some sort of "superbeing" distinguishable from our being. For Tillich God was the "Ground of All Being." By calling

God the Ground of Being Tillich was able to convey the notion of God as anterior to all other beings (i.e., creatures) and as the context which is underneath everything and which gives everything else both existence and intelligibility.[3] Tillich's notion is brilliantly helpful for those who wish to think about God without reference to an idea of a heavenly home somewhere in the sky. Yet the idea of God as Ground is not original with Tillich. He obtained the phrase from the fourteenth-century Rhineland mystics who spoke of God as *Grund*. What Tillich rightly saw was that the term was an important way to speak of God not only experientially (as the mystics did) but also theologically.

There is one other way in which the mystic serves the church and its people. There is a persistent temptation in Christianity to trivialize the idea of God—God as the cultural hero of a given age or God as "the Man upstairs" or God as some sort of Freudian Superego who demands conformity and obedience to the rules. The mystic reminds us forcefully that God can never be rendered down to human intellectual categories; God is always beyond what we can say. Even St. Thomas Aquinas, who spoke more compellingly about God than any other theologian of the Middle Ages, confessed that what he experienced in prayer made all of his writings "seem like straw." For the mystics, with their strainings at language (and their silences!), the reality of God is affirmed but never cheapened. Mystics are never reductionists. In one of the most celebrated passages in all of theology the point is made with awesome power:

> I have learned to love you late, Beauty at once so ancient and so new. . . . You called me, you cried aloud to me; you broke my barrier of deafness. You shone upon me; your radiance enveloped me; you put my blindness to flight. You shed your fragrance about me; I drew breath and now I gasp at your sweet odor. I tasted you, and now I hunger and thirst for you. You touched me, and I am inflamed with love of your peace.[4]

Two Medieval Mystics

It would be impossible in a book this short to list, much less discuss, all of the important mystics who are known to the history of Catholicism. Mysticism is rooted in the New Testament. As we have noted before, early Christianity absorbed the ideas of Neoplatonism by which people attempted to overcome the limitations of the flesh in order to commune with the One. In that sense the goal of the ascetical life was mystical communion with God. The Pseudo-Dionysius,[5] a sixth-century Syrian author, wrote treatises on the ascent to God through sensible and intellectual preparation. His *Mystical Theology* was translated into Latin in the early Middle Ages and had an enormous impact on later theologians. The writings of the Pseudo-Dionysius links the ascetical tradition of the patristic period with that of the Middle Ages. By the high Middle Ages there were flourishing schools of mysticism not only among various religious orders (e.g., the Franciscans) but in various countries such as England and the Lowlands.

We will satisfy ourselves with a brief consideration of two mystics from the late Middle Ages: Julian of Norwich and Meister Eckhart. In that way we can get some idea of the richness and diversity of mystical thought and style. We can also get some notion of the common themes that run through most mystical thought.

Julian of Norwich

The *Showings* of Julian of Norwich (1342–c. 1423) is one of the most strikingly original mystical works of the late Middle Ages. Of the author we know little except what we can deduce from her writings and a few independent historical facts. She was an anchoress,[6] which is to say, a recluse who lived in a small cottage (often called an *anchorhold*) attached to the parish church of Sts. Julian and Edward in Norwich (England). According to her contemporary Margery Kempe (d. 1438), Julian was an experienced spiritual guide. We know that she was living in 1416 (a bequest was made to her in a will that year) and that after 1423 another recluse was living in her anchorhold; so that year is the probable latest year that she could have been alive. Apart from those facts we know only what we can detect in her own writings.

According to Julian's own account, on May 13, 1373, while

she was extremely ill, the Lord granted her a series of fifteen revelations (which she called, in her dialect, "showings"—hence the title of her book) concerning the Passion of Christ, other spiritual realities, and the presence of the Holy Trinity in the individual souls of believers. Shortly after these revelations happened, Julian wrote them down (dictated them?) in a version which is now called simply the "shorter version." Fifteen years later she wrote an enlarged version of the same revelations which was the fruit of her own meditation on the significance of what had happened to her as well as the further light she received from her own prayer and meditation.

The fourteenth century, the golden age of English mysticism, produced such great English mystical writers as Walter Hilton, Richard Rolle, and the unknown author of the celebrated *The Cloud of Unknowing*. Of this group Julian is the one great ecstatic mystic, that is, the one who claimed her experiences were part of an ecstatic vision. Julian's *Showings* were written in English in a nonacademic or scholastic style. Despite Julian's artlessness her book is a treatise of some theological sophistication and much original insight into the life of God in the soul of the believer. Despite the author's claim that she was a poor and unlettered person, the work she has left us reflects a deep knowledge of the Bible and the mystical tradition.

One of the most gripping things about Julian is her deep love for the created world and the root of that love in her love for God. A famous passage on this theme deserves to be quoted at length both to get some sense of her writing style and the passionate depth of her prayer life:

> And in this he showed me something small, no bigger than a hazelnut, lying in the palm of my hand, and I perceived that it was as round as any ball. I looked at it and thought: What can this be? And I was given this general answer: It is everything which is made. I was amazed that it could last, for I thought that it was so little that it could suddenly fall into nothing. And I was answered in my understanding: It lasts and always will, because God loves it; and thus everything has being through the love of God.
>
> In this little thing I saw three properties. The first is that God made it; the second is that he loves it, and the third is that God preserves it. But what is that to me? It is that God is the creator,

and the lover and the protector. For until I am substantially united with Him I can never have love or rest or true happiness; until, that is, I am so attached to him that there can be no created thing between my God and me. And who will do this deed? Truly, he himself, by his mercy and his grace, for he has made me for this and has blessedly restored me.[7]

Julian's most original contribution to mystical literature is her understanding of God in terms of feminine imagery. Other medieval mystics and preachers had used maternal language to speak of Christ, but Julian of Norwich is the first to attempt an openly theological justification for the use of such language. When Julian speaks of God as father and mother, she explains how this unaccustomed imagery can be used in a meaningful way. She says that in her "showings" she learned that the motherhood of God can be understood in three senses: God brings forth creation as a mother brings forth a child; God becomes flesh so that we spiritually are reborn in the Mother Jesus Christ; and, finally, Christ our Mother cares for us like a true mother in his nurturing, protecting, educating, and so on. Julian then concludes with this praise of the Motherhood of God:

> To the property of Motherhood belongs nature, love, wisdom, knowledge, and this is God. . . . The kind, loving mother who knows and sees the need of her child guards it very tenderly, as the nature and condition of motherhood will have. And always as the child grows in age and stature, she acts differently, but she does not change her love. . . . This work, with everything which is lovely and good, our Lord performs in those by whom it is done. So he is our Mother in nature by the operation of grace in the lower part, for love of the higher part. And he wants us to know it for he wants to have all our love attached to him; and in this I saw that every debt which we owe by God's command to fatherhood and motherhood is fulfilled in truly loving God, which blessed love God works in us.[8]

Meister Eckhart

Meister Eckhart (1260–c. 1328) provides a telling contrast to Dame Julian while also allowing us an introduction to one of the most prestigious of the church's mystics; indeed, some have said that Eckhart is, along with St. John of the Cross, the "mystic's mystic." Julian of Norwich was an English recluse who lived a stable life of prayerful retirement. Eckhart was a German Dominican friar who had travelled over most of Europe while pursuing his work as a monastic superior, preacher, and lecturer in theology at the University of Paris. Besides Paris and towns in his native Thuringia we find evidence of Eckhart teaching and preaching in such centers as Cologne, Avignon, and Strausborg. Eckhart the theologian wrote Scholastic treatises in Latin, while Eckhart the preacher left us a large number of sermons in the German vernacular. Dame Julian's influence was limited to the immediate range of her friends, admirers, and disciples, while Eckhart's reputation was such that by the end of his life he had to defend his writing and teaching against charges of heresy at the papal court in Avignon.

Julian's approach to mystical writing was, to use one of her words, homely. She spoke immediately and passionately of the goodness of God, the fiercesome nature of Christ's passion, and the great power of the Trinitarian life of grace. She was an intensely powerful writer, yet free from sentimentality. Eckhart, passionate and powerful as he was as a preacher, used a more restrained and stark vocabulary. Where Dame Julian might speak of the maternity of God, Eckhart is more likely to use words that remind us of the early ascetics: God is Nothing or Desert or Darkness or Wilderness. Eckhart distinguishes between God who is known to humanity in this life through his activity and his revelation and Godhead which is God beyond God, beyond history, beyond speech, and totally different from anything we can think about, imagine, or articulate. Eckhart belongs to that long tradition of mysticism (of which the Pseudo-Dionysius is the most representative early example) which insists on the absolute otherness of the reality of God.

What of the relation of individuals to this God(head)? Eckhart understands each individual soul as coming out from God and destined to return to God. In that broad sense Eckhart is in the great tradition of Augustine. Through sinfulness, both as a state and through sinful acts, we desire the things around us and are snared by the attractions of contingent being. It is only through perfect detachment (Gelassenheit) and disinterestedness (Abgeschiedenheit) that we are drawn back to Godhead. This inner purification is not to be understood in Eckhart's scheme of things as some sort of physical inactivity or withdrawal. He envisions an inner detachment or, as he calls it, an inner silence; in this silent place the soul is fixed back on God, the true ground of his existence. To explain this life of inner silence and outer activity Eckhart uses the image of the stationary center of the axis of a moving wheel, or, as T. S. Eliot calls it variously in *Four Quartets*, "the still point of the turning world" or the "point of intersection of the timeless with time."

Eckhart's doctrine (he was one of the first to use the phrase "mystical theology" widely) is a prime example of the true mystic's concern with the otherness of the reality of God. Drawing as he does on the long tradition of *negative* or *apophatic* theology (i.e., the description of God by negations; God is not this nor that, etc.), Eckhart developed a vocabulary that was so paradoxical as to create doubts about his orthodoxy. Here is one small example; Eckhart is speaking about how one is to love God:

> ... You should love him as if he were a non-God, a non-spirit, a non-person, a non-image. No, even more, as a simple, pure, clear One separated from all duality. And in this One we should eternally immerse ourselves, sinking from something into Nothing. Towards this may God help us. Amen.[9]

Eckhart himself was not insensitive to the reactions of those who found his ideas radical, if not puzzling. He was trying to articulate, not a doctrine (although it was rooted in doctrine) but an experience. In a famous sermon on the Gospel text "Blessed are the poor in spirit" Eckhart went on at some length to argue that the text did not refer to physical poverty (those who thought so were "asses," as he pungently put it) but to an interior poverty so radical and pure that the will did not even desire to seek God; it just was—open to the pull of Godhead. "If anyone does not understand this discourse," he concluded his sermon, "Let him not worry about that, for if he does not find this truth in himself he cannot understand what I have said. . . ."[10]

We have contrasted the mystical doctrine of Dame Julian and Meister Eckhart. What can we say of their common themes? We should briefly note the following:

(a) Both mystics appeal to inner experiences. What they write and speak about derives from their experiences in the life of prayer and not from intellectual speculations alone.

(b) Both insist on a paradox which is common enough in the Christian tradition and in mystical writings but which get a particular emphasis in mystical writing: God is as close to us as our own soul and yet totally and absolutely different from any created reality.

(c) The language by which the mystic speaks of God is a language which, in the words of the poet T. S. Eliot, "cracks, buckles, and strains." Dame Julian reached for the unfamiliar language of maternity to talk about the concern of God for the believer, while Meister Eckhart appealed to the austere tradition which used words like Wilderness or Nothing to describe the God, in the words of Eckhart, who is beyond God. In either case the language is a serious attempt to avoid the obvious, the hackneyed, or the familiar.

Mystics and Reform:
Teresa of Avila and John of the Cross

Teresa of Avila (1515–1582) lived in one of Spain's most tumultuous centuries. During her lifetime the wealth of the newly discovered Americas poured into Spain and it was only six years after her birth that the Protestant Reformation broke out in Germany. Teresa entered the convent in Avila when she was a young woman and spent twenty years as a conventionally pious nun. In 1562 she underwent a sort of "second conversion,"[11] which led her to attempt a far more austere style of religious life and a far greater dedication to a systematic life of prayer. From that time until her death some twenty years later Teresa crisscrossed Spain, founding reformed convents of Carmelite nuns and directing the spiritual life of those in such convents. Teresa combined this active life of religious reform with a deep personal life of prayer and contemplation, the fruits of which are most clearly evident in her writings. In addition to her *Autobiography* (1565), the most notable of her spiritual writings are the two books of ascetical theology: *The Way of*

Perfection (1573) and *The Interior Castle* (1577). The latter work deserves our closer attention.

The Interior Castle was written for the spiritual instruction of her nuns; it was a descriptive guide of the soul's relationship with God. Teresa uses an elaborate central symbol that supplies the book with its title: She imagines a large diamond-bright castle with many rooms or mansions at the heart of which lives the king who is Christ. Teresa describes the passage through the various mansions until the soul reaches the very center of the castle wherein is the Christ; it is there that the soul unites in mystical marriage with the ruler of the Castle.[12] The first three mansions are symbolic of the soul's efforts to root out sin and the penchant for sin as well as the attempt to "work at" a serious life of prayer, sacramental observance, and spiritual reading. Beginning with the fourth mansion it is not the human effort at Christian observance but the compelling grace of God which begins to operate in the soul. At this stage the soul first moves forward under the influence of spiritual consolations given by God (fourth mansion) and then by afflictions, sorrows, dryness, and depression (sixth mansion) as God purifies the soul. In the seventh mansion the soul and God are united in a spiritual marriage. The union is so close that Teresa compares it to the merging of the flames of two candles.

The Interior Castle was written, not by a speculative theologian, but by a woman of immense practical energy who possessed deep personal experiences in the life of prayer. What authenticates *The Interior Castle* is its reflection on lived experience. Theologians who were contemporaries of Teresa were able to clear up an obscure turn of phrase or supply an apposite quote from the Bible, but she alone spoke with authority on the nature of the experiences of the mystical ascent. *The Interior Castle* is uniquely Teresa's book and, apart from its perennial value, in that sense is original. Nonetheless Teresa drew on a great and enduring tradition of mystical language and symbolism to frame the story of her experiences. In that sense the book is part of a classical series of Christian mystical texts. Some of its more traditional formulations include:

(a) Ascent by stages. One of the persistent frameworks in

which mystical treatises are written is that of the ascent. One popular image is the ladder (based on a mystical reading of the significance of Jacob's ladder in the Book of Genesis), the pilgrimage, the journey, or the ascent of the mountain.

(b) Imagery of marriage. In the seventh mansion Teresa speaks of the marriage of the soul with God. This kind of imagery (together with the use of erotic and sexual imagery related to marriage) draws on a very old tradition in spiritual writings whose origins are to be found in the attempts to understand the spiritual significance of the love lyrics in the Old Testament Song of Songs. There is a whole tradition of spiritual treatises giving a mystical interpretation to that book.

(c) Dialectics of consolation and dryness; of joy and spiritual grief. Like most of the great mystics Teresa insists that in the early stages of mystical prayer God grants immense consolations in the form of peace, joy, and contentment in prayer. Prayer is more preferable than any other activity; the hours of contemplation are the happiest of times. As the soul progresses, however, these consolations disappear to be replaced by a sense of aridity, depression, and repugnance. Why? Teresa says that the soul goes through this period of aridity so that one prays not for the consolations but for God. The object of prayer, in the last analysis, is the contemplation of God, not the enjoyment of interior peace; in that contemplation comes peace, not vice versa.

What is the end or purpose of this mystical journey? The first end is the experience of God, which is a foretaste of the vision of God in eternity. But also, Teresa insists, the mystical experience gives the recipient the power to serve the others who are in the Christian community. It is at the heart of the life of service and love for the church. In that insight Teresa links mysticism and apostolic activity. If the faith were to be strong, it would be so because there were those who had experienced God so compellingly that they could lead others to God also. Mystical union provides an inner strength which leads not to quietism but to directed activity:

> It is quite certain that, with the strength it has gained, the soul comes to the help of all who are in the castle and, indeed, suc-

cours the body itself. . . . In this life the soul has a very bad time for, however much it accomplishes, it is strong enough inwardly to attempt much more and this causes such strife within it that nothing it can do seems to it of any importance. This must be the reason for the great penances done by many saints, especially by the great Magdalen, who had been brought up in such luxury all her life long; there was also that hunger for the honour of his God suffered by our father Elias, and the zeal of Saint Dominic and Saint Francis for bringing souls to God, so that he might be praised. I assure you that, forgetful as they were of themselves, they must have endured so little suffering.[13]

In 1567 Teresa of Avila met a young friar in the Spanish town of Medina. She encouraged him not to enter the Carthusians but to use his thirst for a more austere life in the service of reforming the Carmelite Order of which he was already a member. In 1568 Brother John of the Cross (the name he assumed when he decided to join the reforming movement of St. Teresa) and four other friars started the first reformed Carmelite friary. In 1572 John became the spiritual director of the nuns at Teresa's convent in Avila and served as her own confessor. An internal dispute within the Carmelite family led to severe dissension between those who wished to pursue the reform and those who did not. When John of the Cross refused to stop his reforming work, he was arrested by ecclesiastical authorities and imprisoned in the Carmelite monastery at Toledo in 1577 where he served nine months of terrible isolation until he escaped. His last years—he died in 1591—were spent in active work within the reformed Carmelite ranks, though his last year was spent as a simple friar in an obscure friary in Andulasia. At his death he was regarded as a saint by the common folk and soon became renowned for the strength and purity of his mystical teachings. His theology was of such a caliber that he (and St. Teresa) have both been proclaimed "Doctors of the Church."

John of the Cross is regarded as one of the greatest of Christian mystics and one of the finest poets ever to write in Spanish. Unlike Teresa who wrote primarily in prose, John wrote of his experiences in poetry. His prose works are either commentaries on his poetry or treatises which extend and amplify the themes of that poetry.

Some of the poetry of St. John of the Cross, at first reading, seems to be far from religious or mystical. He borrows from the love poetry of Spain and makes use of its pastoral tradition. Some of his mystical verses, in fact, were composed while John was in his monastic prison cell and he heard someone singing a love song out on the streets. His lyrics are extremely spare, unadorned, compact, and, as a consequence, hard to translate. In a poem called "The Dark Night" (which he says was written to celebrate union with God through spiritual negation) we find these simple—yet complex—stanzas:

> Oh noche, que guiaste
> Oh noche amable más que el alborada
> Oh noche, que juntaste
> amado con amada,
> amada en el Amado transformada!

> Oh night, you guide me
> Oh night more lovely than the dawn
> Oh night, you joined
> Lover with loved one
> so the loved one is changed into the Lover.

> En mi pecho florido,
> que entero para él solo se guardaba,
> allí quedó dormido
> y yo le regalaba,
> y el ventalle de cedros aire daba.

> On my flowery breast
> Guarded for him alone
> There he stayed and slept
> I caressed him with airy breezes from cedars.[14]

John's mystical poetry is not all couched in terms of traditional love lyrics; his tendency to spareness can also spill out into a poetry which can be unremittingly austere, an austerity not surprising for a mystic who wrote much on the purgation of the senses as an essential part of the mystical ascent. Some lines on this theme attracted the admiration of T. S. Eliot, who incorporated them in his great religious poem *Four Quartets*. The lines, from John's *The Ascent of Mount Carmel*, play on the paradox of "everything" and "nothing," terms which John used to describe God: God as *todo y nada* ("everything and nothing"). Finally, these lines demonstrate graphically the so-called *via negativa*, or "way of negation," in which the mystic negates the usual impulses of his or her humanity in order to "move beyond" human notions and affections in the search for the experience of God:

> To reach satisfaction in all
> desire its possession in nothing.
> To come to possess all
> desire the possession of nothing.
> To arrive at being all
> desire to be nothing.
> To come to the knowledge of all
> desire the knowledge of nothing.
> To come to the pleasure you have not
> You must go by a way which you enjoy not.
> To come to the knowledge you have not
> You must go by a way which you know not.
> To come to the possession you have not
> You must go by a way in which you possess not.
> To come to be what you are not
> You must go by a way in which you are not.
> When you turn towards something
> You cease to cast yourself upon the all
> For to go from all to the all
> You must deny yourself of all in all . . .
> In this nakedness the spirit finds
> its quietude and rest.
> For in coveting nothing
> nothing raises it up
> and nothing weighs it down,
> because it is in the center of its humility.
> When it covets something
> In this very desire it is wearied.[15]

John of the Cross and Teresa of Avila lived during the up-heavals of the Protestant Reformation. Teresa, more than John, saw her work as an antidote to the incursion of Protestantism into Spain. In order to keep the reformers at bay in Spain the church turned increasingly conservative and suspicious. Indeed, by the next century the finest flowerings of Spanish Catholicism (Neo-Scholasticism, the Jesuits, the mysticism of the Carmelites) were forever in danger from the attention of the Inquisition. Both Teresa and John were the target of church suspicion coming both from within their order and from the Inquisition. Even the paranoid church authorities, however, recognized that internal reform of church structures was as important for church stability as was repressive discipline. One instrument of reform was the nourishment of highly spiritual religious houses which could serve as centers of spiritual renewal and whose lives might inspire the more mediocre or lax religious centers. In short, the reforming efforts of Teresa and John were meant to revive and evangelize. Their method was simplicity itself: They would live as if there was only God in the world. That is a very stern point of departure for a life, but precisely because they took it so absolutely seriously, others, less gifted or less courageous, could measure their own efforts against theirs.

Mysticism and Modernity: *Teilhard de Chardin*

No matter how similar the mystics seem in their doctrine and aims they all reflect their unique religious beliefs and their cultural matrix. That St. John of the Cross should couch his mystical language in explicitly Christian terms and in a language garnered from the love poetry of secular Spain should not surprise us. No mystics of whatever persuasion ever described mystical experiences apart from the matrix of their culture. As an eminent scholar of mysticism has recently written, in order to understand mysticism "it is not just a question of studying the reports of the mystic after the experiential event but of acknowledging that the experience itself as well as the form in which it is reported is shaped by concepts which the mystic brings to, and which shape, his experience.[16]

How do mystics speak in this modern age? How do they reveal the peculiar cultural and religious characteristics of our age? We all recognize that our times are not religious in the same sense that, say, thirteenth-century Germany or sixteenth-century Spain was religious. It should not surprise us that some mystics—Simone Weil (1909–1943) comes immediately to mind—should have a strong sense of the absence of God. Others, given the ease with which we can communicate and learn from other parts of the world, learn from and find help in the mystical traditions of other cultures and other religions. The late Thomas Merton, for example, explained his fateful trip to the Far East as a pilgrimage on which he hoped to learn; he went, as he said, as a student and inquirer, not as a teacher. Of all the mystics who have been touched by modern concerns, however, the most significant must be the late French Jesuit Pierre Teilhard de Chardin (1881–1955), who expressed his strong mystical leanings through the language and ideas of his scientific preoccupations.

Pierre Teilhard de Chardin entered the Society of Jesus when he was eighteen. After his ordination to the priesthood in 1911, he pursued advanced studies in geology and paleontology at the Sorbonne. His education was interrupted by army service during the First World War in which the young Jesuit served with military distinction as a stretcher bearer. In 1921 Teilhard finished his doctorate and began an active career as a research scientist. He worked in China where he was part of the team which discovered Peking Man (Sinanthropos). The outbreak of the Second World War left him stranded in China for the duration of the conflict. After the war he lived in Paris, but moved finally to New York when ecclesiastical authorities denied him the right to assume a professorship at the Collège de France. He died in New York on Easter Sunday, 1955.

During his academic career (from roughly 1915 to his death) Teilhard de Chardin published over one hundred and seventy scientific papers, but not one of his major theological works was available except in typescript for private circulation among friends. In those restrictive days before the freedom of the Second Vatican Council Teilhard was forbidden to publish; it is a sign of his fidelity to the church that he accepted these restrictions. Teilhard's work was judged to be too daring, too distant from the traditional canons of theological language, too near to pantheism, too dismissive of the problems of sin. That Teilhard never got to respond to theological critiques was a direct result of his being forbidden to publish. The case of Teilhard de Chardin is a salutary, if sad, lesson about the repressive side of Catholicism.

There is no doubt that Teilhard's ideas are strikingly original. His whole theological vision was rooted in his ideas about evolution. For Teilhard evolution was not a mere hypothesis; it was the key to understanding all of life and its relationship to the Gospel. The world evolves, Teilhard believed, through a process of what he called "complexification." Through the complexification of molecular life came life; from life came the human mind. These leaps of life and mind did not simply occur here and there on the planet. They formed new layers over the planet; the layer of life Teilhard called "Biosphere"; the layer of the mind he called "Noosphere."

Teilhard then asks: With the emergence of mind on the planet did evolution end? He sees no reason to affirm that it did. Indeed, by a daring leap Teilhard posits a further evolution of both individual consciousness and the layer of consciousness on the planet (Noosphere). Consciousness will eventually turn in on itself into a new consciousness which Teilhard calls the "Christosphere." Consciousness in this sphere will be focused and organized on the Omega Point, which is the final end of all evolution. It is not hard to see that Omega Point is God.

At the center of Teilhard's vision of reality are a number of deeply held convictions. First, Teilhard—rather like Dame Julian of Norwich—had an absolute confidence in the beauty and goodness of the material world; it was in the mystery of material reality that Teilhard first became aware of the reality of God. Unlike some of the mystics Teilhard never felt any necessity of negating the world. On the contrary. It was in the direct contemplation of the material world that he sensed God. God was, to use the title of one of his essays, at the heart of matter.

Secondly, Teilhard was very attracted to that New Testament characterization of Christ which emphasized, not the humanity of Jesus in the Gospels, but the Christ whose presence was in the entire cosmos. Teilhard turned time and time again to those Pauline texts which described Christ in cosmic language:

He is the image of the unseen God
and the first born of all creation,
for in him were created
all things in heaven and on earth:
everything visible and everything invisible.
(Col. 1:15–16)

For Teilhard Christ dwells in the world, sanctifies it, and brings it to completion. He sees the end of time and of history as the culmination of all creation into the cosmic Christ. The presence of Christ in the world is, for Teilhard, rather like the presence of Christ in the Eucharist, though in a different way. Teilhard makes this point in one of his famous meditations, a prayer he called the "Mass on the World." While he was alone in the deserts of China and Mongolia, unable to say Mass, Teilhard loved to meditate on the presence of Christ in the world. As the priest breathes words on the elements of bread and wine, transforming them into the body and blood of Christ, so Teilhard "offered up" the world as he did the Eucharistic Christ when at Mass:

> . . . Once upon a time men took into your temple the first fruits of their harvests, the flowers of their flocks. But the offering you really want, the offering you mysteriously need every day to appease your hunger, to slake your thirst is nothing less than the growth of the world borne ever onwards in the stream of universal becoming.

> Receive, O Lord, this all-embracing host which your whole creation, moved by your magnetism, offers you at this dawn of a new day.

> This bread, our toil, is of itself, I know, but an immense fragmentation; this wine, our pain, is no more, I know, than a draught that dissolves. Yet in the very depths of this formless mass you have implanted—a desire, irresistible, hallowing, which makes us cry out, believer and unbeliever alike, "Lord, make us one."[17]

Teilhard's theological vision has triggered a great deal of argument; his ideas are dismissed at times either as bad theology or bad science. There is no doubt that debate will rage a long time over his accomplishments. One aspect of Teilhard's thought, however, has provided inspiration for creative religious thinkers. Teilhard argues that human consciousness is slowly going through a process of evolution toward a new consciousness which can only be described as religious. Many concerned religious thinkers from both the East and the West think that their efforts at better religious understanding, more intense spiritual dialogue, and greater openness to other spiritual values cannot but help the climate of world understanding and world concern. At a time when tremendous fratricidal wars are waged in the name of religion, Teilhard's ideas remind us that the human spirit needs to move to the Christic, but it does so, as the lessons of evolution teaches, through slow development and not without pain, false starts, and heavy disappointments. Despite that, Teilhard's theory would say, everything is rising in the right direction, that is, toward the Omega Point. To accept that is to make an act of faith not only in the future but in God.

Notes

1. We assume Christian mysticism here. For a fuller discussion of these issues, see Steven Katz, "Language, Epistemology, and Mysticism," in *Mysticism and Philosophical Analysis*, ed. S. Katz (London and New York, 1978), pp. 22–74.
2. Books like Friedrich Heer's *The Medieval World* (New York, 1961) have argued that fourteenth-century German mysticism was a direct forerunner of the Protestant Reformation.
3. For Tillich's discussion, see his *Systematic Theology*, vol. 1 (Chicago, 1951), pp. 235ff.
4. The *Confessions* of Saint Augustine, X, 27.
5. So called because the medieval church thought him to be Dionysius the Areopagite, a convert and companion of Saint Paul. This closeness to the apostolic tradition strengthened the work's authority in the Middle Ages.
6. One of the classics of Middle English prose is the *Ancrene Riwle*, which was a vernacular rule for anchoresses written some time in the very early thirteenth century. That the rule exists also in French and Latin versions attests to its popularity and pertinence.
7. *Julian of Norwich, Showings*, ed. Edmund Colledge et al., Classics of Western Spirituality (New York, 1978), pp. 130–31. This edition makes all earlier versions dated.
8. *Showings* (Long Text), p. 299.
9. From the sermon "Renovamini Spiritu," as quoted in Thomas O'Meara, "The Presence of Meister Eckhart," *The Thomist*, April 1978, p. 181. This issue of *The Thomist* was devoted to Eckhart; it included a very helpful bibliography of studies on Eckhart.
10. *Meister Eckhart: A Modern Translation*, trans. R. B. Blakney (New York, 1941), p. 232.

11. This "second conversion" phenomenon is observable in many of the saints. Mother Teresa of Calcutta, for example, was a teaching sister in India for many years before she felt inspired to start a new life of service to the very poor.

12. Attentive readers will not miss the use of chivalric imagery in the background here. It is common in Teresa who, as she tells us, once ran away to be martyred at the hands of the Moslems after reading Crusader romances as a child.

13. *The Interior Castle of Teresa of Avila*, trans. E. Allison Peers (Garden City, N.Y., 1961), pp. 230–31. There is a more recent translation in the Paulist Classics of Western Spirituality series by Kieran Kavanaugh, O.C.D., and Otilio Rodriguez, O.C.D.

14. My translation. There is a bilingual edition of the poetry in Gerald Brenan's *Saint John of the Cross: His Life and Poetry* (London and New York, 1973).

15. From The *Collected Works of Saint John of the Cross*, trans. Kieran Kavanaugh, O.C.D., and Otilio Rodriguez, O.C.D. (Washington, D.C., 1973), pp. 103–4.

16. Katz, p. 26.

17. Pierre Teilhard de Chardin, *The Heart of Matter* (New York and London, 1978), pp. 120–21.

Readings and Trajectories

The literature on mysticism is immense. Some of the standard books include: Evelyn Underhill, *Mysticism* (London, 1911; with many later editions); W. T. Stace, *The Teachings of the Mystics* (New York, 1960); R. C. Zaehner, *Mysticism, Sacred and Profane* (New York, 1961); Frits Staal, *Exploring Mysticism* (Berkeley, Calif., 1975); Steven Katz, ed., *Mysticism and Philosophical Analysis* (London and New York, 1978). On the kinds of Christian mysticism, see Harvey Egan's "Christian Apophatic and Kataphatic Mysticisms," *Theological Studies*, September, 1978, pp. 399–426. F. C. Happold, *Mysticism: A Study and an Anthology* (Baltimore and Harmondsworth, 1963), is a handy sourcebook.

The Classics of Western Spirituality, published by the Paulist Press (1978–), will provide, upon completion, the major texts of the great mystics of the Western world, complete with introductions from major scholars in the field. Published in both hard cover and paperback, these volumes will be an indispensable source for students of mysticism. To date volumes on mystics like Dame Julian, Meister Eckhart, St. Teresa of Avila, St. Bonaventure, Jacob Boehme, William Law, and others have been published.

A consideration of Sts. Teresa and John of the Cross allows for a comparative study of mysticism and art because of the influence both had on the history of Spanish culture in particular and European culture in general. Two books are of special interest in this regard: Robert Peterson's *The Art of Ecstasy: Teresa, Bernini, and Crashaw* (New York, 1970) and Irving Lavin's monumental study of the Cornaro chapel and the statue "The Ecstasy of Saint Teresa," entitled *Bernini and the Unity of the Visual Arts*, 2 vols. (Oxford and New York, 1980).

The year 1978 was the 750th anniversary of the death of Meister Eckhart; to celebrate that occasion the journal *The Thomist* devoted an entire issue (April 1978) to the study of Eckhart's life and thought. Some of the essays are extremely helpful in tracing Eckhart's influence on both Luther and later German thought, including the existentialism of Heidegger; another essay does a comparative study of Eckhart and Zen. The twenty-three-page bibliography of secondary sources in Eckhart study is especially useful. On the relationship of modern nontheistic thought and mysticism, see the excellent essay of Michael Buckley: "Atheism and Contemplation," *Theological Studies*, December 1979, pp. 680–99. Matthew Fox's *Breakthrough: Meister Eckhart's Creation Spirituality in New Translation* (Garden City, N.Y., 1980) is a valuable addition to Eckhart resources.

Beginning with *The Phenomenon of Man* (New York, 1959) and running through *The Heart of Matter* (New York, 1978), most of the important essays and books of

Teilhard de Chardin have been published. An easy introduction to his thought can be obtained from a reading of N. M. Wildier's *An Introduction to Teilhard de Chardin* (New York, 1968). Two other books, both available in the Image Book series, are excellent synthetic studies: Henri de Lubac's *The Religion of Teilhard de Chardin* (1967) and Christopher Mooney's *Teilhard de Chardin and the Mystery of Christ* (1968). Donald P. Gray, "The Phenomenon of Teilhard," *Theological Studies*, March 1975, pp. 19–51, surveys studies on Teilhard done in the first twenty years after his death. It provides an excellent bibliography and overview. Ursula King's *Towards a New Mysticism: Teilhard de Chardin and Eastern Religions* (New York, 1980) is an important new study. Ewert Cousins' "Teilhard and Global Spirituality," *Anima*, Fall, 1981, pp. 26–30, is a provocative attempt to use Teilhard's ideas in a globally responsible way. *Teilhard and the Unity of Knowledge*, edited by T. King and J. Salmon (Ramsey, N.J., 1982), is a valuable anthology of recent papers on the vision of Teilhard.

6

THEOLOGIANS

There is a hoary academic joke that Jesus, in a vision, asked a modern professor of theology the question he asked his disciples at Caesarea Philippi: "Who do men say the Son of man is?" (Matt. 16:13). The professor replied, according to the story, "Some say you are the Ground of all being, while others insist that you are the ultimate ontological context of reality." Jesus replied, "Huh?" The joke, of course, is a putdown of the dense jargon of academic theology. The stereotype of the theologian is either that of a musty academic in his or her ivory tower writing impenetrable books for other slightly musty professors or gadfly academics (e.g., Hans Küng) who criticize hallowed ideas in the church so much that people are "upset." It is one of the sad realities of our culture that in the real world out there (wherever that may be) theologians are regarded as either irrelevancies fit only for the universities or media personalities to be consumed by *People* magazine or Phil Donahue along with every other ephemeral trend-setter in the country.

The whole idea of theology has a checkered and complicated history in the Catholic tradition. In early Christianity "theology" and "theologian" could mean quite diverse things. For some early Christian writers like Clement of Alexandria (c. 150–220) the word "theology" meant knowledge of divine things. Clement did not hesitate to use the word to describe Homer and his writings since they described the working of the gods. In that usage Clement was following one meaning of the word which had been used for centuries in Greek culture. By the following century most Christian writers had appropriated the term "theology" for specifically Christian purposes, but even then the word was still used in a number of different senses. Theology could mean true doctrine about God or it might signify—as it did for many early monks and mystics—the highest knowledge of God attained by interior illumination of the soul or through the highest state of prayer.

It was only in the Middle Ages that theology began to take on the more narrowly conceived meaning which we now assign to it. What we call "theology," Thomas Aquinas more typically called "Sacred Doctrine" (*sacra doctrina*). What is this "Sacred Doctrine" to which St. Thomas refers? In his day it meant a whole tradition which had evolved over the centuries by which scholars used reasoning (dialectics), grammar, and the other liberal arts to get a better and more coherent understanding of Holy Scripture. Theology was, well into the Middle Ages, synonymous with the disciplined study of scripture. It was inevitable, however, that people would also speculate more philosophically about the content of scripture. Theology became a way of knowing God's revelation more deeply, protecting it from erroneous understanding, and the advancement of some newer understanding of that revelation by the application of human intelligence. That is why St. Anselm of Canterbury (1033–1109) could define theology, in a memorable phrase, as *fides quaerens intellectum*—faith seeking understanding. With St. Anselm, and later in a somewhat different way with Thomas Aquinas, theology became a much more rigorously intellectual tradition in the sense that theology was thought of as the systematic application of human intelligence to the body of revelation. That is why St. Thomas in the very first question of the *Summa Theologica* defends the notion that theology is a science (art. 2) whose proper object is God (art. 7).

When we press the issue of the scope of theology in the church, we find that theology is a very broad category for a whole series of specialized fields of study. One may "do" theology to deepen one's personal faith or to convince a nonbeliever that one's belief has merit. It is obvious that in either case the way theology is done would be quite different. It seems likewise obvious that no theology can be written in a vacuum. Theology must seek, in the words of the Second Vatican Council, "a profound understanding of revealed truth without neglecting contact with its own time."[1]

Some basic motifs in theology are perennial. Christian people today, like those of the sixth or thirteenth century, are anxious about death, preoccupied with human guilt, concerned about the quality of belief, and ready to apply their own faith to the concerns and preoccupations of the age. These issues are at the very heart of being human, and, by that very fact, are constants. Yet every age brings with it its own cultural pressures and its own challenges to the authenticity of belief. Had St. Anselm or St. Thomas known of Freud, Darwin, Marx, or Galileo, their theology would look quite different than it does presently. That Anselm and Thomas did not know these watershed modern thinkers does not invalidate their thought or render it necessarily obsolete. It does force us to be mindful of the ways in which these modern thinkers (and many others) reshape the tradition of theology which has been received from the past masters.

How can we get some feel for the role of the theologian in the church? It would take volumes to even list the major trends in history of Catholic theology so we must be satisfied with a far different, and less comprehensive, approach to the issue. We shall opt for ruthless selectivity working on the principle of *multum in parvo*. We shall look at theologians at work in three vastly different periods of the church's life not with an eye to summarizing their doctrine but to answer questions like these: How did these theologians, to requote Vatican II, gain their profound understanding of revealed truth without "neglecting its own time"? Who was the audience for their theology? How did their theology reflect the pressures of their own age? In the case of the contemporary theologians we shall not focus on this or that particular thinker. We shall concentrate on the issues which the theologians have defined as being pertinent to the "signs of the time."

Thomas Aquinas

No discussion of theology and theologians in the Catholic tradition could dare omit mention of St. Thomas Aquinas (1225–1274). He was not only one of the most influential theologians in the history of the church, but his authority is such that the *Code of Canon Law* legislates that the clergy should receive both their philosophical and theological formation "according to the methods, doctrine, and principles of the Angelic Doctor."[2] St. Thomas, in the words of the late Dom David Knowles, is "not only recognized by all as a figure of importance, one who can stand alongside of Dante as a representative of medieval genius at its height, but he has stood, ever since his lifetime and never more than now, as a master to a large body of thinking men."[3]

Thomas Aquinas was born into a family of minor nobility at Roccasecca in Italy in 1225 or 1226. At a very early age his parents sent him to live at the nearby monastery of Monte Cassino with the fond expectation that someday he would become a monk and eventually abbot of the venerable Benedictine house. In 1239 the emperor Frederick II (who was related to Thomas's mother) expelled the monks from Monte Cassino. Thomas went to Naples and enrolled at the university there. In 1244, despite strong parental opposition, he joined the new Order of Friars Preachers (the Dominicans).

After Thomas entered the Dominicans, he was sent to Paris and then to Cologne for study. At the latter university he was a student of St. Albert the Great (1206–1280), who in time would become his good friend and supporter. Thomas received his doctorate from the University of Paris in 1257. In 1259 he left Paris for Italy where he spent nearly a decade in the service of the papacy following the papal court to the Italian cities of Anagui, Orvieto, Viterbo, and Rome. It was during this period that Thomas encouraged his Flemish friend William of Moerbeke to translate Aristotle's works from the Greek. In 1269 Thomas was back in Paris as a professor of theology, but left the city a second time in 1272 to establish a theological *stu-*

dium at Naples. In 1274, not yet fifty years old, Thomas died while en route to the Council of Lyons.

Of the personal life of St. Thomas we know little. He was corpulent and reticent to such a degree that his companions somewhat unkindly referred to him as a "dumb ox." According to the early biographers, when Albert the Great heard that nickname, he said that one day they would hear the bellowing of that "dumb ox" throughout the world. The Latin verses Thomas wrote for the office of Corpus Christi demonstrate his capacity both for poetry and for emotion, but he rarely let a personal remark slip in his prose writing. The end of his life was poignant to an extreme. On December 6, 1273, Thomas said Mass and failed to go to his writing desk. He never penned another word even though his *Summa Theologica* was unfinished. His closest friend and longtime travelling companion and secretary, Brother Reginald, asked him why he did not write anymore. "I cannot go on," Thomas is reported to have said, "All that I have written seems to me like so much straw compared to what I have seen and what has been revealed to me."[4]

For a person whose active scholarly life was relatively short (from about 1256 to 1273) St. Thomas was an almost unbelievably productive scholar; one modern edition of his writings (the so-called Leonine edition of the last century) runs to twenty-five stout volumes. A glance at the titles of his many treatises reveals the wide interests and obligations of a professional theologian who was at the service of the church through his activities as a scholar and university professor. He produced a polemical and apologetical work, the *Summa contra Gentiles*, for the use of Dominican missionaries who worked in Muslim Spain. He produced a text for theology students at the university which is what his celebrated *Summa Theologica* was intended to be. Like every academic theologian of the day he produced commentaries on various books of the Bible, as well as explanations of various classical authors in the history of theology (Peter Lombard, Boethius, the Pseudo-Dionysius). He wrote nearly a dozen commentaries on newly translated works of Aristotle. The writings of Thomas were educated, unsparing in their learning, and oriented to the needs of church and academy. He wrote, not for the masses, but for an educated elite.

St. Thomas lived at a period of great intellectual ferment; his culture was inundated with new sources of learning coming from the Islamic world. It was Thomas's peculiar genius to grasp the implications of this new learning (especially that represented by the Aristotelean corpus) and use it for his own theological work. Thomas was not afraid of the new; indeed he welcomed the new learning. He was sure that the long-lost works of Aristotle could help deepen and mature the understanding of the faith. He was convinced that human reason led, not away from God, but to him. He taught that human reason could come to a sure knowledge of God by its own powers, just as he was convinced that the same human reason could not come to a direct knowledge of the basic truths of Christianity without a revelation of God. Thomas steered a middle course between those who deprecated reason in the name of faith (e.g., "I believe because it is absurd") and those who would accept nothing that was not verifiable through the logical processes of human reason.

St. Thomas did not just work on "problems" as a theologian. While he wrote on a great number of topics, he was also a person who had a grand, comprehensive vision of all reality. He saw theology as a whole; he had a worldview. The Thomistic vision of Catholic theology has been enormously influential over the centuries not only because of its perceived coherence but also because of the endorsement that Thomism has received from the church. As one reviews the main points of Thomas's theology, it would be interesting to see how much of it still forms part of our own theological presuppositions and images. A Dominican scholar once formulated the main outlines of the theological worldview of Thomas in this fashion:

(1) Beyond the natural order there is an order of supernature about which we know only what God has revealed to us.

(2) The order of supernature cannot be arrived at through human industry; it is a revelation (the word literally means a "pulling back of the veils") from God—a gift; a grace.

(3) Despite the radical distinction to be made between nature and supernature there is no contradiction between reason and faith. Faith is the *perfection* of reason; it does not destroy it.

(4) Reason alone can neither attain to, nor disprove, the supernatural truths of Christianity; e.g., one could never reason to the trinity of Persons in God.

(5) God's causality and providence over the world does not destroy human freedom. Those who are saved, are saved through the free gift of God by grace but those who are damned are damned through their own doings.

(6) Predestination to glory is a free gift of God; it is an act of Divine mercy not something owed to anyone.

(7) The primary reason for the Incarnation is the salvation of fallen humanity. Had Adam not sinned there would have been no Incarnation.

(8) The sacraments of the church are not mere symbols; they are instruments of God's grace. In the final analysis, Christ is the true minister of all sacramental action.

(9) The church, the mystical body of Christ, is the sole custodian of the Faith and dispenser of the sacraments.

(10) Eternal life consists of the vision of God granted to the Saved who, for all eternity, will be in the presence of God.[5]

The theology of St. Thomas Aquinas is rooted in the metaphysics of being. Thomas starts from the fact of existence. It is to the very nature of reality that Thomas, like his mentor Aristotle, makes appeal. This large framework (can anyone imagine a larger one?) starts with the very notion of being and from that start makes large claims. Such a vision has a broad and deep sweep to it even though many moderns find it intellectually dissatisfying. It appears to many today to ignore the more concrete texture of historical reality; its consciousness is too metaphysical, too rational, too abstract. Modern theologians have accused Thomists of creating a theology which is too Hellenic, too far from the earthiness of Hebrew thought, too removed from the historical consciousness of moderns. There is something awesomely ordered and rational about Aquinas as well as something rather impersonal. His achievement is not only that he spoke for his age but for others. That his thought is criticized today is not a diminution of his importance; it is a tribute to its power.

Blaise Pascal

It would be difficult to think of anyone in the history of theology who presents a more dramatic contrast to St. Thomas Aquinas than the French thinker Blaise Pascal (1623–1662). Thomas was a professional theologian who spent his entire adult life as a Dominican friar either as a holder of a theological chair at a university or as a functionary of an ecclesiastical office. Aquinas's writings reflect his professional status as a theologian and his own temperament as a highly rational and disciplined thinker. He wrote theological treatises noted for their austere logic and their monumental sweep. By contrast, Pascal was a brilliantly inventive mathematician and physical scientist whose major theological work is a jumble of notes, outlines, fragments, and quotations left unpublished and unorganized at his death. Thomas Aquinas was a theologian by profession; Pascal was an amateur—in the deepest sense of that word—whose burning faith and intellectual depth made him one of the most original theological thinkers in the history of the church. The great differences in temperament, style, and emphasis between a St. Thomas and a Pascal point up the variety and fecundity of the theological tradition.

Pascal was born in 1623. At the age of eight he moved with his father to Paris where his father wished to pursue a life of scientific study. Pascal showed signs of being a mathematical prodigy, signs which his father encouraged. By the age of sixteen Pascal published an important treatise on the nature of conic sections in geometry. He and his father left Paris in 1640 to live in Rouen where they were to remain for seven years. It was a time of incredible productivity for the young scientific genius. He designed a mechanical calculator to help his father in his tax collecting (it is the ancestor of the computer) and carried out original experiments which proved the existence of vacuums in nature and helped to calculate the weight of air.

Because of his poor health Pascal returned to Paris in 1647 where he soon became part of a wide circle of brilliant thinkers and scientific investigators. In this charged atmosphere he continued his mathematical work (Pascal did pioneering work in the field of calculus), but found himself more closely drawn to questions of religion and the meaning of his own life. He was much influenced by a group of extremely rigid Catholics (called Jansenists) whose purity of life, sense of service, and high seriousness deeply moved him. His own sister had become a nun at the convent of Port-Royal, which was one of the centers of Jansenist theological and devotional thought.[6] The apex of this religious awakening happened on the night of November 23, 1654. After Pascal's death a piece of parchment, with that date on it, was found sewn into his clothes:

Fire

God of Abraham, God of Isaac, God of Jacob,
   not of philosophers and scholars.
Certainty, certainty, heartfelt joy, peace,
God of Jesus Christ.
God of Jesus Christ.
My God and Your God.
Thy God shall be my God.
The world forgotten and everything but God.
He can only be found by the ways taught in
   the Gospels . . . .

In his last years Pascal worked on his various scientific projects, engaged in fierce religious polemics with enemies of the Jansenists (especially the French Jesuits), and labored at a huge theological work, which had the working title of *Apologie de la religion Chrétienne*, a work left unfinished at his death. The notes and fragments of that work were published and make up the famous *Pensées*. It is a mark of his many-sided genius that in the last years before his death Pascal devised a scheme to have large carriages transport people along fixed routes in Paris, thus inventing the first public transport system in Europe. Pascal used the profits from this enterprise to underwrite a number of his favorite charities since he had already dispensed, in the final years, his fortune among a number of worthy causes.

It is the *Pensées* which we wish to consider in some detail. Pascal intended to write a work which would confront the skeptical spirit of his own age, a skepticism he knew at first hand from his social and scientific contacts in the salons of Paris. His age, after all, was one in which the spirit of science seemed at loggerheads with the old faith of the past. Pascal was evidently not impressed with the traditional theology of the schools (he rarely ever quoted St. Thomas, for example); it seems that he felt that their ideology would not make an effective case for belief. Pascal did not have the same confidence as Thomas that reason alone would bring people to an understanding of the reality of God: "All those who have claimed to know God and prove his existence without Jesus Christ have only futile proofs to offer" (189).

What, then, was Pascal's strategy to be? There are two fragments in the *Pensées* which outline his basic starting place:

> First part: wretchedness of man without God. Second part: happiness of man with God. (6)

> . . . Show that religion is not contrary to reason, but worthy of reverence and respect.
> Next, make it attractive, make good men wish it were true, and then show that it is worthy of reverence because it really understands human nature.
> Attractive because it promises true good. (12)

Pascal, then, starts with an analysis of the human condition. He sets out to show that people are finite, hungry for love, uncertain of their future, dissatisfied with their goals, driven toward a satisfaction which they cannot seem to attain. As a second step Pascal intends to show that Christianity (and Christianity alone; it is not one of many options) answers all of the hungering needs that humans have. Christian belief fills up the void which is at the very heart of existence.

But, it may be objected, if Christianity has the answers to human needs, it must be true, but how do we know the truth of Christianity? Pascal answers that the truth of Christ is proved by the fact that he is the perfect fulfillment of all the prophecies of the Old Testament and, further, he shows that fulfillment through the miracles of his life, preeminently the miracle of the Resurrection. These "proofs" in themselves do not compel assent, but like Aquinas Pascal sees such proofs as a preparation for belief; they allow the serious person to become prepared for the gift of faith: "We shall never believe, with an effective belief and faith, unless God inclines our hearts, and we shall believe as soon as He does so" (380).

Those individuals who understand their position in life are poised, as it were, ready to make a choice either for belief and human fulfillment or for a life without faith and, also, without fulfillment. One chooses belief, not as the outcome of evidence, but as an act of faith. This is the character of Pascal's famous "wager." We "bet" that in making an act of faith we have done the better, more perfect, thing:

> . . . Let us weigh up the gain and loss in calling head that God exists. Let us assess the two cases: if you win you win every-thing; if you lose, you lose nothing. Do not hesitate then; wager that He does exist. That is wonderful. "Yes, I must wager, but perhaps I am wagering too much." Let us see: since there is an equal chance of gain and loss, if you stood to win two lives for one you could still wager, but suppose you stood to win three? . . . And, thus, since you are obliged to play, you must be renouncing reason if you hoard your life rather than risk it for an infinite gain, just as likely to occur as a loss amounting to nothing. (418)

There is something very modern about Pascal's thought. Un-like Aquinas who rises to God from a consideration of the order of nature (God as first mover) and the solidity of existence (God as self-subsistent being), Pascal finds God through a consider-ation of human disorder and the fragile nature of human life. He poses two relentlessly stark alternatives for humanity. It is no wonder that many modern existentialists, so preoccupied with the burden of human absurdity and the meaninglessness of life, look to Pascal as an honored ancestor even when they cannot share his theology. It also explains why certain Cath-olics see in Pascal a "religious nihilism of terrifying aspect."[7]

The contemporary Catholic theologian Karl Rahner has writ-ten that all theology begins in anthropology; that was never more true than in the case of Pascal's theology. Whatever his limitations may be, there is nobody (save for the nineteenth-century Protestant theologian Soren Kierkegaard who resembles him so much) who has put the problems of belief in such stern terms. Beyond that, Pascal is one of the most compelling figures in the history of the Catholic tradition. In his person he combined the mind of a scientist, the spirit of a mystic, and the drive of those God-intoxicated people who appear throughout history as challenges to the more leisurely and complacent searchers after religious truth.

Catholic Theology Today

Contemporary Roman Catholic theology is often characterized by two adjectives today: "pluralist" and "historical." Let us say a few words about each term.

Pluralism. There has always been some degree of pluralism in Christian thought. The understanding of Jesus that we find in the Gospel of St. John reflects different concerns than the image of Jesus found in the letters of St. Paul. When St. Thomas taught at the University of Paris, his contemporary the Franciscan friar St. Bonaventure (1221–1274) also held a theological chair. Bonaventure's theology was totally different from that of Thomas in its presuppositions, methodology, and emphases. Franciscan theology to this day stands in tension with that of the Dominicans.

When we use the term "pluralism" today, we mean that the standard textbook theology (often called "Roman theology") in use for decades in all Catholic seminaries has given way to a variety of ways of doing theology; these ways are often in tension with or in opposition to the older textbook theology. Just as Catholicism is no longer rigidly homogeneous and its discipline is no longer uniformly applied, so its theology reflects the hetereogeneity of the contemporary church. It is no longer possible to think of Catholic theology; there are a number of theologies which work within the larger tradition which we call the "Catholic tradition."

Historical. The orientation of contemporary Catholic theology is also historical. Let us be precise in our use of that term. It does not only mean that Catholic theology is more conscious of its discipline as having a historical evolution (although it surely means that); it means that the best of contemporary theology is done today with a keen sense of historical consciousness. St. Thomas thought of theology in terms of existence and the metaphysics of being, while Pascal used as his starting point the nature of human existence. The contemporary theologian is more likely to think of theology as being done from the perspective of people who live in a specific culture at a specific time, who see the world in a set of historically conditioned images, symbols, and metaphors, which, while producing insights of transcendental importance, are insights which come in historical packages and must be understood as such. It is a theology, as David Tracy has written, which is faithful both to Christian texts (i.e., the data of revelation) and to common human experience.[8] Those two components, basic for any theology, need to be in some kind of creative and mutually illuminating tension.

The desire to be close to the processes of history and faithful to the pluralist nature of culture has led to a number of theologies whose very existence was not even explicitly affirmed a generation ago. When one speaks, to cite one example from the North American theological experience, of black theology, the base line is that blacks have had certain kinds of secular and religious experiences in the United States and have related to the larger majority culture (which is largely white and primarily Christian), so that their perceptions and priorities will reflect a particular way of being in American history. A black theology will provide, at the very least, a reflection on the meaning of faith for black believers and, at the same time, serve as a corrective to those other believers who have not shared the historical experience of being black or who, for better or for ill, have shaped the black experience or been shaped by it.

In the contemporary theological world of Roman Catholicism two major historical theologies have had a particular impact on contemporary religious perceptions, both because of their strong challenge to many mainline theological assumptions and also because of their potentiality for radically altering our understanding of the Catholic tradition. I refer to *liberation theology* and *feminist theology*.

Both liberation theology (understood as political theology) and feminist theology (understood either as a political theology or as an alternative approach to theology) have had to fight the mainstream theological schools for a hearing. That they still receive stiff resistance does not obviate the fact that in a relatively short period of time—less than a generation—their ideas have exercised a profound influence not only on the way theology is to be done but about what theological questions are serious enough to be asked.

Theology and Feminism

One of the more extraordinary social revolutions in our times has been the rapid rise and stunning success of the women's liberation movement. To cite a small change: Every attempt has been made in this book to avoid sexual preference language ("mankind" is replaced by "humanity," etc.), whereas books I wrote just ten years ago used such language as the natural order of things. The drive of women (and men of good will) to overcome the historical and social structures which stereotype what women can or cannot do or be as well as the political fight to give women economic and social opportunity and to shield them from explicit or tacit sexual violence has been one of the true political revolutions of our postwar culture.

It was inevitable that such a powerful movement would turn its attention to the status of women in the church and the image of women in religion generally. Feminists who are also committed church people could not but see the cultural and theological ways in which women have been reduced to second-class citizenship in the church. While women have reached great eminence in the Catholic tradition as foundresses, martyrs, mystics, reformers, and thinkers, they have never had access to the sacramental ministry of the church in any full sense of the term nor have they ever had any part in the governance of the church. Church governance was always in the hands of male clerics. Beyond these practical liabilities there is a deep-rooted tradition of misogynism in the Catholic church with women stereotyped as sexual temptresses (e.g., in the writings of St. Jerome) or as defective males (in the thought of Thomas Aquinas). Even the exaltation of the Blessed Virgin Mary is seen by feminist critics as a source of gender oppression in its exaltation of maternity free from the common experience of female sexuality. However much Marian devotion allowed for a feminine element in Christianity, there was still a strong antisexual and distrustful air about it.

Some feminist critics argue that such antifeminine bias is pandemic in biblical religion. Because the God of Judaeo-Christianity is a patriarchical figure who admits of no consort and whose honorific titles (king, ruler, pastor, lord, etc.) are unremittingly patriarchal and masculine, the whole religious tradition that derives from the Bible is, in its essence, beyond the feminist pale. The conclusion to be drawn from such a reading of the biblical tradition is to scrap biblical religion as a hostile force. This radical position has its most vigorous proponent in the writings of Mary Daly. Daly, who trained as a Catholic theologian and still teaches at a Catholic college, sees Christianity in general and Catholicism in particular as hopelessly compromised. In her most recent major work she indicts all male religion and, as a corrective and alternative, proposes an entirely new religious symbol system extrapolated *in toto* from the female experience.[9]

Daly's work is so radical (and, in a certain fashion, so *outré* and sectarian) that it will never gain large acceptance. Her work does provide, however, the outer limit against which other feminist work can be gauged. Those who would opt to remain within (or near to) the Christian tradition as expressed in Catholicism do so while pursuing two strategies, one practical and the other theoretical.

At the practical level women (and men) press for a larger, more equitable, role for women in the life of the church. Within Roman Catholicism this is an awesomely difficult task when even something as trivial as "altar girls" or female lectors is resisted at official levels. The current touchstone of ecclesial ferment in practical feminist circles is the drive for women's ordination to the priesthood. Despite official statements from Rome, most notably the declaration of the Congregation for the Doctrine of the Faith (January 27, 1977) and the many unofficial statements of Pope John Paul II, there is still much active ferment on this question. The Canon Law Society of America and the Catholic Theological Society of America have both worked on scholarly studies on this question, while the

Women's Ordination Conference (founded in 1975) pursues a more activist role in pressing the ordination issue. It is a mark of how difficult this issue is that when women were ordained in the Episcopal church in this country, a number of dissident Episcopalians sought union with Rome based on their perception that Rome would not easily yield on the issue of women priests.

At the theoretical level scholars have undertaken an intense reexamination of the theological tradition to see how masculine triumphalism and male cultural biases in the church have suppressed the freedom of women in the church. New Testament exegetes like Elisabeth Schüssler Fiorenza have focused on the role of women in the early church, while patristics scholars like Rosemary Ruether have tracked the emergence of antifeminine structures in the development of church doctrine and practice.

Feminist theology is not special pleading; it turns a powerful light on the ideologies (i.e., value systems accepted but not acknowledged as such) in the Catholic tradition. It shows that people, wittingly or unwittingly, can "use" the Gospel to sustain or conflate human power, to subjugate others rather than free them, or to inflate one's own power fantasies. A recent writer, surveying the many currents of the feminist debate in theology, sums up the larger theological achievement of theological feminism in this fashion:

> Women's religious protest and affirmation is a grace for our times. In its protest about the clear and real issue of women, it raises to view the scandal of the past and its confident, often idolatrous assertions about God and Christ and human persons. In its courageous iconoclasm and its symbolic association with the other "others" of history and the present, it exposes and denies the splits, dichotomies, manipulation, and exploitation— the sins of our times from a particular and practical perspective. In its new apprehension of God and of Christ, it affirms a vision of human wholeness, integrity, and community, a genuinely new Christian consciousness that extends inclusion, mutuality, reciprocity, and service beyond its own causes. In so doing, Christian feminism transcends itself and enables the tradition to transcend itself, to become the hope, the future, that is promised.[10]

Many feminists (Rosemary Ruether is the preeminent example) link her feminist concerns to the larger issues of political oppression and political liberation. In that sense, at least, they have a natural affinity for the work of liberation theologians who orient their work to an analysis of the social condition from the perspective of theology and theological analysis.

Liberation Theology

Liberation theology is the rubric generally used to describe a way of doing theology that derives from the experience of being Catholic in Latin America. The pioneering Catholic work in this field is Gustavo Gutierrez's *A Theology of Liberation* (1971) in which the agenda of the liberation theologians was set out and the main issues identified.

What is distinctive about liberation theology? First of all, liberation theology is testily suspicious of a good deal of traditional theology. It charges that traditional Catholic theological reflection is too intellectually rarefied and too uncommitted to application and practice. The liberationists see much of traditional theology too concerned with the intellectual agenda of middle class thinkers, but offering no plan or idea about action in behalf of those who are oppressed and so lacking in hope that they have no opportunity to luxuriate in theological thought. Liberationists further argue that too much modern theology reflects the post-Enlightenment bias toward the individual. Given such a bias, these theologians argue, there is an in-built neglect of the social structures which have a shaping influence on human destiny. Traditional theology, in short, is politically and socially deficient.

Secondly, liberation theology reads Sacred Scripture from the vantage point of the urban poor and the peasant class of Latin America. It takes as its basic biblical theme the Exodus motif of liberation from slavery and promise of freedom—a theme which is also basic to the black American religious experience as the black spirituals so readily attest. The New Testament Jesus put forth by the liberation theologians is the Jesus of the poor who promises liberation from oppression by holding out the hope of liberation. Leonardo Boff, a Brazilian theologian, constructs an entire Christology according to a liberationist reading of the New Testament. In his book *Jesu Cristo Liber-atador* (1972; English version, 1980), Boff sets forth a Jesus who liberates from human oppression (unjust laws, evil political order, etc.), alienating powers like sin and sickness, and finally, in the resurrection, liberation from death itself.[11]

Liberation theologians are at great pains to link theology to social reality. In their discussion of the Eucharist, for example, they would insist that the Eucharist not only recalls the passion, death, and resurrection of Christ (a traditional understanding of the Eucharist), but that it is also a sign of how people ought to live in society. The Eucharist symbolizes (and effects) equals before God, under grace, who are reconciled and free from any destructive animus. The emphasis is on community and reconciliation. It is an understanding of the Eucharist which is social and communitarian.

It is not only liberation theology which is communitarian; its practical program of action puts a great emphasis on Christian mutuality. This is most apparent in the development of what are called *communidades de base*—basic communities. These small groups meet to reflect on the scriptures, share the Eucharist, and outline ways of living the Gospel and changing their surroundings based on what they learn from Gospel reflection. These small groups have had an amazing growth in Latin America (there are estimated to be 100,000 *communidades* in Brazil alone) and have become a potent social force. The *communidades* reflect many of the ideas of liberation theology. To compare them with traditional parishes might help also to see how liberation theology differs from traditional theology:

	Parish	*Communidades*
Structure:	hierarchical	democratic
Doctrine:	very important; based on tradition	not important; emphasis on Gospel study
Leadership:	clerics	lay people
Emphasis:	religious practice	moral behavior
Social origin:	middle class	poor and alienated
Sacraments:	means of salvation	signs of salvation
Values:	individual	social
Center:	Rome	the poor[12]

Because of its social and political concerns liberation theology has eagerly read and assimilated scholarship from sociology, economics, and political theory. Many liberation theologians—to the chagrin of its critics—have made ample use of Marxist categories to analyze (and, in some few cases, to prescribe) the social situation of the poor in Latin America. Their argument for doing this is that Marxist thinkers, more than any others, have taken seriously the ways in which systems oppress and alienate people. Dom Helder Camara, the bishop of Recife (Brazil), has said that Catholic thinkers ought to use Marx the same way Thomas used Aristotle in the Middle Ages: as a thinker who sheds light on the contemporary theological situation.

It is much debated about how liberation theology relates to the Marxist idea of social revolution and class struggle, especially in the light of revolutionary violence in Latin America. This is a very difficult issue which must be handled with a certain delicacy given the violence that comes from both right and left in South America and the institutional violence rooted in some state structures—the so-called *violencia blanca* ("white violence") of the state itself. Let us pose the issue in its most stark terms: If the population of a country are totally oppressed by a thoroughly corrupt ruling class, can they violently revolt *in the name of the Gospel?* That they can rebel seems clear; that is how the United States was formed. That they can use self-defense seems equally clear. The question is: Is class violence and class revolution which the Marxists posit as both a historical necessity and a social good compatible with the Gospel? How does revolutionary violence square with the pacifism and passivity of the Gospel? Those are very difficult, and largely unresolved, questions which are not dissimilar to those we raised in Chapter 4 when similar questions about the concept of the historical category of the Christian warrior were studied.

Liberation theology is a fact in the contemporary church. The creativity of the Latin American theologians has spurred the imagination of theologians from other parts of the world, most notably Africa and the Far East, to think of theology in terms of their social experience. Nor should it be forgotten that we are now getting examples of Christian theology (mostly by

Orthodox thinkers) from the Eastern bloc countries where liberation means something quite different from that outlined by these from Latin America.[13] The very ferment produced by these various theologies (many of which may not survive) does signal one clear fact: The day of the hegemony of Roman theology is over: the younger churches are coming of age and their missionary status is now being reversed. They now export ideas rather than import them. The newness of liberation theology should not blind us to its traditional character. In the final analysis liberation theology roots itself in that old biblical idea, characteristic of St. Paul, that Christ came to save, not this or that individual, but the *world*.

Notes

1. Pastoral Constitution on the Church in the Modern World, art. 62, in *The Documents of Vatican II*, ed. Walter M. Abbott, p. 270.

2. Canon 1366, 2; cf. Canon 589, 1 where the same point is made.

3. David Knowles, *The Evolution of Medieval Thought* (New York, 1962), p. 256.

4. J. A. Weisheipl's authoritative biography *Fra Thomas d'Aquino* (Garden City, N.Y., 1974) speculates that Thomas had some kind of physical and emotional breakdown at the end of his life.

5. J. A. Weisheipl, "Thomism," *The New Catholic Encyclopedia*, vol. 14 (Washington, D.C., 1967), pp. 127–28. I have adapted Father Weiseiphl's schema.

6. The nuns of Port-Royal were, as a detractor said, pure as angels and proud as devils. See Ronald Knox's classic study *Enthusiasm* (Oxford and New York, 1950.

7. Frederick Heer, *The Intellectual History of Europe*, vol. 2 (Garden City, N.Y., 1968), p. 131. For a more balanced yet critical view, see Hans Küng, *Does God Exist?* (New York, 1981), pp. 42ff.

8. David Tracy, *Blessed Rage for Order: The New Pluralism in Theology* (New York, 1975).

9. Mary Daly, *Gyn/Ecology* (Boston, 1979) and her earlier *Beyond God the Father* (Boston, 1973).

10. Anne Carr, "Is a Christian Feminist Theology Possible?" *Theological Studies*, July 1982, pp. 296–97. This entire essay is devoted to a *status quaestionis* of feminist theology.

11. Another book from Latin America that makes a similar case is *Jon Sobrino's Christology at the Crossroads: A Latin American Approach* (Maryknoll, N.Y., 1978). Sobrino puts particular emphasis on the Jesus of history, since Jesus, according to Sobrino, lived a life so much like that of the Latin American poor.

12. Adapted from Gottfried Deelen's "The Church on Its Way to the People: Basic Christian Communities in Brazil," *Cross Currents*, Winter 1981, p. 390.

13. See Alexander Solzhenitsyn, ed., *From Under the Rubble* (London and New York, 1975) for a selection of such essays.

Readings and Trajectories

Histories of dogma abound, but a great work is still to be written on the sociology of theologians and their work in the Catholic tradition. For this chapter I was helped by the theoretical work of Bernard Lonergan and David Tracy, but used Yves M. J. Congar's *A History of Theology* (Garden City, N.Y., 1968) for most of my factual information. On more recent theology, see Mark Schoof, *A Survey of Catholic Theology* (New York, 1970) and Gerald McCool, *Catholic Theology in the Nineteenth Century* (New York, 1977).

For a general discussion of medieval thought I still find very helpful the old classic of Etienne Gilson's: *Reason and Revelation in the Middle Ages* (New York, 1938): its clarity and readability make it quite useful for students. The same author's *The Christian Philosophy of Saint Thomas Aquinas* (New York, 1956) is still serviceable. James A. Weisheipl's *Fra Thomas d'Aquino* (Garden City, N.Y., 1974) will win no prizes for style, but is the standard critical biography in English.

Jean Mesnard's *Pascal*, translated by Claude and Marcia Abraham (University of Alabama, 1969), is a handy critical study by a leading Pascal scholar. Also: Jan Miel, *Pascal and Theology* (Baltimore, 1978).

Anne Carr's essay (cited in note 10 of this chapter) has a good bibliography of current feminist writing; for a systematic survey through 1977, see Carol Christ's "The New Feminist Theology: A Review of the Literature," *Religious Studies Review* 3 (1977), pp. 203–12. Also helpful: the anthology *Womanspirit Rising*, edited by Carol Christ and Judith Plaskow (San Francisco, 1979), and Rosemary Ruether's *New Woman, New Earth: Sexist Ideologies and Human Liberation* (New York, 1975). Lawrence S. Cunningham's *Mother of God* (San Francisco, 1982) has a survey of thinking about the Blessed Virgin and feminism. On women and ministry: *Women and Catholic Priesthood*, edited by A. M. Gardiner (New York, 1976), and *Women and Priesthood*, edited by C. Stuhlmueller (Collegeville, Minn., 1978). Elisabeth Schüssler Fiorenza's "You Are Not to Be Called Father: Early Christian History in a Feminist Perspective," *Cross Currents*, Fall 1979, pp. 301–23, is an exemplary introduction of the issues, while her recent book, *In Memory of Her: A Feminist Theological Reconstruction of Christian Origins* (New York, 1983), offers a fuller, more definitive treatment.

Most of the great classics of liberationist thinking—the works of Sobrino, Boff, Gutierrez, Dussel, etc.—are easily available in translation from Orbis Books (Maryknoll, N.Y.), which has specialized in liberation theology titles. A handy sampler of liberation theology may be found in R. Gibellini, ed., *Frontiers of Theology in Latin America* (Maryknoll, N.Y., 1979). Two issues of *Cross Currents* are useful for liberationist thought: *Puebla: Moment of Decision for the Latin American Church*, edited by Gary MacEoin (Spring 1978), and *Learning from Africa* (Winter 1978/79); the latter gives important perspective from a non-Latin American stance. The earlier work *Liberation, Revolution, and Freedom: Theological Perspectives*, edited by T. MacFadden (New York, 1975), has readable essays on a whole range of liberation themes. Walbert Bühlmann's *The Coming of the Third Church* (Maryknoll, N.Y., 1980) is an encyclopedic survey of the church in non-European and non-North American spheres.

7

ARTISTS

Art and Catholic Theology

The Catholic tradition has always been sympathetic to, and supportive of, artistic activity. Catholicism as a historical tradition is unthinkable apart from its churches, paintings, sculptures, works of literature, musical compositions, and finely crafted items of religious and liturgical usage. When Catholic pilgrims gather at St. Peter's basilica in the Vatican, they sense not only the Renaissance grandeur of Michelangelo's dome and the explosive baroque force of Bernini's sculpture; they sense the entire weight of the church's artistic tradition. They learn that there had been a church on that spot since the fourth century built by the emperor Constantine to honor the spot where St. Peter had been buried. That church, and the new one begun in the beginning of the sixteenth century, attracted artists, sculptors, and architects in every age. Present-day visitors can see a medieval statue of Arnolfo di Cambio, a fragmentary fresco of Giotto, statues by Bernini and Canova, as well as bronze doors by the contemporary sculptor Giacomo Manzú. The walls of the basilica echo the chant of the Gregorian tradition as well as Renaissance motets, Baroque masses, and contemporary sacred music. St. Peter's is not a museum; it is a living repository of fifteen hundred years of artistic creativity.

The very splendor of St. Peter's—to cite the most extravagant example of Catholicism's monuments—helps us to focus on some persistent questions: Is the lavish use of art in its various

128

forms a residue of paganism in Catholicism—a form of "idolatry" as some critics charge? Is there an inherent paradox between the artistic tradition of Catholicism and the biblical
injunctions against artistic representations (e.g., Exod. 20:4–6;
Deut. 5:8–10)? How does one reconcile the simplicity of the
Gospel and the Baroque splendors of the Vatican? Is there any
theological foundation that helps us understand the place of
art in the Catholic tradition?

We should note in passing that the Catholic acceptance of
the representational arts (painting, sculpture, etc.) is one way
to distinguish it from the tradition of the Reformation. For the
Protestant Reformation *the* arts were those which emphasized
the preached Word (music, literature), while the plastic arts
were shunned as nonbiblical. It is hard to name one great painter
or sculptor who stood in the Reformation tradition.[1] Even artists like Dürer, Altdorfer, and Cranach who were sympathetic
to the Reformation nourished their iconographical and aesthetical principles on the older Catholic tradition. One could
make the argument that Baroque artistic culture (again, Rembrandt would be the exception) is an expression of the Catholic
Reformation. Baroque art was both an apologetical and a celeb-
ratory reaction against the Reformation. Protestantism's answer to a Bernini was a J. S. Bach.

What, then, is the theological matrix out of which the art of
the Catholic tradition grows?

Toward the conclusion of his monumental two-volume study
on Catholicism the American theologian Richard McBrien in-
dicates three foci which he claims to be characteristic of Catholicism: sacramentality, mediation, and community.[2]

In its sacramentality the Catholic tradition affirms that God
is known through *signs*, both natural (the world itself as God's
creation) and ecclesial signs like the sacraments formally
understood. It is possible to think of the entire Christian reality
in terms of sacramentality. Jesus is a sacrament in the sense
that his Incarnation was a visible sign in the world that God
is real and concerned with the world. The church, in turn, is
also a sacrament because as a visible reality mediating the invisible grace of God it is a sign-extension of the presence of
Jesus in the world. The church is the sign which Jesus gives to

guarantee his work in history. The church, in turn, makes concrete the presence of Jesus through visible signs which the
church numbers as seven.

The natural and ecclesial signs of God do not only *signify*
the reality of God; they *mediate* God's presence to us. Catholicism does not affirm that the usual way of knowing God
is through direct experience even though such an experience
is available to the mystic. God is normally made known to us
through the mediated forms. The constant tradition of the church
is that God is revealed first of all through the work of creation;
as the medieval writer Alan of Lille puts it:

> *Omnis mundi creatura*
> *Quasi liber et pictura*
> *Nobis est et speculum.*
>
> The created world is for us
> like a book, a picture,
> and a mirror.[3]

Along with the world of nature God's work is also known
to us as it is mediated through the unfolding of history, the
social reality of institutions, the goodness and holiness of others, the power and efficacy of the church's sacramental and
liturgical life, and the preaching of God's word.

The reality of God is mediated through community. While
the Catholic tradition affirms the reality of individual religious
experience, it insists that "we are radically social beings: our
use of language is clear evidence of that. There is no relationship
with God, however intense, profound and unique, that dispen-
ses entirely with the communal context of every human relationship with God."[4]

Sacramentality is the theological key for understanding Catholicism's attitude toward sacred art. Artworks are creations;
they are made by those who wish to mediate meaning from the
materials that they shape for their use. Every work of art signals
the ideas of the artist through the medium of her creation. The
sacred artist says, in effect, here is what I have learned about
the presence of God or the words of the Gospel or the actions
of Jesus. The work of art reflects the concern of the artist, but

it also evokes a response from the viewer or reader or listener: "... the work of art encounters me with the surprise, impact, even shock of reality itself. I recognize a truth I somehow know but know I really did not know except through the experience of recognition of the essential compelled by the work of art. I am transformed by its truth when I return to the very day, to the whole of what I call reality ordinarily, and discover new affinities, new sensibilities, for the everyday."[5]

It is obvious that all art is bound to its historical and temporal culture; Raphael would most likely find Op Art puzzling as art. Nonetheless, great art ("masterpieces") not only reflects the time and culture in which it was made, it reaches beyond its culture to speak to us today. Great art is a model and a resource for all times. Michelangelo's "Pietà," for example, speaks eloquently of high Renaissance art, but that same statue provides lessons for today about the nature of beauty, maternity, mourning, sadness, sacrifice, loss, and resignation. We admire it both as a work of art and as a contemporary statement.

In order to specify our discussion about sacred art in the Catholic tradition we will look at some representative examples of the arts from the tradition with a particular focus on these artworks as signs mediating religious meaning.

Icons

One of the oldest art forms in the history of Christianity is the religious icon. Any visitor to a Byzantine church recognizes immediately the characteristic paintings of Christ, the Virgin, and the saints which adorn the walls of the church and which make up the great screen (called the *iconastasis*) that separates the worshipper from the altar. To look at this art is to look at an artistic tradition which goes back to the earliest centuries of the church. The iconic tradition was standard in the Western church until the time of the Renaissance and still is the predominant art style in the East. The figures of the icon face the viewer frontally; they are set against gold backgrounds, and put in poses which are historic and solemn. These images (the word *icōn* is Greek for "image") are solemnly honored in liturgical services with bows, incense, and lighted tapers. To understand icons, one scholar of Orthodoxy has written, is to understand the very nature of Byzantine Christianity.

In the eighth century there was an organized attempt (led by a Byzantine emperor) to rid the church of icons. After a long period of turmoil and unrest the struggle came to an end. The defeat of the *Iconclasts* ("Image Breakers") was considered so crucial to the development of Eastern Christianity that the Orthodox church to this day celebrates the defeat of the Iconoclast movement with a solemn day of religious services called the "Feast of the Triumph of Orthodoxy." The Second Ecumenical Council of Nicaea (A.D. 787) set out the church's teaching on icons and their place in the public life of the church. The council taught that, while adoration, properly speaking, belongs only to God, the icons of the church should be venerated because "honor to the image passes to the source of the image; those who worship the images, worship, in fact, those who stand behind the images displayed." The council, in short, taught that the icons are mediating signs by which we reach out to worship God and venerate his saints.

Theologians link the use of images in the public worship of the church with the doctrine of the Incarnation. They note that St. Paul describes Christ as the image (*icōn*) of God (2 Cor. 4:4) and the followers of Christ as "images of the Son" (Rom. 8:29). In the icons, then, we "see" Christ through the sign which is the painting itself. For Orthodox theology the icon is a testament to the fleshly reality of the Incarnation. Just as Christ truly took on flesh, so the painter "enfleshes" the figure of Christ for the devout believer. John of Damascus (c. 645– c. 750), one of the great defenders of icons, put the matter forcefully:

> Of old God the incorporeal and uncircumscribed was not depicted at all. But now that God has appeared in the flesh and lived among men I make an image of God who can be seen. I do not worship matter but I worship the creator of matter who for my sake became material and deigned to dwell in matter, who through matter effected my salvation. I will not cease from worshipping the matter through which my salvation has been effected.[6]

We must underscore the fact that icons do not serve merely didactic or decorative functions in the church. They are channels of prayer and adoration; they mediate between the earthbound worshipper and the transcendent realities of heaven which "stand behind" the icon. When the believer looks at an icon, it is, as it were, a look through a window into the world of the mysteries of salvation. The iconic presence of the sacred persons are in communication with the believer. The drama of salvation is told and communicated through the icon. It is for this reason that the great Byzantinist André Grabar once described icons as "theology in color."

Icons are the ultimate and uncompromising examples of sacred art in Christianity. Legend has it that St. Luke the evangelist was the first painter of icons. Examples of his painting are shown to the pious pilgrims at the Laterans in Rome as well as the church of the Pantheon and Santa Maria Maggiore.[7] They are all of the type of icon called *Hodegetria* (i.e., the "pointer of the Way"). They depict the Blessed Virgin Mary holding the child Jesus in her left arm and pointing to him with her right hand. Because icons are sacred objects, there is a tremendous resistance to artistic innovation in their production. The icon painter is expected to perfect the basic themes of the icons over and over again much as the master musicians are expected to wrest new meanings from the music of Bach without changing the notes he originally wrote. The painting of icons has always been considered a holy occupation and much of icon painting comes from monastic and convent centers. The names of some of the great icon painters have come down to us, but the better part of the corpus of icons has been done by anonymous artists since it is the finished product, not the fame of the maker, that is central.

We most identify the tradition of icons with the church of Byzantium, but their place in the Western church is also important. Until the dawn of the Renaissance the iconic style was predominant in the Roman church. In the later tradition of Roman Catholic art other functions began to play an important part (decoration, polemics, didacticism, etc.) so that the single idea of sacred mediation was lessened. Nonetheless the ancient idea of art as the medium by which the heart and mind are raised to God has never been completely lost to the Catholic tradition. One still finds it alive every time we see a person praying before a crucifix in a church.

That such sacred mediating art is less compelling today in the West is a sign—for better or worse—that the sacred reality of art has given way to the pressures of secularization. Indeed, it could be argued that the very way we view art (and use it) in the modern church tells us a great deal about the way in which we view our relationship to the Transcedent. The modern French painter Georges Rouault (1871–1958) was one of the few modernist painters who was deeply religious and motivated to paint great Christian art. He was deeply influenced by the iconic tradition. He once said that he wished to paint Christ so compellingly that his pictures would be an occasion for religious conversion. Yet it is a sad fact that his powerful works of religious art are to be seen in museums and private collections. No church, in his lifetime, gave him a major commission to do liturgical work. That is a point to meditate on in this age.

Gothic Light: *Abbot Suger*

In 1124 Abbot Suger (1081–1150) of the royal abbey of St. Denis in Paris decided to rebuild, and lavishly decorate, the abbey church to better accommodate the flocks of pilgrims who came there especially during the trade fairs which were held in the shadow of the abbey itself. In the reconstruction of the church (which was never completed; only the ambulatory and part of the nave was done in Suger's time) Suger decided to take advantage of the new technique of ribbed vaulting to raise the walls of his church higher, lighten the load on them, and, as a consequence, create more space for window openings. By so doing, Suger invented a new style of architecture (which later generations would call Gothic)[8] that would sweep France and give rise to a new culture based on it. Suger is one of those rare persons in the history of art to whom a whole aesthetic movement can safely be ascribed.

While Suger's architectural work was under way, he wrote

two small booklets *On Administration* and *On the Consecration of a Church*. They are goldmines of information on the ideas that stand behind Suger's architectural work. Underlying Suger's whole plan of construction and decoration was a theology of beauty based on the mysticism of light. Suger was heavily influenced by his readings of the Pseudo-Dionysius (whom we mentioned earlier) whose body the abbey was thought to have possessed.

The Pseudo-Dionysius was strongly influenced by Neoplatonic ideas. He believed that every created thing partakes, however imperfectly, in the essence of God. There is an ascending hierarchy of existence that ranges from the grossness of matter to the purity of light. The ultimate light, of course, is God. Everything that is perceived is perceived in the light of its creator, which is God. As light becomes more pure (i.e., as we leave the grossness of matter), we get closer to God.

Suger applied these ideas to his church building. His desire was for people to come in from the profane space of the world and be bathed in a sea of light. This light-filled building would be conceived of as a sort of foretaste of God's light in heaven. It is for that reason that Suger thought of his church as a *porta coeli*—a "gate of heaven." By participating in the created light of the church, one would be led more surely to the light that is God. Suger spelled out this theology of light most clearly in an inscription he composed to appear over the main bronze door of his church. It is worthwhile to note his play on the terms "light" and "door"—two concepts which are central to his theory:

> Whoever thou art, if thou seekest
> to extol the glory of these doors,
> Marvel not at the gold and the expense
> but at the craftsmanship of the work.
> Bright is the noble work: but, being
> nobly bright, the work
> Should brighten the minds so that they
> may travel through the true lights,
> To the True Light where Christ is
> the true door.
> In what manner it be inherent in

this world the golden door defines;
The dull mind rises to truth
through that which is material
And, in seeing this light, is resurrected
from its former submersion.[9]

The most elegant formulation of Suger's light mysticism is
to be found in the stained glass window. It was through the
windows that light was to pour into the church. The light which
flooded the church was, according to Suger, the *lux nova*—the
"new light" is, of course, an allusion to God who is Light according to the New Testament. Furthermore, when one looks
at the scenes depicted on the stained glass windows (which
can be understood and "read" only from inside the church—
a point worth noting), one sees the stories only because light
from the outside illuminates the windows. Suger was quick
to note the deep symbolism of this fact. What we see in the
windows also gives us, however indirectly, a glimpse at the
light which illumines the scene. Readers of Plato's parable
of the cave in the *Republic* will recognize the similarity of this
symbol.

Suger's mysticism of light was to be the great theoretical
statement of Gothic art just as his abbey church became the
prototype of all Gothic architecture: ". . . it became theology
as well, a theology of the Almighty but, still more, a theology
of the Incarnation. In this respect Suger's work created a new
dimension, that of man graced with illumination."[10] The final
expression of that theology came at the end of the Middle Ages,
not in architecture, but in literature when Dante envisioned
the human pilgrimage as ending, after a steep and arduous penitential climb of preparation, in an increasingly effortless attraction to the source of the universe, God, who was conceived
as Light. In the depth of that light Dante, using a brilliant
metaphor to convey the source of revelation (from the books
of nature and revelation), saw "contained by love in one volume
that which is scattered in leaves through the universe, substance and accidents and their relations as it were fused together
in such a way that what I tell of is a simple light (*semplice
lume*)" (*Paradiso* XXXIII, 85–90).

Longing for the Divine: *Michelangelo*

Michelangelo Buonarroti (1475–1564) belongs to that very select group who are universally acclaimed as possessing true genius. His work—painting, sculpture, architecture—is so well known that he epitomizes what art historians call the "High Renaissance." That word "renaissance" conjures up visions of the rebirth of pagan classicism as a reaction against the "otherworldly" Christianity of the Middle Ages. The intermingling of pagan and biblical motifs in such religious works as the ceiling of the Sistine Chapel (in the Vatican) gives currency to the notion that Michelangelo, as an artist of the Renaissance, had moved away from the simple and direct pieties of the Gothic and Italo-Byzantine artists.

That the Renaissance had a different tone from the Middle Ages seems clear enough. The idea that the Renaissance was a simple throwback to paganism must be rejected. One must agree with the judgment of Charles Trinkaus: ". . . the humanists of the Italian Renaissance, as men living in a strongly (if not deeply) religious era, were themselves heavily concerned in their writings with religious questions, and made from their standpoint and through their own humanistic intellectual disciplines some important contributions to the history of Christian thought."[11] What is true of the Italian humanists is, *pari passu*, also true of Michelangelo.

Michelangelo had been in early contact with the very best of Italian humanist thought when, while in his late teens, he enjoyed the patronage of Lorenzo de' Medici in Florence and, through Lorenzo, encountered the ideas of Marsiglio Ficino (1433–1499), the foremost Platonic commentator of the age. It was in that same period that Michelangelo heard, and was mightily impressed by, a less refined thinker and preacher: the hard-line Dominican Savonarola (1452–1498). In his old age Michelangelo told a young friend that after many years the words of Savonarola were still ringing in his ears. At that early age, then, Michelangelo absorbed the intellectual Platonism of Ficino and the unbending medieval piety of Savonarola; they were two influences which would remain with him until his death.

Michelangelo's art can be understood only against the background of his intense piety and the philosophical/theological ideas that he gained from his contacts with the Florentine humanists, his reading (especially the Bible and his beloved Dante), and his deep involvement with a circle of Christian humanists in Rome who were clustered about the figure of Michelangelo's great love, Donna Vittoria Colonna (1490–1547), when he first lived permanently in Rome.

That Michelangelo was more than conventionally pious is beyond dispute; that he related his piety to his calling as an artist is likewise patent. He took very seriously Savonarola's teaching that only the worthiest of artists should attempt to create art for the church. Artists, in this view, had an awesome responsibility because of their role in the salvific function of the church; they were teachers and inspirations for those who would encounter their ideas. Michelangelo held out four criteria for the artist who would approach religious themes:

(1) Artists should be masters of their craft.

(2) Artists should idealize their portraiture, especially those figures which derived from the story of salvation (i.e., Christ, the Virgin, and the saints and prophets).

(3) The ability of the artist should be such that he or she should be able to evoke great feelings of piety in viewers.

(4) Artists ought to be of good moral character in their own right.[12]

Although Michelangelo never wrote a systematic theory of art, it is clear from both his recorded remarks and his poetry (he was one of Italy's most accomplished poets) that he saw the artist as one who combined skills, ideas, and inspiration so as to express the beauty of things in such a way that the artwork hinted at the source of beauty which was God. It was this Platonic ideal of art which Michelangelo sought himself. It was that conviction which is behind his oft-quoted observation that the form of a statue was in the stone waiting only to be released. It also helps explain why Michelangelo himself became so impatient with his own efforts. Toward the end of his life he doubted that he could ever adequately express in the gross matter of stone the ideal of beauty which would lead viewers to God. He expressed that doubt in one of his most beautiful sonnets, a meditation on his art and his inevitable death. The translation is by the American poet Henry Wadsworth Longfellow:

> The course of my long life hath reached at last,
> In fragile bark o'er a tempestuous sea,
> The common harbor where must rendered be
> Account of all actions of the past.
>
> The impassioned phantasy, that vague and vast,
> Made art an idol and a king to me,
> Was an illusion, and but vanity
> Were the desires that lured me and harassed.
>
> The dreams of love, that were so sweet of yore,
> What are they now, when two deaths may be mine,
> One sure and one forecasting its alarms.
>
> Painting and sculpture satisfy no more.
> The soul now turning to the Love Divine,
> That opened, to embrace us, on the cross its arms.

Besides the undoubted originality and power of his work, if there is anything new about Michelangelo, it is that quiet lack of assurance which permeated earlier artists. It is hard to think of a monastic icon painter or the Abbot Suger penning lines such as those above. What one finds in Michelangelo is something approaching the modern religious sensibility (or something traditional for the mystic!), namely, a fierce drive for faith combined with a frustration that faith can be adequately expressed. Like his titanic struggling figures imprisoned in their blocks of marble Michelangelo expresses less the mediating power of art and more its evocative power to relate to human longing for the divine. It is less an art which teaches and more an art that evokes. It says less about the subject than it does about the artist. There is none of the effacement of medieval art. The human ego is there in all its grandeur and fear; it is a sensibility not unfamiliar to our time and place. It is not the order of the universe which is present in Michelangelo; it is the disorder in the human condition along with its deepest longings.

The World Redeemed: *Flannery O'Connor*

The examples of Christian art we have considered to this point conceive of art as a vehicle by which one rises beyond the perception of art to God. This is natural enough given the biblical fear of idolatry. One does not wish to identify the power of the divine with the thing itself. The icon links the worshipper and God just as Gothic light desires to raise the perception of the viewer to the source of light which is God. Sculpture in its idealized form, according to Michelangelo, is an imperfect reflection of the beauty which is God. In a famous metaphor in one of his sonnets Michelangelo writes that behind great sculpture is "that divine hammer which dwells and stops in heaven making other things beautiful. . . ."[13]

There is another Christian aesthetic emphasis by which the very things of creation in themselves shine forth the reality of God if only viewers are able "to see" with the eyes of faith. This tradition, articulated by a number of modern Christian poets and writers, roots itself in the ancient Catholic belief that nature itself is a book of revelation. The nineteenth-century Jesuit poet Gerard Manley Hopkins (1844–1889) is one of the most original exponents of this notion. His poetry is dedicated to the idea that God can be detected in the beauty of the world. His most famous statement on this theme is his incomparable sonnet called "God's Grandeur":

> The world is charged with the beauty of God.
> It will flame out, like shining from shook foil;
> It gathers to a greatness, like the ooze of oil
> Crushed. Why do men then now not reck his rod?
> Generations have trod, have trod, have trod;
> And all is seared with trade; bleared, smeared with toil;
> And wears man's smudges and shares man's smell: the soil
> Is bare now, nor can foot feel, being shod.
>
> And for all that, nature is never spent;
> There lives the dearest freshness deep down things:
> And though the last lights off the black West went
> Oh, morning, at the brown brink eastward, springs—
> Because the Holy Ghost over the bent
> World broods with warm breast and with ah! bright wings.[14]

The American short story writer Flannery O'Connor (1925–1964) has been the most articulate exponent of that sacramental view of the world in our century. O'Connor's conception of the Christian artist is very straightforward. If it is true (as for the believer it most decidedly is) that the world comes into being through the creative act of a good God, that humanity is created in the image of God, that it is fallen and redeemed, that we are free agents under God, then it follows that the way we look at the world is going to be very different from those who do not share that view. The surface appearances of the world hide a deeper significance which is linked to the reality of the Christian fact. Furthermore, if Christians accept the specifics of Christian revelation (all that is implied in the lordship and redemptive work of Christ), they must also recognize that their acceptance appears alien to a large number of people. For that reason modern readers must be shocked out of their ordinary way of thinking. O'Connor writes:

> To this end I have to bend the whole novel—its language, its structure, and its action. I have to make the reader feel, in his bones, if nowhere else, that something is going on that counts. Distortion in this case is an instrument; exaggeration has a purpose, and the whole structure of the novel or story has been made what it is because of belief. This is not the kind of distortion that destroys; it is the kind that reveals, or should reveal.[15]

O'Connor's short stories become more intelligible when one keeps the above quote in mind. Despite the violence in her stories, the oddities of her characters, and the backwoods humor or her narrative there is always something more solemn at work in her stories. Her characters are always defective in their vision or smug in their self-assurance, but their blindness and their smugness almost always lead them into awe-ful revelations. They begin to sense a new way of being in this world which, according to O'Connor, is a redeemed world. Over and over again her characters see mysteries at the edge of things. O'Connor uses the tree line or the horizon or the setting sun to characterize that deeper reality which constitutes the real nature of the world. This mystery is so tightly interwoven into the very texture of her stories that they are almost impossible to paraphrase (indeed, they sound rather still when summarized), yet a few random examples of lines from her posthumous collection *Everything That Rises Must Converge* (1965) might give a small taste of her style. The lines are taken from those climactic moments of stories where, to use her words, manners begin to dissolve into mystery:

> She continued to stare straight ahead but the entire scene in front of her had changed—the tree line was an open wound in a world that was nothing but sky—and she had the look of a person whose sight had been suddenly restored but who finds the light unbearable. ("Greenleaf," p. 52)

> He had ignored his own child to feed his vision of himself. He saw the clear eyed Devil, the sounder of hearts, leering at him from the eyes of Johnson. His image of himself shrivelled until everything was black before him. He sat there paralyzed, aghast. ("The Lame Shall Enter First," p. 190)

> Until the sun slipped behind the tree line, Mrs. Turpin remained there with her gaze bent to them [i.e., some pigs] as if she were absorbing some lifegiving knowledge. At last she lifted her head. There was only a purple streak in the sky, cutting through a field of crimson and leading, like an extension of the highway, into the descending dusk. She raised her hands from the side of the pen in a gesture hieratic and profound. A visionary light settled in her eyes. ("Revelation," p. 217)

What stands behind this powerfully evocative writing? It is the tactile sacramentality which we discussed at the very beginning of this chapter. It is a view that is not only not common but one which stands in tension with much of literary modernism. O'Connor is not insensitive to this fact nor is she smug in her faith. Her fiction (and her theory about fiction) bears the double weight of modernity and belief; that may be precisely why she is such a compelling artist in the Christian tradition. Her sense of the reality of God in the world accompanied a deep sense of the modern estrangement from God as this short credo she once wrote in a letter makes clear:

... I am a Catholic peculiarly possessed of the modern consciousness, that thing Jung describes as unhistorical, solitary, and guilty. To possess this *within* the church is to bear a burden, the necessary burden for the conscious Catholic. It's to feel the contemporary situation at the ultimate level. I think that the church is the only thing that is going to make the terrible words we are coming to endurable; the only thing that makes the church endurable is that it is somehow the body of Christ and that on this we are fed. It seems to be a fact that you have to suffer as much from the church as for it but if you believe in the divinity of Christ, you have to cherish the world at the same time you struggle to endure it.[16]

Religion, Art, and Modern Culture: A Postscript

We have discussed some Catholic novelists who still affirm the sacramental vision of life and who still believe that an art derived from and founded on Christian premises is still possible. There are many such writers today including some (preeminently Aleksandr Solzhenitsyn) who loom up from rather unlikely places to challenge the comfortable assumptions of our secular world. Nonetheless, no novelist committed to the Christian vision is complacent about the challenge that faces them. The very best novelists (and other artists) who have faced up to the problem of modernity have understood unflinchingly the secularity of our culture. Walker Percy has put the problem pungently and directly:

> The Christian novelist nowadays is like a man who has found a treasure hidden in the attic of an old house, but he is writing for people who have moved out to the suburbs and who are bloody sick of the old house and everything in it.[17]

Percy's point is that modern culture is immune to the traditional Christian vocabulary; the culture is not convinced that the words have meaning. The old forms and the old words are exhausted. If this is true of the literary arts, it is all the more true of visual arts where the exhaustion of traditional Christian forms seems nearly total. If one surveys the modern masters from, say, Braque and Picasso at the beginning of the century to the "art scene" today, it is difficult to find any substantive number of explicitly religious works of art or works which are consciously indebted to the Christian vocabulary. Very few works take their inspiration from the historical tradition of Christianity and those that do, often do so for formal rather than religious reasons. When Picasso did studies of the Grünewald crucifixion in the thirties, it was for studies in form, not because Picasso had an interest in the passion of Christ.

One could argue that many painters and sculptors are devoted to the expression of some of the most primordial religious truths: the sense of cosmic wonder, the questions of finality, meaning, existential context, and so on. These questions are raised, however, without specific reference to the traditional vocabulary of Christian belief or theology. The traditional vocabulary of Christianity is often turned into a privatized language for the artist alone. "Instead of making cathedrals out of Christ, Man, or 'Life'," the abstract of expressionist Barnett Newman once wrote, "We are making them out of ourselves, out of our own feelings." This deep-felt sense of wonder, anxiety, desire, and exploration may very well be understood as religious. Indeed, a case may be made that it is in fact religious, but its religious content is cast, more often than not, in terms of problems rather than solutions.

The great artists of our time have wrestled with the consequences of a world in which belief is no longer a possibility. The critic George Steiner has said that postmodern culture is posttheological. Anyone who is seriously interested in the Catholic tradition must understand that fact and come to grips with it. It is one of *the* issues for the believer today.

It does not suffice to say that art and literature are "highbrow" and their concerns are beyond those of the average Catholic. Smugness, Flannery O'Connor once said, is the besetting sin of Catholics. If the church proposes itself as a guardian of the revelation of Jesus, it must be concerned about the interest (or lack thereof) evinced by those who spend their lives creating significant human works which the world calls great art. The Catholic tradition must stand in judgment on the consequences of unbelief in our culture (that is the prophetic function of belief) and contribute to the building up of the human enterprise by speaking to the world of culture in a reasoned and caring way. To neglect either task is to retreat into a sectarianism which is alien to the universality of the Gospel.

The very lack of formal religiousness in so much of contemporary culture presents an acid test for the credibility of the teaching church. William Barrett has written that "For anyone who has been exposed to modern art and literature 'loss of being' will not appear as an empty and remote term borrowed from a philosopher like Heidegger. It is a condition against which poet or artist, beyond the wrestle with his craft, has to struggle in order to find a foothold somewhere, to draw a breath, and to stand in some relation to life and nature that permits him to be what he is."[18]

The question is: Can we point out a foothold or provide a whiff of oxygen to both artists and their audiences?

Notes

1. The single exception—a great one—would be Rembrandt. There is some scholarship that would suggest that artists like Michelangelo were in contact with reformed ideas but their main inspiration was Catholic.

2. Richard McBrien, *Catholicism*, vol. 2 (Minneapolis, 1980), pp. 1180–82. McBrien's work is an invaluable compendium of Catholic belief and practice to which this work is indebted.

3. Alan of Lille, as quoted in M. D. Chenu, *Nature, Man and Society in the Twelfth Century* (Chicago, 1968), p. 117.

4. McBrien, p. 1181.

5. David Tracy, *The Analogical Imagination: Christian Theology and the Culture of Pluralism* (New York, 1981), pp. 111–112.

6. John of Damascus, as quoted in Timothy Ware, *The Orthodox Church* (Baltimore, 1969), p. 41. John Damascene, as he is also called, did not live to see Nicaea II, but his thought was influential in its formulations about icons and against iconoclasts.

7. Paintings alleged to have been done by Saint Luke are also housed in several monasteries in Greece.

8. The term "Gothic," meaning barbaric, was applied to medieval architecture in the eighteenth century to distinguish it from classical architecture. It was not meant to be a flattering term at the time.

9. Abbot Suger, as quoted in Erwin Panofsky, *Abbot Suger: On the Abbey Church of Saint Denis and Its Administration* (Princeton, 1946, p. 23). This volume translates and comments on both of Suger's little books.

10. Georges Duby, *The Age of the Cathedrals* (Chicago, 1981), p. 108.

11. Charles Trinkaus, "The Religious Thought of the Italian Humanists," in *The Pursuit of Holiness*, ed. C. Trinkaus and H. Oberman (Leiden, 1974), p. 340. Trinkaus's *In Our Image: Humanity and Divinity in Italian Humanist Thought*, 2 vols. (Chicago, 1970) exhaustively demonstrates this point.

12. See Robert Clements, *Michelangelo's Theory of Art* (New York, 1961), and David Summers, *Michelangelo and the Language of Art* (Princeton, 1981).

13. Michelangelo, as quoted in Clements, p. 78.

14. *The Poems of Gerard Manley Hopkins,* ed. W. H. Gardner and N. H. McKenzie (Oxford, 1967), p. 66.

15. Flannery O'Connor, *Mystery and Manners,* ed. Sally and Robert Fitzgerald (New York, 1962), p. 162. A similar point is made by the Catholic novelist Walker Percy in *The Message in the Bottle* (New York, 1975), pp. 101–17.

16. Flanner O'Connor, *The Habit of Being: The Letters of Flannery O'Connor,* ed. Sally Fitzgerald (New York, 1979), p. 90.

17. Percy, p. 116. Percy calls this situation the "devaluation of Christian vocabulary."

18. William Barrett, *The Illusion of Technique: A Search for Meaning in a Technological Civilization* (Garden City, N.Y., 1979), pp. 241–42.

Readings and Trajectories

The classic Catholic statements on art from a Scholastic point of view are Jacques Maritain's *Art and Scholasticism* (New York, 1943) and *Creative Intuition in Art and Poetry* (New York, 1953) and Etienne Gilson's *The Arts of the Beautiful* (New York, 1965). A more recent study is Hans Küng's *Art and the Question of Meaning* (New York, 1981).

Two books which are very useful studies of the literature and methodologies of literary/theological studies are Vernon Ruland's *Horizons of Criticism* (Chicago, 1975) and Lynn Ross-Bryant's *Imagination and the Life of the Spirit* (Chico, Cal., 1981).

The standard study of theology and culture which stands behind a good deal of modern theorizing is Paul Tillich's *Theology of Culture* (New York and London, 1959). Nathan Scott's *Wild Prayer of Longing* (New Haven, 1971) is very helpful in defining sacramentality in the context of literary study. Vincent Buckley's *Poetry and the Sacred* (London, 1968) is the best work on the relationship of poetry and the religious sense. The same discussion is much advanced in Justus George Lawler's magisterial *Celestial Pantomime: Poetic Structures of Transcendence* (New Haven, Conn., 1979).

David and Tamara Rice-Talbot's *Icons and Their History* (Woodstock, N.Y., 1974) is an elegant stylistic interpretation of icons by world-famous authorities. Otto Demus's *Byzantine Art and the West* (New York, 1970) shows the continuing influence of Byzantine art on the Latin church right into the Renaissance period; this is an important work with a scholarly bibliography.

The classic work on Gothic architecture remains Otto von Simpson's revised *The Gothic Cathedral* (New York, 1964).

No systematic study of Flannery O'Connor's theological thought exists, but critical studies of her fiction abound; one of the more theologically sophisticated recent works is John R. May's *The Pruning Word: The Parables of Flannery O'Connor* (Notre Dame, Ind., 1976): May's work also has a fine bibliography.

An excellent study of the interaction of critical secularity and Christian symbols can be found in Theodore Ziolkowski's *Fictional Transfiguration of Jesus* (Princeton, 1972).

Rosemary Haughton's brilliant rethinking of the Catholic tradition in the light of aesthetical principles is set out in *The Catholic Thing* (Springfield, Mass., 1979) and *The Passionate God* (New York, 1981).

8

HUMANISTS

Humanism as a Problem

One of the more powerful buzzwords in our contemporary political discourse is "humanism" or, more specifically, "secular humanism." Many conservative critics, especially those identified with the "new religious right" blame a whole range of modern problems—declining literary, erosion of moral values, flabbiness of civic purpose, lack of discipline, rise in crime, corruption of family strength—on a pervasive philosophy (the religious right claims it is a crypto-religion) which they call "secular humanism."

Humanism is one of those words which admits of a wide variety of meanings. At its most benign it means the study of the traditional liberal arts as opposed to the sciences. It can also mean a sense of values when it is used as the adjective "humane." Its most pejorative meaning for the religious right means a glorification of human values without reference to, or actively antagonistic toward, transcendental religious ideas. The religious critics most often refer to a series of humanist manifestos issued in this country beginning in the 1930's as a source of secular humanist thinking. Underlying all of these documents, the critics would argue, are certain basic propositions which are antithetical to everything that traditional religion would stand for. These propositions would include:

(1) A bias against any notion of supernaturalism. Secular humanism is naturalistic.

(2) A denial of any dualism of the human spirit (body/soul/spirit) with the concomitant denial of immortality and a belief in the singularity and importance of this life alone.

(3) A denial of any detectable purpose to the universe. The secular humanists would argue that the universe evolves without any plan or final end.

(4) A strong affirmation of rationalistic and scientific methodologies as *the* way to understand the world and human destiny. A strong conviction that education can solve most human problems.

(5) An affirmation that the individual is the ultimate source of human value. The realization of the individual personality would count as the highest good.

(6) A strong sense of social concern expressed in a form which is traditionally seen as "liberal" in its social and political aspiration.

(7) A philosophy which is humanocentric not theocentric; religion is a human enterprise with a human object and based on human values.[1]

Humanism defined in that fashion derives historically from ideas first formulated in the Enlightenment period in the eighteenth century when the scientific method, democratic theories of politics, and reflections on the "Rights of Man" began to get their clearest articulation both in thought and in action (e.g., in both the French and the American Revolutions). Part of that Enlightenment program, as the noted scholar Peter Gay has argued, was a conscious reaction against the received tradition of historical Christianity.[2] Much of Enlightenment thinking was in reaction against, and in resistance to, the older ecclesiastical traditions, both Protestant and Catholic, which seem to represent the stranglehold of the dead past.

The question of whether all humanism is, by its very nature, antagonistic to religious values depends very much on who is speaking about humanism. The humanism we have discussed above claims (at least some of its adherents claim) to be religious without necessarily being theistic. Marxist humanism and the existentialist humanism of Jean-Paul Sartre, to name but two examples, are programmatically atheistic. Indeed, Sartre, in his famous essay "Existentialism as a Humanism" (1946), stated that his entire philosophy was an attempt to work out a philosophy of life derived from the serious implications of atheism. The late French philosopher Jacques Maritain in his work *True Humanism* (New York, 1954) attempted a humanistic construction based on theocentrism and a serious appropriation of Christian categories. Maritain argued that humanity could develop fully only in a right relationship with God since humanity was created in God's image and likeness. Lack of theocentric perspective brought with it, inevitably, an antihumanism.

Religious humanism (Maritain), Atheistic Humanism (Marx), and Secular Humanism (that we have described above) all share this in common: They try to deal with the final end of humanity and the structures of human life and happiness; they all attempt to articulate the yearnings and aspirations of the human condition. It is also evident that the critique of religion made by the secular humanists has helped to underscore the deficiencies and the weaknesses of religion just as the religious critique of secular humanism has been a salutary warning against the smug confidence in science to solve all problems and a naïve belief in the sovereign value of education.

The Catholic tradition has expressed a certain ambivalence about humanism. There is a certain thread which runs through Catholicism which is openly antagonistic to human achievement and human values. "What has Jerusalem to do with Athens?" asked Tertullian in one of his more testy moods. "Paris has destroyed Assisi!" cried the late medieval Franciscan poet Jacopone da Todi. In both cases the disfunction is between classical learning (Athens) or "highbrow" learning (Paris, i.e., the university) and the straightforwardness of the Bible (Jerusalem) or the simple piety of a St. Francis (Assisi). The late medieval *Imitation of Christ* says that the true Christian should "rather experience compunction than know how to define it." We have also seen a certain bias against urban culture, human comfort, created beauty, and the works of humans in the ascetic tradition. The most open antagonist to the Roman humanist spirit were the desert ascetics and their most faithful followers.

Against this strong antihumanist bias, of course, is another tradition that runs parallel to the first. It is that tradition by which the second-century writer Justin Martyr could claim that all culture is under the Incarnate Word, Christ, or by which the medieval St. Thomas could appropriate the classical ideas of an Aristotle for Christian purposes. It is that tradition which, in the words of the Second Vatican Council, provides direct sanctions for the building of human society: "For when, by the work of his hands or the aid of technology, man develops the earth so that it can bear fruit and become a dwelling worthy of the whole human family and when he consciously takes part in the life of social groups, he carries out the design of God."[3]

These two strains of the Catholic tradition have always stood in some kind of creative tension; they are more corrective than antithetical. The ascetic ideal reminds the Catholic that the world is "not all there is"—that we have a final end as individuals and as a community. The humanistic ideal (and I use the term "humanistic" in its widest and most benign sense) corrects any tendency of the ascetic to denigrate totally the goodness of the world which is, as we have already said, from the hand of God and sacramental or to forget that we are created in the image and likeness of God. The ascetic bids us focus on our eternal home, while the humanist directs our attention to our condition as wayfarers and pilgrims in this world. A rare figure like Dante encourages us to see both strains at the same time, but less gifted folks tend to oscillate between the two. It could be argued that the Second Vatican Council, with its strong incarnational bent, was a humanist reaction against the stern otherworldliness of the Tridentine church. The current emphasis on contemplation and spirituality may be seen as a corrective to the excessive activist tendencies of the last two decades.

In this chapter we will examine with some care two explicit attempts at synthesizing human learning and divine revelation into a program of life which can fit under the rubric of "Christian Humanism." Interestingly enough, both of these synthetic attempts happened at crisis points in the church's history: Erasmus was active at the outbreak of the Protestant Reformation, while Pope John Paul II was elected at a time when many felt that the church was undergoing a crisis of nerve following the Second Vatican Council. We use those two figures not because they are the only examples of Christian humanism (we could have equally compared Thomas More and Teilhard de Chardin), but because they manifest so many basic similarities. Despite their strongly diverse cultural backgrounds, their far different personalities, and their gaping intellectual differences, both of them, despite the separation of centuries, are passionately intellectual figures who felt a strong need to take the best learning they could acquire and put it at the service of the Gospel. They both desired to appeal to the intelligentsia of their day for a serious reexamination of the claims of the Gospel.

Erasmus of Rotterdam

Born illegitimate in 1466 (or 1469), Erasmus was educated in the schools of the Brethren of the Common Life at Deventer in Holland. Later, with some reluctance, he entered the monastery of the Augustinians and was ordained to the priesthood in 1492. In 1494, partially to escape the rigors of monastic observance, Erasmus became personal secretary to the bishop of Cambrai, but left his service after a year to study theology at the University of Paris. From that time, until his death some forty years later, Erasmus moved from place to place, as need and circumstance dictated, shunning any appointment which would hold him long. For periods he lived in England, once as a guest of Sir Thomas More and another time as a lecturer at Cambridge. He travelled in Italy and spent some time living in Venice with the Renaissance printer and humanist Aldus Venutius; he had a similar post with the printer Froben in Basle. He spent time as a teacher at Louvain, as a writer in Fribourg, and, finally, settled in Basle (Switzerland) where he died in 1536.

During this restless life of travel and change Erasmus poured out a steady stream of writing on every conceivable topic of humanistic interest. He composed schoolbooks for beginners, translations of Greek plays, editions of the Fathers of the church, an edition of the Greek New Testament, treatises on theology and spirituality, works of piety, pamphlets of polemical topics, and scores of letters. He was, in his mature years, one of the most famous persons in educated Europe. He carried on—not always peacefully—a correspondence with every important person of his day from Pope Leo X to St. Thomas More (who was an intimate friend) and Martin Luther. His ideas were so influential that well into the next century one finds echoes of Erasmian Christianity. Indeed, some scholars (like the philosopher Richard Popkin) regard him as a singlehanded intellectual revolutionary who, without desiring it, contributed significantly to the later tradition of European skepticism.

Erasmus was not a systematic theologian, a professional literary critic, or a spiritual writer. He is usually described as the most important Christian humanist of the Renaissance era. The word "humanist" in that period is to be understood as a man of letters who devoted himself to the *studia humanitatis*, i.e. the great classical tradition of the West with its roots in Latin and Greek culture. To understand what it means when we say that Erasmus was a *Christian* humanist requires that we note the predominant concerns of his life and the basic themes that run through his work.

First, Erasmus was passionately committed to the ideals of an interior Christian piety. Appalled by the degeneration of popular Catholic piety in his age into superstition and formalism, Erasmus was a stern and merciless critic of pilgrimages, the cult of relics, the formalism of the monasteries, and the more vulgar manifestations of popular piety with respect to images, fasting, etc. He regarded much of that kind of religion as a shade away from fraud and magic. Deeply influenced by the *devotio moderna* of his native Netherlands which he learned from the Brethren of the Common Schools, a pious group of layfolk and clerics dedicated to education, Erasmus preached a Christianity with Christ as model and exemplar and with the cultivation of purity of heart and standards of Christian ethical behavior. This strong sense of interior piety undergirds all of his Christian teaching and is at the heart of all of his ideological writing. His famous *Handbook of the Christian Knight*, first published in 1501 but with many further editions during his lifetime, is filled with pleas for an interior conversion free from mere formalism and superstition. What Erasmus wrote of relics in the *Handbook* is a microcosm of his entire vision of Christianity:

> When you venerate the image of Christ in the paintings and
> other works of art that portray Him, think how much more you
> ought to revere the portrait of His mind that the inspiration of
> the Holy Spirit has placed in Holy Writ. No artist could possibly
> reproduce those words and prayers of Christ that represent him
> so exactly in the Gospel. . . . No relic of Our Blessed Lord can
> possibly approach the strength and the beauty of his very
> self. . . . You are convinced that it is advantageous to have a
> small particle of the true cross in your home, yet this is nothing
> compared with carrying the mystery of Christ in your mind.[4]

In the *Handbook of the Christian Knight*[5] Erasmus states
that the two basic weapons of the Christian are prayer and
knowledge. It is the latter weapon which occupied so much of
the attention of Erasmus, both in his life and in his writings.
Erasmus was much taken with, and a passionate student of,
the "New Learning" (as classical humanism was called) coming
from Italy. He loved the new discoveries in classical literature,
revelled in the formulations of classical philological study, and
devoted himself to the study of both Latin and Greek, languages
which he soon mastered completely. Although Erasmus was
an indifferent student of Hebrew, he was a strong advocate of
its study and an unflinching supporter of Johannes Reuchlin
(1455–1522), the greatest non-Jewish Hebrew scholar of the age.
While at Louvain (1517–1521), Erasmus vigorously supported
the *Collegium Trilingue*, which was devoted to the study of
biblical languages. During his own scholarly career he published a number of critical editions of the Latin Fathers, while
his critical edition of the New Testament in Greek (first published in 1516) with its dedication to Pope Leo X was one of
the most important milestones in the history of biblical scholarship. Although not a good critical edition (Erasmus was able
to consult too few manuscripts), it forced scholars to look at
the text of the New Testament in a new way.

What is crucial for an understanding of Erasmus's contribution to the Catholic tradition is to note his firm conviction
that learning and scholarship were a powerful instrument both
for the cultivation of personal piety and also for institutional
church reform. He lived at a time when much of Scholastic
theology and philosophy were viewed as exhausted and reduced

to a game of logic. It was also an age when ignorance among the clergy was rife and corruption ubiquitous. Erasmus, like other Christian humanists of the age (Vives and Ximenes in Spain; D'Etaples in France; Colet, Linacre, More, and their circle in England), believed that if people could get back to the pure doctrine of the Bible and the ancient commentators (like Jerome and Augustine), they would see the Gospel in all its vigor. Like his contemporaries, the various Protestant reformers, Erasmus wanted the scriptures in the hands of everyone (now a real possibility since printing was a practical reality and literacy was on the increase) including, as he once said in a paraphrase of the Gospels he once wrote, "the farmer, the tailor, the mason, prostitutes, pimps, and Turks."[6]

Today we tend to associate the name of Erasmus with his work *The Praise of Folly* (the original title *Encomium Moriae* contains an Erasmian pun; it can also mean "In praise of More"), written in 1509 when he was a guest of Sir Thomas More in England. The book was immensely popular in its own day, going through dozens of editions in the sixteenth century. It was, however, a sort of "throwaway" book which Erasmus wrote to amuse More and his circle while flaying the stupidities of the age in the bargain. For all its humor it did have the underlying serious purpose (never distant from Erasmus's mind) of being an intellectual critique of the follies of the age.

One of the main targets of *The Praise of Folly* was the church and its institutions. Because Erasmus was such a bitter critic of the church and so liberal in his practical proposals for church reform (he favored a vernacular liturgy, a married clergy, a severe limit on the growth of monasticism, etc.), it has often been asked why Erasmus did not join the reformers after Luther broke with Rome. Erasmus had a good number of things in common with the major reform figures: They both excoriated the failures of monasticism and the religious life: they both deplored the weakness of Scholastic theology and the corruption of the hierarchy. Both the reformers and Erasmus shared a passionate love for scripture study and the researches into patristic literature. They both agreed that much of popular religion was externalized, mechanical, and far from the spirit of Christ. A wit once said that Erasmus laid the egg which Luther hatched. It is also a fact that after the Reformation break came, there were many in the Catholic camp who doubted Erasmus's allegiance to Rome.

Erasmus remained in the church partly because of temperament (he was more at home in the church than he was in any single country) and partly because of deep-felt religious reasons. Erasmus, true humanist that he was, did not share the reformer's pessimistic view about the sinful state of humanity nor did he reject totally the place of good works in the scheme of justification. Luther and Erasmus debated these points in their famous controversy about free will. Beyond those specific concerns Erasmus saw the historical church as the traditional *locus* of the Christian consensus of history, the place where, over the centuries, people came to an understanding of the Christian Gospel and defended it against deformation and heresy. Erasmus argued that even if some of the ideas and beliefs held by the church were not arguable from a scriptural point of view, they should not, on that account, be rejected. Erasmus wrote:

> As it is Christian prudence not lightly to believe anything not expressly stated in Scripture, so it is the part of Christian modesty not to reject petulantly what the religious contemplation of pious men has given for the solace and the enlightenment of believers.[7]

How does one finally assess the significance of Erasmus? His life seems to illustrate both the possibilities and the limitations of any attempt to construct a Christian humanism. He saw the New Learning not as an exercise in intellectual nourishment for the very few, but as a powerful tool to aid piety and energize reforming movements. It seems odd to us today to think of philology (the study of words and language) as revolutionary, but that is exactly what his contemporaries thought. A true intellectual discipline for the study of the Bible was just beginning and it was beginning precisely at the time when printing was making books possible for the masses. Without the careful scholarship of Erasmus neither the German translation of the Bible done by Luther nor the King James Version in English would have been thinkable. Erasmus's emphasis on the serious study of the Bible and its classic commentators helped focus the church's attention on what could be legitimately claimed as an authentic part of the Deposit of Faith.

Erasmus held up as a model for life what he called the Philosophy of Christ (*Philosophia Christi*). In his reaction against the externalism of late medieval piety he set forth Christ who was exemplar and model: "Take care that you do not move the eyes of your heart away from your example, Christ. You will not err if you follow the leadership of truth. You will not cast yourself among the shadows while you walk through the light. You will not imitate the blindness of the multitude."[8]

Such an emphasis, directed as it was to Christ as one who teaches the truth for people, while moving and just in its own right, is not a full picture of the Christ of the Catholic tradition. In reaction against the abuses of his day, one finds in Erasmus little emphasis on the sacramental Christ or the Christ of the liturgy. In fact, in all of his writings, Erasmus never mentions saying Mass although he was a priest for nearly forty years. Erasmus shied away from those aspects of Christian liturgical life in favor of an interiorized and private form of piety. While such an emphasis is understandable, given the culture in which he lived, it is a deficient view nonetheless.

Whatever his deficiencies, Erasmus stands as one of the great intellectual figures of the Catholic tradition. He failed to stem the onslaught of the Protestant Reformation with its deep appeal to the masses, but he did demonstrate that human learning was not only compatible with a reformist impulse in the church, but could serve as a creative and deeply spiritual way of being Christian. He was convinced that the church did not have to be at odds with the intellectual tradition of Europe; he was serene in his conviction that Christianity was compatible with the deepest aspirations of human intellectual life. Despite his serenity of conviction the Reformation was a fact and many of the practical reforms of which he dreamed did not happen. They were too close to the Reformation spirit and the ancient church resisted them. What he did accomplish was no mean achievement in its own right: "The revival of traditional patristic culture made new again so that Scripture too should be rediscovered, and be at the heart of a reform of the church entirely from within."[9] That fact was not much appreciated in the Catholic

Reformation (his works ended up on the *Index* or accessible only in heavily censored form), but it is much admired today.

Pope John Paul II

On October 16, 1978, Karol Wojtyla, cardinal archbishop of Crakow (Poland), became pope assuming the name of John Paul II. It was a historic occasion for the church for a number of reasons. The new pope was the first non-Italian pope elected in centuries (Adrian VI, a Dutchman, died in 1523 after one year as pope) and the first from the Slavic lands of Eastern Europe. He is the first pope in this century who had first-hand experience with some of the major social and intellectual conflicts of our era. He lived under the Nazi occupation of Poland as a youth and exercised his priesthood in a country ruled by a hostile and repressive Marxist regime. Having served as a university professor of philosophy, the pope has had intimate scholarly contact with the strains of contemporary thought (he reads over a half-dozen languages) and as a published poet and performed playwright he knows our literary culture well. It is hard to think of a churchman who could have had wider or deeper experiences as a preparation for the papal office.

Soon after his election and installation the new pope began to speak and write as head of the church. What became clear from the first was that Pope John Paul was not going to be a spokesperson for ghost-written theology nor was he going to hand on traditional formulas (although, it should be noted, the pope is a very conservative theologian by any contemporary standard). John Paul has a total vision of humanity which is rooted in his own profound studies of philosophy and his deeply spiritual understanding of Catholic theological tradition. As both an intellectual and a spiritual leader, the pope is trying to formulate and articulate a comprehensive view of humanity that will ring true to human experience and, simultaneously, be faithful to, and reflective of, the revelation of the Gospel. To understand that comprehensive view (and to get a firm base for understanding all of his major addresses and writings), one must understand the pope's thinking on three topics: the nature of the human person; the character of human culture; and the person of Christ as the perfection of the person and the key to the meaning of culture.

The year 1979 saw the publication in English of *The Acting Person*,[10] a book the pope had published originally in Polish in 1969, but which was now revised into its definitive form. It is a densely theoretical work and far beyond the concerns of this book. We do note, however, that its basic purpose is an attempt to construct a portrait both of the human community and the moral conscience of the community (and individual) by an intensive analysis of the value and the uniqueness of the individual person. The book is less concerned with who a person is; it is centrally concerned with how a person acts and how "acting" constitutes both individual, social, and ethical norms of living. This unflinching focus on the individual, not as an abstract principle, but as an acting (i.e., thinking, willing, doing, etc.) person is at the basis of both the pope's notion of philosophical ethics and his religious vision. The papal religious message is grounded in a humanistic anthropology developed from his study of philosophy and his acceptance of the Gospel in faith.

What Pope John Paul understands by the notion of person can be intuited from a close reading of his first major encyclical, *Redemptor Hominis (The Savior of Man)*,[11] published on March 15, 1979. Part III. 14 of the encyclical explicates the papal notion of "man" (papal language and the available translations are hopelessly sexist in language; I use the papal language, but I think it is instructive to note its pervasiveness) in some detail as an "unrepeatable reality of what he is and what he does . . . and because he is a person, a history of his life that is his own and, most important, a history of his own soul that is his own." The personal history of each individual, the pope continues, is written as a personal history, not in isolation, but "through numerous contacts, situations, and social structures linking him with other men, beginning to do so from the first moment of his existence on earth." In the development of humanity humans feel the same contrary tidal pulls in their "continued inclination to sin and at the same time in their continual aspiration to truth, the good, the beautiful, justice, and love. . . ."

This vision of the individual, as an individual, with a personal history and as a social being linked to other human bonds and as a pilgrim caught between the forces of good and evil, is not some abstract intellectual construction. For a person who suffered under the Nazis and the Communists, who was a working person, and who lived for the world of art and culture, the pope is more aware than most that every personal story is told in the particular setting of culture. Culture, as the future pope said in 1964, is an "acquisition of facts by the exclusive means of which man expresses himself. The products of culture are a testimony to his spiritual life, for the spirit of mankind not only lives through its mastery over material things but also lives within itself, through themes to which it alone has access and which only it can understand."[12]

The papal understanding of culture is not that of an aesthete; he knows that the structures of culture, as human inventions, share all the ambiguity of human work, capable of alienating and repressing the acting person. As the pope pointed out in *Redemptor Hominis*, humanity can (with good reasons) fear its own creations; the inventions of culture, after all, can destroy, dehumanize, or exhaust the world. The political and social structures which derive from human political reflection can ignore the individual with his or her unique personal history in the name of abstract ideologies (profit, revolution, the future, etc.), just as they can crush the individual by an unwillingness to face up to massive poverty or social powerlessness. These very woes fall on a hapless humanity when the demonic possibilities of human culture remained unchecked. To avoid this lamentable state of affairs persons must take precedence over the things (i.e., the culture) that they create. The pope writes:

> Man cannot relinquish himself or the place in the visible world that belongs to him; he cannot become the slave of things, the slave of economic systems, the slave of production, the slave of his own products. A civilization purely materialistic in outline condemns man to such slavery even if, at times, no doubt, this occurs contrary to the intentions and the very premises of the pioneers. (III. 16)

The pope expends great effort in an analysis of the human condition and of the "acting person" because he realizes that as the head of the church he must think of the church as it was established for the good, indeed, the salvation, of humanity. The encyclical *Laborem Exercens* (*On Human Work*) makes note of the wide way in which the pope intends to understand the human condition, a way which makes use of all the humanistic disciplines as well as the data of the Gospel:

> The church is convinced that work is a fundamental dimension of man's existence on earth. She is confirmed in this conviction by considering the whole heritage of the many sciences devoted to man. . . . But the source of the church's conviction is above all the revealed word of God and therefore what is a *conviction of the intellect is also a conviction of faith*. The reason is that the church believes in man: she thinks of man and addresses herself to him not only in the light of historical experience . . . but in the light of the revealed word of the living God.[13]

The papal analysis of the human condition is preparatory in the sense that to understand humanity is a necessity prior to an understanding of what the Gospel adds to, or contributes toward, the needs of humanity. In the papal view the Gospel does not free-float like some set of abstract mathematical formulas; it is a revelation, eternally true, that is addressed to human history. The individual is precious because he or she is made "in the image and likeness of God"; persons are to be honored and freed from exploitation because of the redemption of Christ; the physical world is not to be abused because we are given stewardship over it by God; we must avoid a materialist view of history because we have a transcendental end; and so on.

In what sense is this a religious humanism? Or, to use a language more congenial to the papal usage, a Christian personalism? It is a humanism in the sense that Pope John Paul sees Christian revelation not as an alien force superadded to humanity but as a gift which completes and perfects an already good humanity. At the core of the pope's philosophy is the unique, unrepeatable individual, already redeemed by Christ and at least potentially aware of that redemption.

The humanism of an Erasmus was instrumental. He deeply loved and faithfully learned the humanistic disciplines coming from Renaissance Italy. He used them to engender piety, reform the church, and clarify what he understood to be true Christianity. John Paul's humanism is both instrumental and substantive. It is instrumental to the degree that he quite comfortably utilizes contemporary philosophical categories (especially phenomenology) in order to clarify his views and to ground them in the matrix of human intelligence and common experience. It is a substantive humanism in the sense that the pope has a comprehensive view of humanity deriving from the instrumentality of humanistic study and the insights of his Christain faith. It is not a humanism that is as explicitly cosmic as that of the late Teilhard de Chardin (see Chapter 5), but it does discuss humanity as a historical reality in all of its social, political, cultural, and ethical complexity. After Pope John Paul had visited the United States in 1979, the Jesuit weekly *America* underscored the papal conviction that "the welfare of the human person must be the final measure of all relationships among the nations of the world, of all economic and political systems, and of all negotiations over regional boundaries or military superiority."[14] That succinctly states the humanistic bias of his entire orientation: the human individual, the one who, in the pope's words, "has a personal history."

Does the pope propose a humanism adequate for the complexity of the human situation? There is no doubt that his presence on the chair of Peter has provided a stability and an integrity for the church. His analysis of the human situation is profound and fertile for both reflection and action. Critics within the church have been less inclined to criticize his analysis of human affairs and the human condition while they are more prompt to point out the rather traditional character of his theology. They see his theological views as resistant to any discussions of the problems raised by the world of the postmodern. They see a pope so profoundly attached to the tradition of the church as to be unwilling to see the critique brought to that tradition by the growth of historical consciousness. His theology, his critics would argue, is too heavily metaphysical and innocent of that nuance which one finds in such thinkers as Bernard Lonergan and Karl Rahner. Some contemporary American theological writers, openly devoted to Rahnerian methods, have put the pope's theology in the context of his own background:

> John Paul's theology is not fundamentalist, but it is not sophisticated to the level his intellectualism would lead one to expect. Rather, it is as though he has not allowed his philosophical and literary studies to impinge on his traditional faith. That faith has been too valuable, too clearly the core of survival in communist Poland, to be fully subjected to critical scrutiny.[15]

That criticism has been made before. Whether the "traditional" theology of the pope's Polish experience is adequate or not is an issue for history. The bearer of the Petrine ministry must teach the whole church and preserve the tradition handed down to him. In that position it is obligatory for the pope to be a conservative (which is quite another thing from being an obscurantist—something nobody accuses the pope of being) in order to contend with (and be a guide for) the centrifugal forces of both the right and the left in today's church. At this stage all we can say is that the starting point of his thought—the actually existing individual person who not only is but who acts—seems an unimpeachable starting point.

Christian Humanism as a Problem

Catholicism has always regarded humanism with some ambivalence. The Catholic tradition has been so concerned with the supernatural content of its revelation at times that human accomplishment seemed somewhat suspect; almost an alien and decidedly naturalistic religion. When, in 1852, John Henry Newman gave a series of lectures which were to become later his celebrated book *The Idea of a University*, he took precise notes of that problem. Newman made an elegant plea for the university as a place where learning could be pursued disinterestedly, that is, for its own sake and according to its own discipline. Newman envisioned theology as the core of that education, underpinning all other learning and giving it ultimate coherence.

Because of Newman's conviction (not then widely shared in

Catholic circles) that human learning had its own autonomy, it would be theology which would give the university its peculiar character as a "Catholic" university. Without theology the end product of humane education, rounded by the humanities, sharpened by the sciences, and educated to ethical behavior, is the gentleman,[16] the *beau idéal* of the world, as Newman calls him. Newman saw quite clearly that such an education would never produce a religious person since, as he noted, in the fourth century both Saint Basil and the emperor Julian the Apostate "were fellow students at the school of Athens; and one became the saint and doctor of the church, the other her scoffing and relentless foe."[17]

In a brilliantly original study Brian Wicker has pointed out that in the final analysis there was a basic tension in Newman's notion of the university.[18] Behind the pleasant façade of the former Oxford don Newman was an unflinching apologist for the faith who would not shield himself from the fact that knowledge would not save nor would being a gentleman. The tension, in the last analysis, is part of a larger tension. No matter how far the works of the human intellect take us philosophically, socially, or aesthetically in the Catholic tradition, there is still another strand in that tradition which stands in skeptical judgment on all human achievement. It is that strand which impelled Michelangelo to fling his chisel at his last "Pietà" in frustration at trying to capture the pathos of the Redemption. The perfection of human effort always remains under the shadow of the cross just as all the works of humanity will one day see the Son of Man coming in his power and glory.

There is, then, no contradiction between the humanistic spirit and the Gospel, but there is a tension. Luther understood that tension as Erasmus perhaps did not. John Henry Newman, himself a trained humanist, understood it clearly and made it explicit in his lectures on university education. After all, Newman's hero is not the gentleman but St. Philip Neri (1515–1595), for St. Philip decided to spend his life in a particular way: not as a hunter of souls but as one who "cast in his net to gain them; he preferred to yield to the stream, and direct the current, which he could not stop, of science, of literature, art, and fashion, and to sweeten and to santicfy what God had made very good and man had spoilt."[19] It was not learning, but sanctity that attracted the mind of Newman to his patron, St. Philip.

Along that same line Pope John Paul has a very sophisticated defense against the limits of humanism. His vision of the person is perfected in the light of the Gospel; it is a vision informed by humanism and something more. For John Paul it is the character of redemption which explains the enigma of the human situation. In that case the human is asked to accept mystery as the last piece in the puzzle of life.

At bottom humanism is a problem for the Christian in two ways. First, the very notion of humanism is colored today by an understanding of the term either as it links to classical humanities or as an ethical and philosophical alternative to religion that the word is muddied (John Paul, after all, does not use the word as much as he does use the term "personalism"). Beyond that, the new social sciences have pointed out how flawed and ideological our understanding of humanism has been; it has had very large components of sexism and social elitism as the liberationist thinkers have pointed out. Beyond those intellectual difficulties is the theological position that would argue for an understanding of the Gospel which would affirm humanistic values but always stand in some sort of tension with them so as not to absolutize the culture of a given period or the achievements even of the ages. That is not to say that a Christian humanism is not possible; it is possible. It is to say, however, that such a humanism should have a tentative character given the limits of the human in the face of the divine.

Notes

1. For this analysis I am indebted to Michael A. Schuler's PhD dissertation: "Religious Humanism in Twentieth Century American Thought" (Florida State University, 1982).

2. In Peter Gay, *The Enlightenment: An Interpretation* (New York, 1968).

3. Pastoral Constitution on the Church in the Modern World, art. 57, in *The Documents of Vatican II*, ed. Walter M. Abbot, p. 262.

4. *Handbook of the Christian Knight*, in *The Essential Erasmus*, trans. John P. Dolan (New York, 1964), pp. 66–67. There is also a complete translation of the *Enchiridion* by Matthew Spinka in *Christian Classics*, vol. 14 (Philadelphia, 1954).

5. The original title has a pun, of the type much loved by Erasmus. *Enchiridion* can mean in Greek either a "handbook" or a "short sword."

6. Erasmus, as quoted in Roland Bainton, *Erasmus of Christendom* (New York, 1969), p. 141.

7. Erasmus, as quoted in Bainton, p. 195.

8. *Handbook of the Christian Knight,* in *The Essential Erasmus,* p. 73.

9. Louis Bouyer, "Erasmus and the Medieval Biblical Tradition," in *The Cambridge History of the Bible,* vol. 2, ed. G. W. H. Lampe (Cambridge, 1969), pp. 504–5.

10. Part of the series *Analecta Husserliana,* it appeared simultaneously in Holland and the United States.

11. My quotes from the papal encyclicals are in the translations of the National Catholic News Service (NCNS), which appear in the Catholic press soon after the date of their release. The Daughters of Saint Paul, a Boston religious publisher, has made a whole series of the papal writings and addresses available; see "Readings and Trajectories" at the end of this chapter.

12. Archbishop Karol Wojtyla, as quoted in George Blazynski, *John Paul II: A Man from Krakow* (London, 1979), p. 151.

13. *Laborem Exercens,* I. 3; the emphasis is mine. The encylical was dated 14 September 1981. At the end of the document the pope notes that he had finished it in May but it was delayed by his stay in the hospital (i.e., after the attempt on his life).

14. Editorial in *America* 141 (1979), p. 185.

15. John Carmody and Denise Carmody, *Contemporary Catholic Theology: An Introduction* (San Francisco, 1980), pp. 146–47.

16. Women did not attend the university in nineteenth-century England. For a fiercely intellectual reaction to that kind of discrimination the reader is directed to Virginia Woolf's classic works: *Three Guineas* and *A Room of One's Own.*

17. John Henry Cardinal Newman, *The Idea of a University* (Garden City, N.Y., 1959), p. 219.

18. Brian Wicker, "Newman and the Idea of Education for Gentlemen," *Cross Currents,* Summer 1980, pp. 167–80.

19. Newman, p. 239.

Readings and Trajectories

The humanism of Erasmus must be seen against the background of Renaissance humanism generally. The classic studies on that topic are those of Paul Oskar Kristeller: *Renaissance Thought: The Classic, Scholastic, and Humanist Strain* (New York, 1961) and *Renaissance Thought II: Papers on Humanism and the Arts* provide good summaries of his researches. The major study of Italian humanism and religious thought is: Charles Trinkaus, *In Our Image and Likeness: Humanity and Divinity in Italian Humanist Thought,* 2 vols. (Chicago, 1970).

Besides the works on Erasmus cited in the text I also found useful Lewis Spitz's *The Religious Renaissance of the German Renaissance* (Harvard, 1963) and two books by E. E. Reynolds: *Thomas More and Erasmus* (New York, 1965) and *The Field Is Won: The Life and Death of St. Thomas More* (Milwaukee, 1968). The University of Toronto is now publishing the edited works of Erasmus; Yale those of Thomas More. For recent research on humanism in Western vistas, see Keith Robbins, ed., *Religion and Humanism: Studies in Church History XVII* (Oxford, 1981).

The best book on the thought of Pope John Paul II is that of George Huston Williams, *The Mind of John Paul II: Origins of His Thought and Action* (New York, 1981). Mieczyslaw Malinski's *Pope John Paul II: The Life of Karol Wojtyla* (New York, 1979) is the memoir of a close friend; it suffers from being a bit too adulatory. The pope's discourses and speeches are made available in English in handy volumes from the Daughters of St. Paul in Boston; some selected titles: *Pilgrimage to Poland* (1979);

U.S.A.: The Message of Justice, Peace, and Love (1979); *Talks of Pope John Paul: Ireland* (1979); etc. Of more substance: *Sign of Contradiction* (New York, 1979), which was the Lenten conferences Cardinal Wojtyla gave at the Vatican; *Foundations of Renewal* (first published in 1975; San Francisco, 1980) was the future pope's study of the post-conciliar church. *Love and Responsibility* (New York, 1980) and *Fruitful and Responsible Love* (New York, 1979) are examples of his thinking on Christian ethics. Gregory Baum's *The Priority of Labor* (Ramsey, N.J., 1982) is a study of John Paul's economic thought.

For various aspects of humanism as a religious problem: José Miranda, *Marx and the Bible* (Maryknoll, 1974); Avery Dulles, *The Resilient Church* (Garden City, N.Y., 1977); Hans Küng, *On Being a Christian* (Garden City, N.Y., 1976). On humanism as a counter to religion there is much material in Küng's *Does God Exist?* (Garden City, N.Y., 1980). Martin D'Arcy's *Humanism and Christianity* (New York and Cleveland, 1969) is a classicist approach to humanism done with minimal reference to the Second Vatican Council. Claude Geffre, ed., *Humanism and Christianity* (New York, 1973), is the *Concilium* volume on the topic; its essays show a sophisticated understanding of humanism in existentialist and Marxist circles.

9

ACTIVISTS

William A. Clebsch makes the argument that the social consequences of the French Rvolution made possible the Christian activist when "men and women liberally took over the divine functions of the creation and redemption and mastery of their history."[1] In the long history of Catholicism there have been many figures who have attempted to alleviate the sufferings of the poor or who protested the evils of rulers in the discharge of their office. It is likewise true that many Catholic writers envisioned ideal societies based on theological as well as political ideas (Dante comes to mind immediately) or actually constructed an alternative society based on their understanding of the Christian tradition. John Calvin did it with his theocracy in Geneva, just as the Jesuits did it with the *Reducciones* for the Indians in Paraguay.

What happened after the French revolution was much more radical. In the aftermath of that revolution the old Christian absolutes about the stability of society and everyone's place in it were in profound disarray. No matter how absolute the resisters of revolution might attempt to be, the old order had been swept away. Political activism was on the rise with many and diverse ideas. The fact that the church resisted this change officially (as it did in documents like the *Syllabus of Errors* of 1867) only means that it did not see the handwriting on the wall. One result of this upheaval—a result important for our study—is the conviction that no state government is above or beyond the judgment or the discernment of the informed Christian. While all people are called to the duty of citizenship, there is no reason why they cannot take exception or fight for change in the predominant structures of the sociopolitical order. These structures do not belong to the order of the divine.

Who (or better, what) is an activst? For our purposes we mean a person devoid of constituted authority who, from specifically Christian impulses, publicly works for sociopolitical change. Unlike the prophetic figure (though the work of the activist has a prophetic ring to it), the activist does not only denounce present evils "in the name of the Lord." Nor does the activist like the servant of charity do the works of mercy alone indifferent to the political or the social milieu. The activist combines elements of the prophetic, the charitable, and the revolutionary role. A concrete example might help to specify the distinctiveness of the activist: Mother Teresa of Calcutta works with the poorest of the poor indifferent to the political systems of the countries in which she works; indeed this political indifference is often raised as a criticism of her. By contrast, the late Dorothy Day of the Catholic Workers also labored with the poorest of the poor on the lower East Side of New York, but she did that work in tandem with her role as a pacifist, political critic, agitator for labor causes, and so on. Mother Teresa is a servant of charity; Dorothy Day an activist. The comparison is not meant to be invidious; there are a diversity of charisms in the church.

Catholic activists have related to the tradition of the church in a variety of ways. Some, like Dorothy Day, and many of the other Catholic Workers, combine an extremely traditional Catholicism with a radical social vision drawing on anarchist, personalist, and pacifist sources. Even a highly controversial activist like Daniel Berrigan gained his notoriety not for the hetereodoxy of his theological ideas but for the daring of his public protests. When one examines Berrigan's own writings (they are often in the form of prose-poems, short meditations, stories, etc.), the explicit sources he calls upon are the Bible, the writings of the great mystics, and, as he says, the example of such subversive Jesuit forebearers as the English Jesuits of the Elizabethan Age. It is quite possible to go to jail for ideas which are found in the New Testament. Still other activists, with a background in Catholic social thought, operate at a level of social or political work in which their Catholic commitment is more background and less visible in their work.

The many ways of being a Christian activist reveal some thread of continuity. The late Peter Maurin (1877–1949), founder of the Catholic Workers, spoke often about the "dynamite of the Gospel." He meant that the Gospel not only impels to heroic charity but also commits to change. In the popular mind the activist is seen primarily as a doer. Activists are active about activities! Religiously speaking, however, what distinguishes activists from the simple doer is—and here is a great paradox—the quality of their prayer life and their capacity for contemplation. Commenting on just one aspect of Christian social action (militant nonviolence), James Hanigan has argued that such activity not only demands a spirituality but constitutes one. It is rooted in the life of the Gospel since, he wrote, "to commit oneself to a spirituality is to commit oneself to a method or a means, to a process, to a way of life."[2]

The purpose of this chapter is to examine some contemporary examples of Catholic activism, not to proselytize for their way of life or to endorse their ideas (many of which are admirable and require no endorsement from us), but to note the deep Catholic underpinnings of their life and the ways in which they draw on the old treasures of the Catholic tradition to make all things new in Christ.

What will concern us in particular is the ways in which activists are able to retrieve from the traditional spiritual and theological insights in order to use them for the social situation at hand. The life of the activist is a peculiarly good study for such an endeavor. The activist is, as we have noted, a relatively recent development in the church. In the past people had, as a culture, faith strong enough to accept poverty as a way of life. It was in the order of things that there should be poor and rich since all would be made clean in the life to come. With our present sense that the Kingdom is to be made real in the here and now, the plight of the poor (this to cite one example) is not to be seen as part of the schema of reality. We now have a sense that some may elect poverty as a way of living the Gospel, but it is not in the spirit of the Gospel that many should be impoverished. This is hardly a new insight; what is new is the conviction that the change from destitution to plenty can be gained not only by being charitable but by creating new forms of social order. That change may be done in a manner that is purely secular; the Catholic activist is convinced that there is a Christian way. It is that latter conviction which we shall explore in the lives of some exemplary Catholics.

Dorothy Day

Born in 1897, Dorothy Day's early life reads like a fictionalized account of American bohemia at the turn of the century. Politically radicalized while still a college student in Illinois (her best friend Rayna Simon, died in Moscow in 1927 after a career as a Communist organizer in China), she left school after two years to become a writer. Going to New York City, Dorothy proved herself an able (and politically committed) journalist working for papers such as *The Call*, *The Masses*, and *The Liberator*. She was an intimate friend of the American Communist Mike Gold and a social friend of Eugene O'Neill, the great American playwright. In her New York days she also was on close social terms with Hart Crane, the poet (they lived in the same apartment building), Malcolm Cowley, the literary critic, John Dos Passos, the novelist, and Allan Tate, the poet, and his wife, the writer Caroline Gordon.

In 1927 she had a child (named Tamara) while living in a common law marriage with an old-line political anarchist, Forster Battingham. For reasons that perhaps she herself little understood, Dorothy Day had her child baptized as a Catholic and soon converted herself. Such a religious change put a strain on her relationship with Battingham (though they remained close friends until her death in 1980) which eventually ended. Dorothy provided for herself and her child as a freelance journalist, sometime screen writer, and novelist.

In 1932 Dorothy Day met Peter Maurin, a gentle Frenchman who had passionate ideas about the reformation of society and the work of the church in that reformation. Maurin had once been a Christian Brother in France and, for a time, a wandering laborer in Canada and the United States. From his own reading and study Maurin developed an idea about the possibility of social change on ideas based on the Gospels and Catholic social teaching which would provide an alternative both in capitalism and communism. His alternative vision was rooted in the philosophy of personalism: Individuals are to take responsibility for other individuals. With this idea and the Gospel imperative to give everything for others Maurin began to preach a way of living in order to make the world, as he used to say, a place where it was easier to be good. In many ways Maurin was a utopian romantic who envisioned a small, rural, and decentralized culture based on manual production, held together by worship and prayer, and producing a culture as the common effort of scholars and workers. Like many of the English Catholic social critics of the time (e.g., Vincent MacNabb, Eric Gill, etc.) he had an antiurban streak in him. Maurin preached "Cult, Culture, and Cultivation." He dreamed of houses of hospitality to serve the poor and communal farms where people could live from the work of their hands and develop a genuine Christian culture. These rural communities were to be, in his rather quaint phrase, "agronomic universities." They were to be, in reality, rather like Benedictine monasteries except that they were to be for all.

What saved Peter Maurin from being just one more addlepated visionary was his very real commitment to the poor, his passionate love for Christ, and his single-minded desire to help those who were in need. "The coat that hangs in the closet belongs to the poor," he used to say. Many people who knew him were moved by the Franciscan simplicity of his life and the generosity of his spirit. Dorothy Day herself, no sentimentalist in these matters, thought him to be a saint. Peter died in 1949, but Dorothy Day referred to him constantly in her later writings as one of the basic inspirations for her own work. What Maurin wrote about St. Francis of Assisi in one of his "Easy Essays" (a simple style of writing he developed) was just as surely applicable to his own life:

St. Francis desired
that men should work with their hands.
St. Francis desired

that men should offer their services
as a gift.
St. Francis desired that men should ask
    other people for help
when work failed them.
St. Francis desired
that men should go through life
giving thanks to God for His gifts.[3]

Dorothy Day was heavily influenced by Maurin's ideas about the integration of religious living and service to the poor. More than intellectual and spiritual inspiration Peter Maurin gave Dorothy Day a suggestion which was to change her life and create the Catholic Worker movement: He encouraged her to start a newspaper. On May 1, 1933, the first issue of *The Catholic Worker* appeared on the streets just in time to compete with the communist *Daily Worker* at the May Day rallies in New York. Until her death in 1980 Dorothy Day was a regular contributor to that paper; the best source to follow in order to keep up with her reading, her prayer life, her ideas, and her current activities were the columns which, in later years, went under the rubric "On Pilgrimage." Unlike Peter Maurin who had a profound mistrust of large-scale social protest ("Strikes don't strike me," he once wrote), Dorothy Day—probably reflecting her early days as a socialist and suffragette—espoused and worked for a number of social causes. She was a resolute pacifist (her pacifism in World War II cost her readers and supporters), a dedicated supporter of civil rights causes long before it was fashionable to do so, a fighter for labor justice (her last arrest was in 1973 while picketing for the farm workers of Caesar Chavez in California; her first had been for the woman's vote in 1915), and a zealous opponent of nuclear arms.

It would be fair to assume that Dorothy Day was a "liberal" and, as such, applauded all that was liberal in the Catholic church. She certainly approved of all of the social teachings of the church, but on matters of sexual ethics, church discipline, and doctrine she was staunchly conservative. In 1966, during the heady days of the Second Vatican Council, she wrote of her distrust of the excesses in the new liturgy (she wanted no masses celebrated with coffee cups and ordinary bread, she said) and ringingly reaffirmed her faith: "I believe we must render most reverent homage to Him who created us and stilled the sea and told the winds to calm, and multiplied the loaves and fishes. He is transcendent and immanent. He is closer than the air we breathe and just as vital to us. I speak impetuously, from my heart, and if I err theologically in my expressions, I beg forgiveness."[4] The turmoil of the church in the 1960's bewildered her (although it never shook her faith), just as the sexual revolution horrified her. Her own early life (which included love affairs and an abortion) may have given her a great feeling for personal discipline and tradition.

If one were to describe Dorothy Day's spirituality, one would have to say that it took the form of traditional piety rooted in the liturgy, the reading of the Bible (the *lectio divina* of the monks—reading to form oneself in Christ), and the example of the lives of the saints. What made her such an extraordinary spiritual person was her ability to see the spirituality of the church as an endless resource for personal growth in holiness and as an agent for social change in this world. She had an absolute conviction that the Gospel was the Word of God, that it was to be believed, and to be acted upon. She was, in the best sense of the word, a biblical fundamentalist. She accepted the idea that the Gospel was the foundation of life and it was to be accepted in all of its demands. She believed—really believed—that one should give away all one's possessions to feed the poor just as she believed that one should turn the other cheek and do good for evil done. Her social activism was an outpouring of her life of prayer. She always kept the activism of her life in tandem with her appropriation of the Gospel: "Every time hand bills are passed out, every time one walks in a picket line, or sits down in a factory or before a factory gate . . . these acts are expressions of faith, hope and charity."[5]

For many years Dorothy Day and her fellow workers maintained houses of hospitality where she took in, gave shelter to, and fed, the most abject castoffs of our urban society. She received the addicted, the senile, the insane, the alcoholics, the maimed, and all of the other "street people" who are the shame of our cities. It was an exhausting work sustained over the decades by the command of St. Paul that the "love of Christ compels us."[6] These houses of hospitality as they were called were meant to be practical expressions of the command to help the poor. Over the years hundreds of people—many of whom would later go on to lives of activism and scholarship both inside and outside the church—came and served these houses. There are over twenty of these houses today in the United States keeping alive the Catholic Worker ideal.

There was a radiant directness in Dorothy Day. From Peter Maurin she learned the rather simple idea (but the very hard practice) of stepping outside one's door, looking around, and starting to do good. She believed in simple action, not grand schemes. During the days of the war in Vietnam an Indian Jesuit said to her that the war was necessary because without it all of Asia would end up in the communist camp. Her response reflected her knowledge of the lives of the saints:

> I could only point to the example of Saint Ignatius who first of all laid down his arms, then went to support himself by serving the poor in hospitals, and then went back to school to study. Peter Maurin not only emphasized such a "simple" program but pointed out that we should study history by reading the lives of the saints, which throw light on what is happening in the present day.[7]

This directness sprung from Dorothy Day's utter seriousness about a radically committed life, a seriousness anchored in her own early political experiences, her attraction to the call of the Gospel, and her conviction that there were abundant resources in the tradition of the church for social change that needed to be read with an eye to the present. Although Dorothy Day knew all of the great figures of modern social activism (A. J. Muste, Martin Luther King, Jr., etc.), her models for the life of committed action were gleaned mainly from the spiritual tradition of the saints: the radical poverty of St. Francis, the mystical activism of St. Catherine of Siena, the abandonment of St. John of the Cross, the "little way" of St. Thérèse of Lisieux.

The personalist philosophy of Dorothy Day and the Catholic Workers emphasized direct contact with the individual. It was not poverty that was to be fought but poor people who were to be aided; humanity was not to be loved but this or that human, no matter how naturally unlovable that person might be. Because of that direct approach it never bothered Dorothy Day that her works and her ideas did not get general acceptance. She recognized that many officials of the church were cool to her ideas even though the most obdurate of them gave her grudging respect for her selfless charity. She was not afraid of joining picket lines to protest the Catholic Archdiocese of New York's unwillingness to negotiate with gravediggers, although she always pledged her obedience to the hierarchy of the church. It was not in her to contest the authority of the church; she often said that if the archbishop of New York asked her to close the Worker house, she would do so. From what one can learn even the toughest bishops (like the late Cardinals MacIntyre and Spellman) were reluctant to fool with a woman whom many (much to her amused disgust) regarded as a saint.

Dorothy Day died on November 29, 1980. She was buried in a grave opened at the expense of the Catholic Archdiocese of New York. At her funeral there was an incident recalled by her biographer; it may have been an epiphany illuminating her life:

> At the church door, Cardinal Terence Cooke met the body to bless it. As the procession stopped for this rite, a demented person pushed his way through the crowd and bending low over the coffin peered at it intently. No one interfered, because, as even the funeral directors understood, it was in such a man that Dorothy had seen the face of God.[8]

Adolfo Perez-Esquivel

On October 10, 1980, the Nobel Committee announced that its peace prize would be awarded to Adolfo Perez-Esquivel of Argentina. The award was a complete surprise to the world given both the large number of well-known nominees (fifty-seven of them including the then president of the United States, Jimmy Carter, in recognition of the Camp David Accords bringing peace between Israel and Egypt) and his own obscurity. Reporters had to scramble to get information about this obscure person. He was not well known even in his native Argentina except to the military government, which was chagrined by the choice and made little of it in the press. Perez-Esquivel certainly had none of the recognition of the previous year's winner, Mother Teresa of Calcutta.[9]

Born in 1931, Adolfo Perez-Esquivel, a trained sculptor and art teacher, is married, the father of three children and a resident of a pleasant suburb of Buenos Aires. A voracious reader and pious Catholic, Perez-Esquivel was "converted" to a life of religious activism by his reading of the writings of Mohandas Gandhi (1869–1948), the classics of St. Augustine like the *Confessions*, the writings of the French mystic Charles de Foucauld, and the writings of the Trappist writer Thomas Merton (1915–1968; see Chapter 2). In 1971 he became a founding member of the *Servicio de Paz y Justicia* ("Peace and Justice Service"), a militantly nonviolent group of lay activists, clergy, and others who dedicated themselves to work with peasants, working-class people, and victims of human rights violations in Latin America. In 1973 he started a monthly magazine *Paz y Justicia* in his native Argentina and a year later was named head of the *Servicio* for all of Latin America. In that capacity he has travelled all over the Southern Hemisphere and lectured both in North America and in Europe. His organization is an ecumenical one, but has the close support of the Latin American hierarchy. Perez-Esquivel has also been received in audience and been encouraged by Pope John Paul II.

For the last decade Perez-Esquivel has visited many Latin American countries to study specific instances of repression and encourage projects for social reform, the latter ranging from the defense of the native Indians of Ecuador to aiding the peasant land leagues of Paraguay in their problems with an unsympathetic government. In his native Argentina Perez-Esquivel has been particularly concerned with the so-called *desaparacidos* (the "vanished ones") —the estimated ten to twenty thousand persons who were taken either by the military government or by the Rightist death squads during the turmoil of the late 1970's and from whom nothing has been heard since. Most are presumed dead.

Those who know Latin America only fleetingly will recognize that activities of the kind that engage Perez-Esquivel are not without grave risk. He knows those risks at first hand, having been arrested both in Ecuador (1975) and in Brazil (1976) during the course of his work. In 1977 he was detained by the Argentinian police, kept in jail for fourteen months, and tortured. He refuses to go into detail about his experiences in the hands of the police, but some remarks he made about torture (and his torturers) reveal a good deal about his personalism and his evangelical Catholicism:

> When you experience this extreme situation of being between life and death, you try to understand what Christ said on the cross: "Father, forgive them for they do not know what they are doing." This was very contradictory for me and I tried to understand more deeply . . . what was it that Christ was trying to say to us in this supreme moment? . . . What I discovered little by little was that what (the torturers) they did not know was that they were persons and that we were persons. They had lost their identities.[10]

Although Perez-Esquivel has been reticent about his own spiritual formation, we do know that he formed his interior life from an intense personal encounter with his Catholicism and his militant peace philosophy gleaned from his study of Gandhi. There is little evidence that he has openly identified with the ideology of the political left (he certainly does not accept the notion of revolutionary violence) or the more militant strains of the political theologians. He does draw sustenance from liberation themes in the Latin American theological tradition (cf. Chapter 6). His spiritual program has some affinity with that of Dorothy Day, although he does not reflect the more rigorous ideological bent of the Catholic Workers. Nor does he seem to propose or endorse unified political solutions, although he is an avowed enemy of the military governments of Argentina. He does say that he wants the dehumanizing elements of traditional politics in Latin America stopped. Like his hero (and fellow activist) Archbishop Helder Camara of Recife (Brazil), he sees the poverty of Latin America as the root evil of all human rights violations. He has noted that from poverty a vicious cycle starts: Poverty breed violence, which, in turn, creates oppression, which then creates more poverty.[11]

Like most of the great Christian activists of our times (e.g., Martin Luther King, Jr., A. J. Muste, Daniel Berrigan, Dorothy Day, Lanza del Vasto, etc.), Perez-Esquivel invokes the figure and thought of Mohandas Gandhi for his programmatic ideals. Gandhi (1869–1948) is regarded as the father of the modern nation of India. His determination to get Indian autonomy and nationhood led him to pit his energies against the British colonial power of India. His success in creating a free India would have insured him a rightful place in world history in its own right, but his method for doing this has been vastly influential and of worldwide application in a number of social settings. In South Africa (where he first worked after studying law in England) and later in India Gandhi developed and applied ideas which he had developed from his profound meditations on the Hindu tradition and its scriptures as well as his studies of the Russian novelist Tolstoi's radical Christianity and Henry David Thoreau's theories of nonviolent protest. The basic concept in Gandhi's spiritual and social vocabulary was *satyagraha*—"truth-force." Gandhi passionately believed that a passive nonviolent resistance to any great evil would prevail over that evil because of the force of truth itself. Good would win over evil. In struggles with the English government in India, for example, Gandhi encouraged thousands of people to allow themselves to be manhandled by the police, beaten, arrested, and so on without complaint and without any resistance. Eventually, Gandhi believed, the sheer force of nonresistance and not striking back would exhaust those who tried to prevent Indians from having their civil rights or whatever goal that was sought. Gandhi, of course, was proved right. Martin Luther King, Jr., would try the same tactics (e.g., lunchroom sit-ins, boycotts of segregated transportation, etc.) with the same success in the United States.

The Gandhian notion of *satyagraha* was not simply a political strategy based on an analysis of power. It was not the Indian version of a strike or a factory occupation. It was a passionate religious conviction based on Gandhi's idea that truth would prevail as long as there was no admixture of violence or strife. In fact, in his autobiographical work *The Story of My Experiments with Truth* (Boston, 1968), Gandhi wrote in the preface, as a partial explanation for the book's title, that he identified

God with truth—a notion not alien to readers of the New Testament. *Satyagraha* was a religious way of being nourished by an appropriation of the Hindu scriptural tradition (especially Gandhi's study of the *Bhagavad Gita* which he both translated and commented upon) and the ethical Christianity of the Sermon on the Mount (Matt. 5–7) which had so impressed the Socialist Christians with whom he had come in contact in England. Goodness won over evil when a person was true and acted in truth. *Satyagraha* was a life philosophy that was equal parts the Hindu doctrine of *ahimsa* (nonviolence) and the imperative of Jesus to "turn the other cheek."

It is easy to see how Perez-Esquivel and other activists would be attracted to Gandhi's ideas. His teachings not only resonated the best of the Gospels, but they had been "field-tested" with success both in South Africa and in India. It is fascinating to see the complex interaction and voyage of Eastern and Western religious ideas in the whole history of Gandhi's spiritual development: He goes to England where his Hinduism comes in contact with ethical Christianity. The blend of these ideas goes back to India where they are put to use there and in the struggle for Indian independence. The ideas, in turn, come back to the Americas and Europe where they are readopted by those of the West for their struggles for justice and peace.

This cross-fertilization of religious ideas from widely disparate religious traditions is something that one sees quite clearly in the lives of a number of activists. It is an example of what the American theologian John Dunne has called "crossing over" or "passing over." While one remains true to one's own religious tradition, one can pass over "by sympathetic understanding from his own religion to other religions and come back again with new insights for his own. Passing over and coming back, it seems, is the spiritual adventure of our time."[12] Thus, Gandhi obtained a deeper insight into the Hindu notion of *ahimsa* by passing over to a consideration of the Sermon on the Mount, just as Martin Luther King, Jr., developed a better grasp of the prophetic tradition of the Bible by a consideration of the Gandhian idea of nonviolent resistance. Perez-Esquivel, of course, did just the same with respect to his own commitment to evangelical Catholicism.

The point that Dunne argues with such conviction is that the process of passing over does not mean a kind of religious syncretism (a little of this, a little of that, etc.) or a resistance to any commitment. It means rather a willingness to be open oneself to religious insights in order to deepen one's own convictions. Such a process, Dunne argues, provides a sense of human solidarity and a grasp of self-worth: "In the moment of passing over you see your oneness with other men and with God, but in the moment of coming back you see your own concreteness and individuality."[13] The Christian activism of a Perez-Esquivel, then, is ecumenical not only in his willingness to cooperate with Catholics and other Christians in Latin America but because of his willingness to "cross over" to gain religious insights from outside his culture. That might explain why he has such a strong sense of personal mission and a firm sense of human solidarity. His life, to borrow a phrase from Gandhi, is an experiment in truth.

Activists: Signs of Contradiction

In the Decree on the Apostolate of the Laity the Fathers of the Second Vatican Council declared that the laity (and, by extension, the clergy and religious) "everywhere and in all things must seek the justice characteristic of God's kingdom . . . outstanding among the works of this type is that of Christian social action."[14] Those are noble sentiments which have been reiterated by most of the popes since the Second Vatican Council, relying on papal teachings which stretch back to the great social encyclicals of Pope Leo XIII in the latter part of the last century. The problem, of course, is not with the need for a program of social action but the preferred method of implementing a vision of social betterment. The question of implementation becomes all the more vexatious when social issues impinge on existing political structures. A cursory look at congressional debates in the United States will reinforce the point apart from any question of religious exigency.

What distinguishes the activist from other Christian workers vis-à-vis the social order is that the activists often find themselves in direct conflict with the powers of the established social, economic, or political order. A concrete example might help us to understand the point. In 1979 the winner of the Nobel Peace Prize was Mother Teresa of Calcutta. Except for her unbending stand against all abortions (and the carping of some American nuns who thought too much was made over this very traditional woman), Mother Teresa is a public person freed from the criticisms of the press. It is hard to find fault with a woman who devotes her total energies in helping the most unfortunate people in the world. She is also a totally unpolitical person devoid of any great social or political scheme to save the world. Her work is done where it is possible to do it irrespective of the reigning social order. She works in India unhampered by official interference because what she is engaged in is direct service to the very poorest and most destitute of India's cities. It is a timeless labor. Were she allowed to set up a foundation in Moscow (highly unlikely), we know that she would spend little time in ideological conflict; she would simply gather in the needy.

By contrast, the 1980 winner Adolfo Perez-Esquivel tries to succor the needs of the unfortunate in a more structural manner. He is concerned with the powers that render people destitute and it is those powers that he wishes to address. Those structures are politically reinforced and, as a consequence, his work brings conflict and resistance. That explains why a Perez-Esquivel may be arrested and a Mother Teresa most probably would never be. Their work is different; the risks are diverse. The church has need for both; the Gospel provides models for both.

The social activist always risks abrasions from the established order. The social activist also runs more subtle risks and some persistently alluring temptations. Activists can mistake their social ends for the will of God. It is one thing to say that people are not to be oppressed or left in starvation, but it is quite another thing to say that this or that particular political solution is the *only Christian* way to end such oppression. Confusions of this kind can turn the activist into an ideologue or monomaniac. It can cause Gospel energies to be weakened or diffused in the pursuit of purely philosophical goals. The activist must cultivate a rarefied sense of discernment to avoid this temptation. Those who come in contact with the activist, in turn, must allow for his or her preoccupations and prejudices to be challenged so they also fail to read the signs of the times. In the work of activists and their perception by others openness to the Spirit is of the essence.

In the turmoil of the late 1960's and early 1970's we saw such clashes of perception in Catholic reactions to the activism of the two priest brothers Daniel and Philip Berrigan. They had a long and idealistic history of struggling against prejudice and bigotry. Their concerns for civil rights led them (as it did many activists including Martin Luther King, Jr.,) into the antiwar movement as strife in Vietnam increased. Their highly symbolic acts of protest (nonviolent but destructive of material) against the war included raids of selective service offices where records were either burned with napalm or doused with blood. Such activities led to their arrest, conviction, imprisonment, and, in the case of Daniel Berrigan, fugitive status before entering prison. That two priests (Daniel is a Jesuit; Philip, a Josephite priest, later resigned from the priesthood) should destroy property, be arrrested, and enter prison seemed improbable, if not scandalous, to most Americans. Their activities raised a storm of heated controversy about the role of activists in the American church. What was to be made of these two contentious brothers? William Van Etten Casey set out the polarities of opinion quite clearly:

> Are they prophets pointing to the disintegrating fabric of a corrupt society? victims of ruthless bureaucrats and soulless judges? martyrs in a just cause? Or are they self-righteous fanatics? arrogant nihilists? grandstanders on an ego trip?[15]

Some Catholics did regard the Berrigans as prophetic voices, but the majority of Catholics, one suspects, were more bewildered than offended by their activities. Others, of course, judged them as thriving on media attention in their desire for martyrdom at the hands of very reluctant authorities. Who is right? How does one even attempt to assess their work and its significance? On specific issues it is very hard to make a judgment. Did their protest shorten or prolong the war? Were they naïve or realistic about the Vietnamese, given Vietnam's recent abyssmal track record on human rights? We cannot begin to answer those questions; they are too woven into the skein of our present history. From the distance of history we can say this: At the root of the Berrigan's protest was the desire to stop killing, bombing, violence, and destruction. That much of what they did seems, from a religious perspective, unimpeachable. It can be argued that to ask what their results were is not to ask the correct question. There may exist another yardstick to measure the value and the efficacy of the activist.

If the activists draw at least part of their spiritual sustenance from the prophetic tradition of the Bible (as they most surely do), it is then the deliverance of the message which becomes paramount. The Hebrew prophets were not conspicuous for their success; indeed, Jesus notes that their reward for speaking to Israel was violent death. Their mission was to deliver the "Thus saith the Lord." Gary Wills, commenting on the religious activists of the United States, makes the point trenchantly:

> It is this responsibility to the people that certifies the prophet. Some try to use "prophet" (or poet or seer) to mark a person off as eccentric, having private urges that take him away from the rest of us. Nothing could be farther from biblical standards, by which the prophet exists for the message, and the message exists for delivery, for those it addresses. God sends the prophet to his people; rejection of the message is rejection of the source.[16]

We respond to the activist by asking if the message is true? Does it correspond to what the Gospel urges? How we discern that truth or how we read that Gospel is a consistently mysterious process for most of us. In the midst of our own times and our own history it is often difficult to discern the truth. To this day the Berrigan brothers continue to resist nuclear war without conspicuous success or notable audiences. Only time will tell whether they are right or not; whether they were clear-headed prophets or fanatics. The one thing that always nags at us is this: They may be right.

The activist often rises up in our midst as a sign of contradiction. We tend to admire the prophetic voice in direct proportion to the voice's distance from us. We can praise a Pastor

Dietrich Bonhoeffer (1906–1945) for being a martyr to the Nazis because he was so obviously right. But what of the untold thousands of decent Germans who could not see that in 1944? It is easy for us to say with a Perez-Esquivel that torturing people is wrong and contrary to the Gospel. But our affirmation that people should not be tormented in the name of public order or political stability only raises for us more vexatious questions: What are we to do about the fact of torture? To what degree can we cooperate with governments who do such things? How are we to judge a *Realpolitik* which says that we must look for the lesser evil, that is, better a torturer who is a friend than a totalitarian government which is an enemy? To what degree is such thought complicity in evil? Must we, in the name of the Gospel, say that to torture is to be outside Christ? Concrete questions of that kind are far more cutting than abstractions. The activist tests our willingness to move from the abstract to the concrete. Peter Maurin used to declare that the coat in the closet is the one that belongs to the poor. How literally are we to understand that? To the degree, one suspects, that we act on that is the degree to which the Gospel is appropriated in our lives with totality. In that sense, we have a yardstick, for seeing how far we must go in the following of Christ. For that purpose at least the activist is sent by God.

Notes

1. William A. Clebsch, *Christianity in European History* (New York, 1979), p. 233.

2. James Hanigan, "Militant Nonviolence: A Spirituality for the Pursuit of Social Justice," *Horizons*, Spring 1982, p. 13.

3. Peter Maurin, as quoted in Marc Ellis, *Peter Maurin: Prophet in the Twentieth Century* (New York, 1981), p. 69.

4. Dorothy Day, *Meditations* (New York, 1970), p. 73. Originally published in *The Catholic Worker* in March 1966.

5. Dorothy Day, *On Pilgrimage: The Sixties* (New York, 1972), p. 172. This volume is an anthology of Day's columns in *The Catholic Worker*.

6. In 1975 I heard Dorothy Day invite students to come and help as volunteers while warning them not to come with any ideas about the "romance" of poverty. She asked for those who could stand dirt, poverty, misery, and violence "for the love of God."

7. Dorothy Day, *On Pilgrimage*, p. 257.

8. William D. Miller, *Dorothy Day: A Biography* (San Francisco, 1982), p. 517.

9. Interestingly enough, Perez-Esquivel had been nominated by Mairead Corrigan and Betty Williams, the two peace activists from Northern Ireland who had won the award in 1979 for their efforts against sectarian violence in Ulster.

10. Perez-Esquivel, as quoted in "Perez-Esquivel," *Current Biography* (1981), p. 323.
11. See the interview with Perez-Esquivel in *Newsweek*, 27 October, 1980, p. 78.
12. John Dunne, *The Way of All the Earth* (New York, 1972), p. ix. Father Dunne's volume has an excellent discussion of Gandhi.
13. Ibid., pp. 220-21.
14. Decree on the Apostolate of the Laity, art. 7, in *Documents of Vatican II*, ed. Walter M. Abbott, p. 298.
15. Preface to *The Berrigans*, ed. W. V. E. Casey (New York, 1971), p. 8. The contributors to the volume thought them heroes and models. Father Andrew Greeley's article, not in the volume but part of an earlier symposium published by Holy Cross College, thought the Berrigans arrogant, ideological, anti-American, rigidly doctrinaire, and, by their highly publicized protests, prolonging the war that Greeley deplored. On Greeley's judgment, see John Kotre, *The Best of Times, The Worst of Times* (Chicago, 1978), pp. 175ff., and Noam Chomsky's essay in Casey's anthology.
16. Gary Wills, *Bare, Ruined Choirs: Doubt, Prophecy, and Radical Religion* (Garden City, N.Y. 1972), p. 267.

Readings and Trajectories

The Catholic Worker Movement has touched the lives of most Catholic activists in America in the last fifty years. Dorothy Day's own writings provide much information: *From Union Square to Rome* (New York, 1939); *The Long Loneliness: The Autobiography of Dorothy Day* (New York, 1952); *Loaves and Fishes* (New York, 1963). The two studies of William D. Miller are fundamental: *A Harsh and Dreadful Love: Dorothy Day and the Catholic Worker Movement* (New York, 1973) and *Dorothy Day: A Biography* (San Francisco, 1982).

On Peter Maurin there are two biographies: Arthur Sheehan, *Peter Maurin: Gay Believer* (New York, 1959), and Marc Ellis, *Peter Maurin: Prophet of the Twentieth Century* (Ramsey, N.J., 1981). An anthology of Maurin's *Easy Essays* (Chicago, 1975) updates the earlier *Easy Essays* (New York, 1936) and *The Green Revolution* (Fresno, Calif., 1961). The indispensable source is, of course, *The Catholic Worker*, which still sells on the street for one penny a copy. For a broadly historical context for the Workers, see Neil Betten, *Catholic Activism and the Industrial Worker* (Gainesville, Fla., 1976).

Adolfo Perez-Esquivel's *Christ in a Poncho* (Maryknoll, N.Y., 1983) is a collection of his occasional writings together with documents of the nonviolent movement in Latin America.

John Dunne's books deal profoundly with spirituality and activism; see especially *The Way of All the Earth* (New York, 1972); *Time and Myth* (Notre Dame, Ind., 1973); and *The Reasons of the Heart* (Notre Dame, Ind., 1978). The influence on activists exerted by Thomas Merton has been deep. On the relation of his spiritual doctrine and the "world," see: *Contemplation in a World of Action* (Garden City, N.Y., 1973); also; *Gandhi on Non-Violence* (New York, 1965).

A great deal of Catholic activism has been indebted to Emmanuel Mounier either directly or indirectly; see his *Personalist Manifesto* (London, 1938) and John Hellman's *Emmanuel Mounier and the New Catholic Left* (Toronto, 1981) and the same author's "John Paul II and the Personalist Movement," *Cross Currents*, Winter 1980/81, pp. 409–20.

10
OUTSIDERS

Toward the end of *A Portrait of the Artist as a Young Man* the hero, Stephen Dedalus, and his friend Cranley have a lengthy conversation about Stephen's rejection of his Irish Catholicism. Cranley could not understand why Stephen, given his virulent rebellion against his childhood faith, did not receive Communion as a simple gesture to please a request of his dying mother. If Stephen did not believe in the Real Presence of Christ in the Eucharist, what harm was there in going through a rite which would have comforted his own mother? Stephen admits to an irrational fear of the sacred (but, he hastily notes, he also feared thunder, firearms, etc.) and then adds: "I fear more than that the chemical action which would set up in my soul by a false homage to a symbol behind which are massed twenty centuries of authority and veneration."[1]

In that one passage, in a novel transparently autobiographical, Dedalus (Joyce) encapsulated his relationship to the Catholic church of his infancy and youth. He resolutely refused its discipline and worldview, but could not escape its influence. In that short novel and in subsequent works like *Ulysses* (1921) and *Finnegans Wake* (1939) the echoes of the Catholic tradition are insistent and deep. Although Joyce remained bitterly estranged from the Catholic Church throughout his life,[2] his imagination was saturated in its symbols, images, metaphors, and, I think it could be argued, its sensibility.[3] Joyce himself described his desire to be a "priest of the imagination," one who would "transsubstantiate" gross material into art by the use of words.

James Joyce would qualify eminently for that category of Catholic that we here understand as the "outsider." Outsiders either leave the Catholic tradition after having been born into it or approach it as prospective converts but never make a gesture of allegiance or they convert and then, in time, leave it. In all of these cases, however, the outsiders draw sustenance from that tradition or react against it dialectically so that the tradition is illumined or they share its values even though they may do so, as in the case of Joyce, in a grudgingly inverted manner. The outsiders may be persons like the British novelist Graham Greene, once a convert,[4] who now describe themselves as "Catholic atheists" (the term originated, I think, with the Harvard philosopher George Santayana) or like the fictional hero of Walker Percy's Love in the Ruins who makes an outsider's act of faith:

> I, for example, am a Roman Catholic albeit a bad one. . . . I believe in God and the whole business but I love women best, music and science next, whiskey next, God fourth, and my fellow man hardly at all. Generally I do as I please. A man, wrote John, who says he believes in God and does not keep his commandments is a liar. If John is right, then I am a liar. Nevertheless, I still believe.[5]

Catholic outsiders need not be only those who are in tension with their faith. They may well be those who, for a variety of reasons, feel the power of the Catholic tradition, borrow from it, hymn its accomplishments, or find nurture in its spirituality, yet find themselves incapable of joining the church. That incapacity may spring from a number of reasons, moral, cultural, and/or intellectual.[6]

In today's church there is yet another kind of outsider. In the period before the Second Vatican Council the discipline of the church was such that one either chose for the church in a rather narrowly ascribed way or was out of it. There were quasi-empirical tests to distinguish the practicing Catholic from the one who was a "nonpracticing Catholic" (did one make one's "Easter duty," i.e., receive the sacraments of Penance and Communion during the Easter season?). There was an intellectual understanding that provided an interior criterion for one's Catholicity. One either accepted the "entire package" or one was estranged from the church. It was unthinkable for a person thirty years ago to advocate and practice birth control and claim to be a Catholic, or dispute magisterial statements and remain a "Catholic in good standing." Today, as research clearly shows, Catholics do not leave the church simply because they feel at odds with a particular facet of the church's teaching. For many Catholics such selectivity is not seen as rebellion but as an act of what Hans Küng calls an "internal emigration."[7]

Relationships to the church can be extremely complex. There are those who break with the church in bitterness and finality; others who look back on their Catholic days with nostalgia and wry humor often mixed with some anger; again, others who look to the church with admiration and respect, but never approach it. Some find an aesthetic fascination with the Catholic tradition. "If the basic claims of Catholicism were not so outlandishly preposterous, I'd join tomorrow," a friend of mine said one day when she had accompanied me to Mass on a weekday morning. Her aesthetic sense of Catholic sacramentalism and liturgy is as keen as her distaste for Catholic doctrine. If she sustains that aesthetic interest (with its strong leanings toward spirituality), she would have to be included in my category of the outsider.

There is a temptation to label the outsider either a simple apostate, a selective heretic, or an obdurate but egotistical romantic. There was a time when those who left the church felt this dismissal in palpable ways. We should remember that only in recent years has it been possible to buy Joyce's major works in his native Dublin. The prohibition was based not only on Joyce's vivid sexual imagination but on the virulent sentiments expressed against the Irish church. In a similar manner, those who expressed publicly an admiration for the church but did not join were (a) praised for their insight and sagacity, (b) dismissed as dilettantes, or (c) patronized for their lack of the "gift of the faith."

It seems obvious that "outsiders" can teach us much about our own Catholic tradition since the outsider, almost by definition, stands as a critic of the church. Criticism always helps. Certain classes of outsiders remind us with force that, on occasion, the church has been grievously remiss in its treatment of its members. There are many outsiders who are there because rigidity, insensitivity, harshness, or neglect has driven them there. Such persons remind us of the demonic element in the church. The history of the anti-Modernist purges conducted in the early years of this century (during the pontificate of Pope St. Pius X) is a dreary catalogue of bigotry and cruelty toward faithful Catholic scholars who were either silenced during their entire scholarly life or who were driven from the church. It was an episode which, in the words of one historian, poisoned the atmosphere of the church and had dire consequences for later generations of Catholics.[8]

For those who simply left the church but who have been formed by its *ethos* there are lessons to be learned (as there are from other Catholics) in the ways in which their thinking or sensibilities develop out of their acknowledged Catholic matrix. In the previous chapter we spoke at some length about the Catholic Worker movement and Dorothy Day. One alumnus of that movement is Michael Harrington who is the most prominent American exponent of Democratic Socialism. Harrington's pioneering book *The Other America* (1962) is generally credited with giving the impetus for the great social welfare programs of the Kennedy and Johnson administrations. In his autobiographical memoir Harrington pays a generous tribute to his Catholic upbringing, his indebtedness to his Jesuit mentors in high school and college, the formative influence of his years with the Catholic Workers, and his departure from the church. It was a transition which is described with ease and not without a wistful tribute to his memories of the church:

> By the time I arrived at the church I had decided that I could not go to communion since I no longer believed in the faith, not even by way of an existential leap. . . . I was not, as I had anticipated, racked by a Dostoevskian sense of loss. The whole experience was, I am afraid, about as tragic as getting off a streetcar. What I did not know then was that twenty years later, as the Church began to come unstuck, I would become an atheist fellow traveller of moderate Catholicism.[9]

Harrington is more forthright than many in recognizing the ways in which the church shaped the main contours of his thinking (he even credits his Jesuit education for the critical manner in which he has read and assimilated Karl Marx). He is also shrewder than most in his conviction that the radical Catholicism seen after the Second Vatican Council may not be the dawn of a new day but the final spasm of the church as a recognizable historical entity. That analysis may not be correct, but it is sobering in its implications and chastening for those who tend toward facile optimism. Those who cherish their religious tradition ignore the friendly insights of outsiders like Harrington at their own peril. After all, they never announce their bad news with glee. One reads Harrington (and many like him; Wilfred Sheed and Gary Wills come to mind immediately) with a sense that they feel an infinite sadness at the sight of an institution in decline when that very institution and its tradition so nurtured their youth.

Communal Catholics

The American priest-sociologist Andrew Greeley has identified a group of American Catholics who are self-consciously Catholic and reflectively concerned with the Catholic experience in this country but who relate either marginally to the institutional church (they may or may not go to church with regularity; they are indifferent to both episcopal and papal pronouncements) or selectively committed to the ecclesial structures (they typically ignore strictures about birth control, but favor the parochial school system and make use of the church's sacramental ministry). They appreciate the Catholic church as a collectivity, which is to say that they identify themselves as Catholics and they are appreciative of its worldview and *ethos:* they share the Catholic love of tradition, its sacramental view of life, its view of human nature, the richness of its symbolic life. They are unlikely to become "professional" Catholics who work directly or indirectly at church concerns. Father Greeley calls these people "communal Catholics."[10]

Who are these communal Catholics?

They tend to be well educated, pragmatic, and professional

in their social status. They are high achievers who come from a Catholic background, feel little anger at the church, and hence are distinguishable from radical critics and reformers. They sense, however indirectly, that the Catholic tradition still has resources worthy of serious consideration. They would identify themselves as Catholics and would not seriously consider being anything else.

The paradox of communal Catholics, Greeley asserts, is that their loyalty to the institutional church is "soft," but their defense of many Catholic values is very strong, if somewhat selective. They recognize the nativism of mainline American culture with its resistance to "their kind." They tend to resist the last socially acceptable form of bigotry: anti-Catholicism.

Both the professionalism of the communal Catholics and their pragmatic attitudes make them suspicious of the ideologies of both right and left, although Greeley's research, *pace* the conventional wisdom, finds most educated Catholics a bit left of center politically. They tend to be irritated about the amateurish nature of much Catholic social analysis. They wish for a better educated clergy and more intelligent sermons (many of the communal Catholics are clerics and/or religious), as does everyone. They are anxious to shape the American experience and their own from ideas, impulses, symbols, and matrices which they have discovered in their own Catholicity. They resist those who would denigrate the family or family values and would encourage a more just social order reflective of the Catholic concerns for community, proportionality, and tolerance of failure. They understand that certain Catholic symbols speak deeply to the limit situations of being human and applaud efforts to mediate those symbols with seriousness and relevance.[11]

Is there a recognizable body of communal Catholics in America? Harsh critics of Greeley's work have suggested that Greeley's typology is a thin apology for what once was called a "fallen-away Catholic," while more whimsical critics regard the communal Catholic as a sociology of Andrew Greeley's friends.

Neither critique seems adequate or, it must be said, totally without merit. Greeley seems to have put his finger on a type of Catholic who does exist in the contemporary church. One could name prominent Catholics in public and professional life who would fit Greeley's description. Their confession of their Catholicism is public and their worldview is transparently rooted in a Catholic *ethos*, but their connection with the concerns of the church seems fragile at best. They do not fight the church; they tend to ignore it while still drawing on their own inherited Catholic values. They are different from those who self-consciously write themselves outside of the Catholic tradition. Although some may be tempted to be censorious toward such Catholics, it seems both priggish and unhelpful to do so. They, after all, contribute to the commonwealth from a Catholic perspective. Their rootedness in Catholicism moves beyond mere nostalgia or tribal loyalty.

To identify communal Catholics is not, of course, to canonize them. Father Greeley himself, basically sympathetic to communal Catholics, can be critical of their very real shortcomings. While most of them look back with nostalgia to a Catholicism that once was, the communal Catholics tend to blithely ignore present church realities. Greeley deplores this tendency to romanticize their own past, while professing an arch indifference to the staggering erosion of the present-day institutional church.

Greeley makes this criticism *en passant*, but he may have put his finger on a problem that should merit more than half a page.[12] Such indifference is not only shortsighted; it is, in the long term, fatal. Communal Catholics exist today because they were the beneficiaries of a strong tradition of Catholicism which was mediated to them through a disciplined church, a Catholic school system, a firm sense of tradition, a demand for allegiance—all of the things which today are in a parlous state of decay.[13] For all of the deficiencies of traditional American Catholicism, it produced a body of Catholics from whom the communal Catholic now comes. If the trend of current ecclesial decay continues—and most signs point in that direction—the communal Catholics of today may represent a single generation. To put it another way: What are the structures (present or future) that will mediate the values which will produce the next generation of communal Catholics? If the present structures are eroded as badly as everyone thinks, the future of the communal Catholic seems dim indeed. They may be a one-generation phenomenon.

The communal Catholic may turn out to be nothing more than a slightly alienated intellectual or professional, conscious of his or her own roots, but not really passionate enough a Catholic to fight for those reforms in the church which will hand the next generation a Catholic heritage. People cannot live on nostalgia and they cannot forever draw on a bank of capital which is not somehow being replenished.

At its best Father Greeley's typology reminds us that there is an older generation of Catholics in the present Catholic population which roots itself in the old discipline of Catholicism and still finds nourishment in that connection. Whether there is another generation of these Catholics to come (is there a communal Catholic under the age of forty?) is questionable. They may be more smug than realistic. Communal Catholics remind us of two facts about the church: There once was a very clear vision of what Catholicism was and what it wanted; today we grope for that vision again, but have not yet articulated what it is. The communal Catholic draws on that part of Catholicism which Rosemary Haughton calls *Sophia*—the wisdom that flows in the tradition and which acts as a corrective to the structures of the church in its visible form. Without *Sophia* the church can become oppressive; without the church *Sophia* can become arch, gnostic, sentimental, romantic.[14] The communal Catholic flees the church for *Sophia*, but, as Haughton reminds us, wisdom comes only in relationship to the church. It is that latter lesson which the communal Catholic still must learn, assuming, of course, that he or she wishes to pass on the tradition of Catholicism to his or her children and grandchildren.

At the Threshold: *Ignazio Silone and Simone Weil*

The history of European Catholicism in our century has been exceedingly complex and fascinatingly vital. This century has seen the reactionary spasm of the anti-Modernist crisis, the horror of Catholics killing Catholics in two world wars, the rise of communism with its triumph in Eastern Europe and its threat in some Western democracies which lay at least a cultural claim to being Catholic, the renovation of theology after the Second World War with its triumph at the Second Vatican Council, and, finally, the emergence of a world Catholicism increasingly resistant to the older thought patterns and cultural roots of what Hilaire Belloc once called the "Europe of the Faith."

In the midst of that complex panoply there have been some extraordinary personalities who have been deeply touched both by the church and by the great currents of cultural modernism. Their stories illuminate both the crises of our era and the ways in which the church reacted to them. They specify in their particular lives the larger phenomenon much noted by intellectuals: the capacity of modern culture to alienate some very sensitive persons. Modern consciousness is inevitably touched by a culture where values seem to strain under the weight of history and the demonic power of inhumanity can reach the fevered pitch of Auschwitz and the Gulag. It should not surpirse us that both people of the church and those outside of it react to the "acids of modernity" (to use Walter Lippmann's phrase) in quite different ways. Pope John Paul II, after all, can testify with first-hand authority about Nazism and Communism, war and repression, alienation and community. He represents one reaction to modernity. Some "Catholic" outsiders represent another. We intend to look at just two of them.

Ignazio Silone (1900–1979), whose original name was Secondo Tranquilli, was born a Catholic and educated by the Jesuits in his youth. He left school without finishing an undergraduate degree. In the 1920's he worked with left-wing political groups and ended up being a founding member of the Italian Communist Party (PCI). He left the party in 1930 out of digust with Soviet duplicity and inhumanity. In 1931 Silone went into exile in Switzerland because of his resolute antifascism; the reality of the danger can be seen by the fact that his brother was later tortured to death by the fascist police. It was while he was in exile that Silone began to publish some of his major novels: *Fontamara* (1931), *Bread and Wine* (1937), and *The Seed Beneath the Snow* (1942). At war's end he returned to Italy where he was practically unknown (his novels had been forbidden in fascist Italy). It was only in the last decades of his life that he received the honors in Italy which he had already received abroad.

Silone was the quintessential outsider. He was passionate in his devotion to socialism, but belonged to no party; he was devoted to Christianity, but estranged from the church. He was an Italian writer who was first published (in German) in Switzerland. As an exile, he was a physical outsider. When he returned to Italy, neither Christian, Marxist, nor formalist critics could approach his work with total sympathy.

The social and philosophical estrangement of Silone kept him free of parties (he was deeply suspicious of all major institutions), while leading him to a view of social justice which emphasized the struggles of the solitary individual. He sought a new kind of individual, purged of all egotism, who would say with total dedication a resounding "no" to all the forces which would dehumanize or alienate humanity. In novels from *Fontamara* and *Bread and Wine* in the early part of his career to his final work in the 1960's Silone sought to sketch out a new kind of "saint" who would incarnate human and Christian values to combat the powerful structures which enslaved and degraded people.

In that search to define a new kind of person Silone makes abundant use of Christian language and symbol. This is not merely a literary ploy. It is an attempt to understand the power of Christianity in a new and compelling manner. In his novel *Bread and Wine* the hero, Pietro Spina, in hiding from the fascist police in Italy, disguises himself as a priest. It is clear, as the novel builds, that Silone regards him as a new kind of priest who discovers that in the sharing of the peasant food of bread and wine (hence the title with its direct eucharistic references) one finds a new sense of community, transcendence, forgiveness, and the true face of Christ as he is incarnated in time.[15]

Silone has always been fascinated with the underground stream of Catholicism in his native Italy which erupted in the Middle Ages as an apocalyptic sectarianism standing in opposition to both the papacy and the civil authority. He believes that such a tradition always lives even if it runs underground for periods. In his drama *The Story of a Humble Christian* (1968) Silone appeals to this tradition in his story of Pope Celestine V (1210–1296), who became pope but tendered his resignation within the year. For Silone Celestine was a hero precisely because he relinquished power.[16] Celestine had a suspicion of power (in the play he said that it was the temptation which Satan offered to Christ in the desert) because he understood how power can corrupt. Celestine preferred to align himself with the poor disenfranchised radical Franciscans who looked for an apocalyptic end to the powers of this world.

Silone's vision is, as he himself admitted, a utopian one. That is what gives it its mythic power: It looks beyond the realities of history to something more. Pietro Spina, in a sequel to *Bread and Wine*, gave voice to the kind of person who might save the world: "A new type of saint will be born, a new type of martyr, a new kind of man. . . . I do not believe that there is any other way of saving one soul today."[17] This kind of saint would not live a life apart, but would exist in the very struggles of humanity. Those words sound abstract today, but must be seen against the realities of Nazism and Fascism where solitary struggle was a life and death exercise.

Of late, it has been fashionable to dismiss Silone as a regional writer who reflects the Fascist period but whose ideas are as dated as his concerns. With the emergence of liberation theology, however, his paradigms take on a new urgency. Latin American theologians should appreciate his emphasis on the hidden face of the poor Christ, his analysis of powerlessness, his concern with the socially aware believing community, his orientation to a kingdom of God ahead of us in time and beyond the present powers of the world.[18]

Silone never rejoined the Catholic church of his youth, even though he was greatly heartened by the work of Pope John XXIII and the Second Vatican Council. He remained an outsider to the end. He felt free to draw upon the Catholicism of his youth just as he felt free to draw on the social activism of that same period. He believed that both in Christianity and the social praxis of this century there were resources to overcome the terrible alienation of his time. Silone created a vision of an activist church which appeared in its time to be romantic and eccentric, but today, given the powerful currents of liberation theology, now looks prescient.

Simone Weil's life stands in startling contrast to that of Ignazio Silone's even though both of them share the common status of cultural and religious outsider. Both of them also faced the same cultural pressures brought to bear on those who, in the twenties and thirties, sought in the left an answer to the horrifying spector of Fascist totalitarianism. One an Italian, the other a Parisian, they both rejected the Marxism of their formative years, both thirsted for a transcendence in the midst of the horrors of European history, and both prized the ability to act as a witnessing individual in the face of collective madness.

Born in 1909, Simone Weil was the only daughter of well-to-do French Jewish parents. Her father was a successful doctor and her brother (André) would go on to become a world class mathematician who would eventually find a home in America at the Princeton Institute for Advanced Studies. Precociously brilliant, she finished her degree in philosophy at the École Normale Supérieure in 1931 where she had as a classmate Simone de Beauvoir. In the thirties Simone Weil held a series of teaching positions in provincial schools in France while spending her spare moments as an activist and writer for leftist causes. Her activism earned her in one provincial newspaper the title of the "Red Virgin of the Tribe of Levi"—a testament both to the bourgeois smugness and the open anti-Semitism of the times. In 1934–1936 Simone Weil actually left teaching to work as an unskilled laborer in various factories and in agriculture. In 1936 she went to Spain to fight for the Republican forces in the civil war, but scalded herself after only a few months (her clumsiness was proverbial) and had to return to France.

The decisive years for Simone Weil's spiritual development were 1937–1938. Raised in an essentially secularized family, Simone Weil had ideas about religion that had been basically academic in her youth. During a spring visit to Italy in 1937 she visited Assisi, the birthplace of St. Francis of Assisi, where in the little romanesque church of Santa Maria degli Angeli (housed in one of the most vulgar and ill-conceived church buildings in the Western world) she felt compelled to kneel and pray by a force, as she was to write later, stronger than herself.

The following year Simone Weil decided to spend a week at the Benedictine abbey of Solesmes, famous for the quality of its chant and the purity of its liturgy. Her visit, during Holy Week, was basically an exercise in aesthetics. While she was there, an English guest gave her a copy of the metaphysical poet George Herbert's poem entitled "Love." The poem made a profound impression on her. Tormented by violent headaches (they plagued her all of her life) and soothed by the poem, she appears to have had a mystical experience which she later described in an autobiographical memoir:

> I used to think that I was merely reciting a beautiful poem, but without my knowing it the recitation had the virtue of a prayer. It was during one of those recitations that, as I told you, Christ himself came down and took possession of me.[19]

By 1941 Simone Weil was living in Marseilles out of reach of the anti-Semitic policies of the French Vichy government which was then ruling Nazi-conquered France. It was there that she met the holy and energetic French Dominican priest J. M. Perrin. He served as her spiritual advisor and friend during her years there; it was to him that a number of precious essays, later collected in *Waiting for God*, were sent. In 1942 she left France for the United States since she could not live safely any longer beyond the reach of the Gestapo. From New York Simone Weil left almost immediately for London where she went to work with the Free French who had there a government in exile. By 1943 her health had completely broken. On August 24, 1943, she died of self-inflicted starvation and pulmonary tuberculosis. She had refused to eat more than those who were forced to live under Nazi rule in France. The coroner's report said that the "balance of her mind was disturbed." She lies buried today in a cemetery in Kent.

From 1937 until her death Simone Weil became more interested in Catholicism and invested enormous energies in the study of Catholic mystics, the relationship of Catholicism to Greek culture, the mystical tradition of Hinduism, and the

Catholic life of prayer. She also led an intense spiritual and ascetical life. Yet she never entered the church. She explained to Father Perrin why she did not request baptism. The first four essays which make up *Waiting for God* and a later work which she wrote while in New York[20] offer basically three reasons for her hesitancy concerning entrance into the church.

First of all, in an act of self-deprecation, Weil outlined her deep faith in the power of the sacraments and her own feeling that she had not reached that level of spiritual maturity which would allow her to participate in the sacramental life of the church at a spiritual level she felt they demanded. She would leave it in God's hands to guide her; she stated that God would guide her infallibly to one form of baptism or another. So, she concludes, "Why should I have any anxiety? It is not my business to think about myself. My business is to think about God. It is for God to think about me."[21]

Because of her inability to consider approaching the sacraments in a formal way, she envisioned her vocation to remain outside the church as an "anonymous Christian." She saw her life as a way of being hidden in the mass of alienated crowds tenaciously holding on to faith in God despite all of the counter pressures not to believe. She does not develop the theme, but one finds in it a sentiment not unlike the calling of contemporary religious like the Little Brothers and Little Sisters of Charles de Foucauld who attempt a life of contemplation in an indifferent and hostile atmosphere. Nor is her idea all that different from the "solitary witness" praised by Ignazio Silone in his very first novel *Fontamara*. Weil wrote to Father Perrin that a life lived in the manner she described would permit her to live out a life of sacrificial service and a witness of love, since, as she wrote, "I long to know them so as to love them just as they are. For if I did not love them as they are, it will not be they whom I love and my love will be unreal."[22]

Besides these rather theological reasons Weil also adds another one, this more socially critical. Weil sees the church, as an institution, as an instrument of power, and, in that sense, like Silone, an instrument capable of oppression and evil despite its connection with the Gospel. Her distaste for the institutional church centered on the church's willingness to excommunicate dissidents as well as its acquiesence to secular power. Her distaste reflects, at least in part, her undying hatred of the Roman Empire (after all, her criticism was directed at the *Roman* Catholic church) as a locus of power, force, and the conquering spirit.

Weil distinguished being a Catholic *by right* from being a Catholic *in fact*; in the former sense she made claims on the church (it has a mission to all of humanity), but did not think of herself in the latter sense. Weil states her position in a passage which has been criticized as dramatically egocentric, praised for its deep spirituality, and admired as a hymn to the best of the church:

> I love God, Christ, and the Catholic faith as much as it is possible for so miserably inadequate a creature to love them. I love the saints through their writings and what is told of their lives— apart from some whom it is impossible for me to love fully or to consider as saints. I love the six or seven Catholics of genuine spirituality whom chance has led me to meet in the course of my life. I love the Catholic liturgy, hymns, architecture, rites, and ceremonies. But I have not the slightest love for the church in the strict sense of the word, apart from its relation to the things that I do love.[23]

Nearly a generation ago Karl Rahner envisioned the future of Christianity as being in a diaspora situation with Christians being such a numerical and cognitive minority that they would be, in his phrase, "anonymous Christians."[24] Postmodern culture and the sheer growth of the world would emarginate Christianity in large sections of the planetary culture. There is, of course, another kind of anonymity, the anonymity of the Christian who cannot even identify with the diaspora church. They are rare souls who challenge the assumptions of those who never reflect on their comfortable place in the church. Persons like Simone Weil and Ignazio Silone never entered the church, but they understood its riches as many who are in that church never can. Their high seriousness makes us uncomfortable— and that is as it should be. They belong to that rather select company—Pascal and Soren Kierkegaard come to mind immediately—who remain forever at the edge defining the limits of belief.

Outsiders/Insiders

The people we have discussed to this point—both communal Catholics and the more severe outsiders like Silone and Weil—are defined in relation to the institutional church. The communal Catholics essentially "tune out" the official structures of the institution; the Silones and Weils, by contrast, are more conscious of the church as a historical and social institution. They both criticize the church as an institution, but they are equally appreciative of the church as an essential and formative part of the development of Western culture. From that vantage point they are not unlike other European intellectuals like the Marxist theoretician Antonio Gramsci (1891–1937) and the Spanish critic and philosopher Miguel de Unamuno (1864–1936) who, while diffident about the church and conscious of its demonic side, wrote with insight about its positive place in European culture. To borrow the distinction we have used before, they sensed the *Sophia* of the Catholic tradition, but rejected the constraints of the institution.

Since the Second Vatican Council there have been numerous attempts to "redefine" the meaning of the church or (to borrow from Avery Dulles's influential book) to propose different models of the church.[25] The range of this redefinition has even led some to understand "church" in such a way that what has been historically understood as church is now to be considered not only passé, but counterintuitive. To cite the most obvious example from our contemporary experience: Recent experiments both in Europe and in the Americas (especially Latin America) have envisioned the church as discrete ecclesial communities (*communidades de base*) which are not just different models of the parish but real alternative communities often in dialectical tension with the official church.

These ecclesial communities take many different forms. Some in Europe arose out of disputes between parishes and the local bishop most often over political questions. Every close observer of the North American Catholic scene knows of alternative communities which have to greater or lesser degrees opted out of episcopal authority. These groups range from charismatic intentional communities which have taken on sectarian qualities to liturgically oriented communities centered around priests who have married or otherwise alienated themselves from the larger ecclesiastical structures. While the late sixties saw an explosion of experiments in alternative church structures,[26] the slight flurry of these house churches and floating parishes did not take on any permanent significance; most of them have died out. That some of them still persist reflects unhappiness with the monarchical concept of the church or impatience with the slow pace of ecumenical reconciliation.

About the *communidades de base* little needs to be said[27] except to note that their existence is a fact, their growth a wonder, and their significance a subject of intense debate. Many who are critical of the *communidades* see them as undermining church authority and as flirting with sectarian separatism or degeneration into political cells. Concerning these criticisms there are few ways to respond except to say that the standard parish structures are not *de jure divino* nor is history innocent of other sectarian groups who have come to naught. To put it another way: There is no way now to say whether the *communidades* are a passing fancy or the wave of the future. We obviously need to follow these developments with care and compassion with the New Testament advice as background: If this is of human invention, it will pass; if of God, nothing can stop it.

What, in the last analysis, must be said of the outsiders? For those who prize unity (as opposed to mere uniformity) above all, the outsiders are a source of either pain (because they are outside of the church) or hope because they may come into the church. That much is obvious. The outsider, however, serves two other functions: that of teacher and prophetic critic.

From the outsider we can deepen our own grasp of the Catholic tradition. For all of his vehement anti-Catholicism James Joyce is still an excellent (indeed, preeminent) guide to the riches of Catholic language and ritual. To read his dense pages is to see unpacked the deepest lines of our common liturgical, iconographical, ascetical, and symbolic life. *Propriora vilescunt*, the old Latin writer said: "We spurn the things closest to us." We also accept them as our due without reflection or appreciation. Many—and not all of them hidebound reaction-aries—have lamented the ease with which the post-Vatican II church chucked out so much of our valuable past. Are the vapidly pious ditties sung in our parishes really a step forward from the tradition of Gregorian chant?

The outsider, of course, does not only testify to the "glories" of the past; the outsider serves as critic and prophet. No one has meditated more seriously on the meaning of the cross in our era than Simone Weil, just as no one has more clearly seen the potentiality of Christian witness in the face of organized evil than Silone. The outsider tells us, in brief, that we possess the pearl of great price, but, often, because we possess it, we undervalue it. The outsider chides us for our smugness and demands that we be serious.

Notes

1. James Joyce, *A Portrait of the Artist as a Young Man* (New York, 1960), p. 243.
2. His wife refused the offer of a priest to perform Joyce's funeral service; she said she could not do that to him. Interestingly enough, on his desk at the time of his death were a Greek lexicon and Oliver Gogarty's book *I Follow St. Patrick*; see Richard Ellmann, *James Joyce*, rev. ed. (New York, 1982), p. 755.
3. See the excellent article of Mary Gerhart, "Resentfulness Transformed: Joyce from *Dubliners* to *Finegans Wake*," *Cross Currents*, Summer 1981, pp. 194–213.
4. Greene's most recent novel, *Monsignor Quixote* (New York, 1982), reflects how deeply he is still involved in questions of faith and doubt from a Catholic perspective.
5. Walker Percy, *Love in the Ruins* (New York, 1972), p. 6.
6. We should note that we are not talking about those who simply admire tradition. We are concerned with those who draw from that tradition in one way or another.
7. Hans Küng, *The Church Maintained in Truth* (New York, 1982), p. 77. For conservative responses to this kind of thinking, see, among others, George A. Kelly, *The Battle for the American Church* (Garden City, N.Y., 1979), and his *The Crisis of Authority: Pope John Paul II and the American Bishops* (Chicago, 1982).
8. *History of the Church*, vol. 9: *The Church in the Industrial Age*, ed. Hubert Jedin (New York, 1982), pp. 455–66, deals with the integralist suppression of modernist or suspected modernist tendencies in Catholic intellectual life.
9. Michael Harrington, *Fragments of a Century: A Personal and Social Retrospective of the Fifties and Sixties* (New York, 1972), p. 25.
10. Andrew M. Greeley, *The Communal Catholic* (New York, 1976). For a less polemical and more substantive treatment, see Greeley's *The American Catholics: A Social Portrait* (New York, 1977).
11. See Andrew M. Greeley, *The New Agenda* (New York, 1973), for an analysis of these symbols; it is one of a number of books Greeley has written on this subject.
12. Greeley, *The Communal Catholic*, p. 16.
13. Most of Greeley's research points in this direction.
14. Rosemary Haughton, *The Catholic Thing* (Springfield, Ill., 1975).
15. It would be instructive to compare Silone's new understanding of the priest with

that of James Joyce in *A Portrait of the Artist as a Young Man*. For Joyce the new priest is an artist; for Silone, a social revolutionary.

16. For Dante he was a villian because by his *gran rifito*, as Dante calls it in the *Inferno*, the infamous Boniface VIII came to the papacy. The church sides with Silone; Celestine V was canonized a saint.

17. Ignazio Silone, *The Seed Beneath the Snow* (New York, 1942), p. 185.

18. See the shrewd remarks of Wayne Lobue, "Ignazio Silone's Politics of Charity," in *The Bent World: Essays on Religion and Culture*, ed. John R. May (Chico, Calif., 1979), pp. 191–202.

19. Simone Weil, *Waiting for God*, trans. Emma Craufurd (New York, 1952), pp. 68–69. This volume contains a series of autobiographical letters and an autobiographical essay. Most of Weil's work was published posthumously.

20. Later published as *Letter to a Priest*, trans. Arthur F. Wills (New York, 1953).

21. Weil, *Waiting for God*, pp. 50–51.

22. Ibid., p. 48.

23. Ibid. pp. 49–50.

24. See Karl Rahner, *The Chrisitan Commitment* (New York, 1963), pp. 3–38, and Anita Röper, *The Anonymous Christian* (New York and London, 1966).

25. Avery Dulles, *Models of the Church* (Garden City, N.Y., 1974).

26. See Malcolm Boyd, ed., *The Underground Church* (Baltimore and Hammersmith, 1969), for a dated but interesting discussion of some of these experiments.

27. See Alvaro Barriero, *Basic Ecclesial Communities: The Evangelization of the Poor* (Maryknoll, N.Y., 1982).

Readings and Trajectories

Theodore Ziolkowski's *Fictional Transformations of Jesus* (Princeton, 1970) is a fascinating treatment of Jesus as he appears in literature in our century. Ziolkowski treats of Jesus as outsider. His discussion of Silone (in a chapter called "Comrade Jesus") is especially apt.

In addition to Michael Harrington's work cited in the text, his article "The Search for Transcendental Values," *Cross Currents*, Winter 1981/82, pp. 407–22, is valuable for what he understands to be the need to replace traditional religious faith. The entire article is in implicit dialogue with Catholic thought. For a more traditional view of Catholicism (and an interesting piece to contrast with "communal Catholicism"), see John Noonan's article "American Catholics and the Intellectual Life," in the same issue of *Cross Currents*, pp. 433–38.

For an intellectual biography of Andrew Greeley, valuable for the evolution of his thinking toward the idea of the communal Catholic, see John Kotre's *The Best of Times, The Worst of Times: Andrew Greeley and American Catholicism 1950–75* (Chicago, 1978).

Gregory Baum has edited a collection of autobiographical essays by prominent Catholic intellectuals entitled *Journeys* (New York, 1975), which gives insight into both the communal Catholic and the outsider. Francine du Plessix Gray's *Divine Disobedience* (New York, 1970) is a somewhat precious but informative study which is helpful to understand the outsider who is equally a social activist (cf. the previous chapter).

Mary Gordon's two brilliant novels *Final Payments* (New York, 1978) and *A Company of Women* (New York, 1980) have striking things to say about women and alienation in relation to the church. The same topic can be traced in Mary Daly's revised *The Church and the Second Sex* (New York, 1975), and in *Women of Spirit*, edited by Rosemary Ruether and Eleanor McLaughlin (New York, 1979). Charles Fracchia's *The Second Spring* (San Francisco, 1980) is a good, if journalistic, survey of the turmoil and tension in contemporary Catholicism. It provides background for an understanding of both the communal Catholic and the outsider.

Books on Simone Weil continue to multiply even though her own books are continually in and out of print. George Panichas's anthology *The Simone Weil Reader* (New York, 1977) is a generous introduction to her major writings. There are two major biographies of Simone Weil: Jacques Cabuad, *Simone Weil: A Fellowship in Love* (New York, 1965), and Simone Petrement, *Simone Weil: A Life* (New York, 1976). E. W. F. Tomlin's brief *Simone Weil* (New Haven, 1954) is a model of good sense. George Abbot White, ed., *Simone Weil: Interpretations of a Life* (Amherst, Mass., 1981), is extremely helpful both for the quality of the essays and for the bibliographical material.

The wider issue of the cultural outsider (e.g., Camus's *L'Etranger* is better translated as *The Outsider*, as it is done in England, than as *The Stranger*) has been much discussed since the advent of existentialism as a cultural force. Some of the more readable books on this topic include: Colin Wilson's *The Outsider* (New York, 1956); William Barrett's *Irrational Man* (Garden City, N.Y., 1958); and Nathan Scott, Jr., *Mirrors of Man in Existentialism* (New York and Cleveland, 1978). Diogenes Allen's *Three Outsiders* (Cambridge, Mass., 1983) is an interesting study of Pascal, Kierkegaard, and Weil.

11

SAINTS

The word "saint" has many meanings in the Catholic tradition. The word is used in the New Testament to refer to those who are members of the church. A saint is also defined as anyone who enjoys the vision of God in eternity; in that sense sainthood is the designated end of the Christian life and the vocation to which all are called. At first blush those two meanings of the word "saint" seem a bit strange because the more popular reflex is to consider the saint one who has lived (or lives) in a way beyond the common experience of ordinary life. Our experience of saints—save on those rare grace-filled moments when we might actually meet one—tends to be in the rather hieratic and artificial context of stained glass windows, edifying stories of doubtful credibility, or those austere marble figures in churches displaying their instruments of torture or emblems of holiness. Those saints who are officially recognized either by immemorial custom (papal canonization did not begin until the medieval period) or by canonization (the official act of putting a person on the list or *canon* of those who can be publicly venerated in the church) tend to be distant from us in time, status, and culture. Most, in fact, are European and members of religious orders, while most Catholics are layfolk who work and raise families or pursue vocations and live lives untouched by professional connections with the church. In vast areas of the Catholic world the main task of life is to acquire food and secure shelter for one's family.

The "problem" of saints is further complicated by an inquiry into their role and function in Catholic life. Some traditional saints, with their lives lost in the mists of legend, fiction, or obscurity, serve only as sources of religious power: St. Christopher is the patron of travellers, but about his life we know nothing. Others serve as models or paradigms of the Christian life as the impact of St. Francis of Assisi so clearly shows. A third category is seen primarily as a spiritual resource, that is, their ideas seem more important than their person. Most educated Catholics would not like to live like a Carmelite, but most would be greatly nourished by the experiential teachings of St. Teresa of Avila and St. John of the Cross.

For our purposes we will devote our attention to the saint as a resource or paradigm, not as a miracle worker. In another place I described the saint as anyone who was so grasped by a religious vision that the person's life was radically changed and that changed life then served (or serves) as a model for others.[1] The point is that a saint is not merely a very devout Catholic but that a particular person has received such an insight into the "liveability" of the Christian Gospel and has so followed through existentially on that insight that others see new possibilities for their own lives. As Karl Rahner has written, people can look at the saint's life and see that there is a particular means of being Christian: "They create a new style; they prove that a certain form of life and activity is a really genuine possibility; they show experientially that one can be a Christian even in 'this' way; they make a certain type of person believable as a Christian type."[2]

Without presuming on the right of the Vatican congregation for the Causes of the Saints, I would describe Mother Teresa of Calcutta as a living saint. I think that she is recognized as such by a good part of the world. It should be remembered that Mother Teresa had been a nun for about twenty years before she experienced a second conversion experience which set her on a new path. In that she is very much like the great St. Teresa of Avila who also spent some rather conventional years in a convent before she began her life among the poor in earnest. While Mother Teresa was on a train trip in India, she experienced a deep and abiding conviction that the destitute poor (whom she could see at every moment from the train window) should be served in a direct fashion. She soon received permission to leave her own order (the Sisters of Loreto) and began to take in the destitute dying from the streets of Calcutta. That work has burgeoned in every direction so that today her Missionaries of Mercy (there are both male and female branches) work on practically every continent and various works of charity and help.

Note carefully what Mother Teresa experienced and what she then did. She felt compelled to serve and she went out and began to do it. Her ministry is as old as the corporal works of mercy, which is to say nothing new either in her style of work or in the institutional framework within which she operates. Quite the opposite; she is as traditional and observant a person as one could hope to find in the Catholic church today. About her work a number of observations are pertinent.

First, and most obviously, Mother Teresa has shown that the perennial injunctions of the Gospel to see the needy as the person of Christ (see Matt. 25:31–46) is still a part of our tradition and that the injunction can be fulfilled. She so enfleshes this work of the Gospel in such a traditional and time-honored way that one wonders why it is so much a subject of interest to the news media. That it is news is a tribute to her capacity for demonstrating that the most basic imperatives of the Gospel must be learned and relearned anew.

Secondly, Mother Teresa gives testimony that the older forms of traditional religious life still have a certain vitality in them. Mother Teresa has provided no new model of formal religious life. She has taken a traditional model (her sisters live like "old-fashioned nuns" in their external rule) and breathed life in it. At a time when women's religious life (as well as men's) is in a parlous state of decline, there must be some practical lesson in what Mother Teresa has done.

If Mother Teresa "reassures" the conservative Catholic (as she most decidedly does) by her artfulness in showing the vitality of the traditional form of the religious life, there must be a cautionary word entered at this point. It is very easy to see figures like Mother Teresa as surrogates for the Gospel work to which, in fact, all have been called. This is not to say that everyone is called to work in the slums; it is to say that the duty of being a Christian is not discharged by simply giving material support for those who do so. Furthermore, it is easy to overlook some very painful lessons when we view Mother Teresa as simply a holy nun doing a holy nun's traditional work.

A close look at Mother Teresa's life points to the demands of the Gospel in the starkest of terms: She gives up all for the sake of others. Those with whom she works remind us of the vast number of ill-used and pathetically poor people there are in the world. Her persistence in her work (a nonromantic work; there is nothing uplifting about disease, squalor, sickness, or abandonment to death) reminds us of the grace needed for the saintly life. Saints, unlike social workers and others, do not "burn out." They are sustained to do the same things every day with care, compassion, and no sense of routine or tedium. In that sense at least even the "traditional" saints like Mother Teresa render a judgment on us. We may shrink from the full implications of the heroic Christian life, but the lives of the saints tell us that it is possible to live in that fashion.

The Catholicity of Sanctity

Catholicity means universality. Traditional theologians have said that Catholicism can be understood as *de facto* universality (Catholicism is present in all of the world) or *de jure* Catholicism—Catholicism has an obligation to enter into all cultures and to speak to all peoples. That latter sense of catholicity means that the Catholic tradition cannot restrict itself to certain geographical areas, parochial kinds of thought patterns, or particular social structures. "While she transcends all limits of time and of race, the church is destined to extend to all regions of the earth and so to enter into the history of mankind."[3] The story of the church as it unfolds in history through its various types of Christian life is the story of its striving after Catholicity. Catholicity, in short, is the *telos* of the church, not its actual state.[4]

In this book we have used the term "catholic" not in the dogmatic sense but in the historical sense of that tradition which distinguishes itself from the Reformed and Orthodox tradition even though we recognize that, theologically speaking, they use the term "catholic" (in the creeds, for example) with perfect theological justification. In a more particular sense we also think that there is a catholicity of sanctity in the Catholic tradition.

We have also been careful not to structure our work according to class, rank, gender, or status in the church. We have emphasized that diversity of gifts which cuts across all such distinctions remembering with St. Paul that "there is a variety of gifts but always the same spirit; there are all sorts of service to be done, but always to the same Lord; working in all sorts of different ways in different people, it is the same God who is working in all of them" (1 Cor. 12:4–7). This reluctance to treat "prelates" as opposed to "laity" is not meant to minimize the hierarchical differences in the church but to underscore another, more basic, notion in the Catholic tradition: Everyone in the church—from prelate to peasant, from theologian to illiterate—is called upon to respond to the grace of Christ. It is the way that response is made (as opposed to peculiar vocational calls—the two overlap at times) which has been the particular concern of this work.

Consider the papacy. The efficacy of a pope, apart from his functional powers, depends in part on the degree to which he incarnates the Gospel given the status which he possesses in the church. In the execution of his office(s) as pope he may reflect *seriatim* the role of theologian, mystic, pilgrim, or ascetic—all modes of being adopted in one way or another by pontiffs of recent memory. Popes may also be called upon to profess their faith with their lives (the line of papal martyrs is an honorable one) or they may choose to attempt to combine the role of pope and warrior (as did Pope Julius II—the *papa terribile* immortalized in Raphael's portrait) to no great spiritual advantage. In the last analysis, however, it is the pope as exemplary Christian—as a paradigmatic figure—that instructs us most fully about the power and potentiality of the Petrine ministry.

The idea that the papacy helps us to understand more fully the potentialities of the Catholic way of life is indicated by the large number of modern novels that have attempted to create fictional popes who manage to render outstanding service both to the church and to the world. In the English language alone there has been a tradition of such novels from Morris West's extremely successful *The Shoes of the Fisherman* (1963) to the more recent novel of W. F. Murphy *The Vicar of Christ* (1979) to say nothing of a large number of lesser known novels, short stories, and dramas which imagine the ideal pope—with the story usually set in the future.[5] What all of these fantasies have in common is that the pope heroes have a powerful life of faith and a penchant for mysticism combined with their life of activism. They may be pragmatic Americans, East Europeans, or even medieval hermits but at the core of their being is an unshakeable faith and a life of prayer which is at some level in tension with the world with which they have to deal. They incarnate the transcendental ideals of the Gospel in a world where they have constant contact.

Hans Küng has gained such notoriety by his persistent criticisms of the papacy that it is easy to forget that when his criticisms are all made, he still argues for the biblical warrant for a Petrine ministry. He envisions that ministry not as the office which bears the crust of centuries of privilege and tradition but as a truly ecumenical office which offers a core of stability for the pilgrim church. Küng does not understand the Petrine ministry as being validated by historical succession but by a succession of the spirit which has behind it "The Gospel of Jesus Christ . . . this legitimacy is higher than any other for the Petrine ministry."[6] And what does that mean in the concrete? It means that the papacy or Petrine ministry must exert a "pastoral primacy of spiritual responsibility, of moral guidance, and active provision for the welfare of the church as a whole."[7]

What is true of the exemplary nature of the papacy is equally true of every estate in the church. The pope may have definite functions appropriate to his position, but above all he should be a model of pastoral care for the church as a whole. History has called upon popes to defend civilization itself (Leo the Great), judge it by prophetic action (Celestine V who resigned the papacy), or die for its values as many early popes did. It is the paradigmatic figure of the truly holy pope who teaches us the most about the church at its finest as the memory of the late revered Pope John XXIII so amply showed in his life. He combined simple piety, peasant shrewdness, genuine humor, love of people, a subtle intelligence with a vision of the church as it could be. To him we owe the great vision of the Second Vatican Council.

We have discussed a great variety of ways in which a person lives in the Catholic tradition or has lived in its past history. Every one of those types has produced extraordinary persons whom we call saints. Each type we have discussed is best exemplified by their saints. Since this study is at least partially historical, our saints come from the past tradition. Even many of those whom we feel free to call saints today live essentially no differently than the saints of the past. The life of Mother Teresa of Calcutta would be essentially the same had she lived four hundred years ago. Only rarely does a saint appear whose style of life is so radically different that an entirely new way of being a Christian appears. For the early biographers of St. Francis, to cite an example, Francis was a new type of man, the *novus homo* whom some thought would usher in the final eschatological age.

If sanctity is truly Catholic, however, it must not only be found in every age and place but in every cultural situation. When I was very young, I heard the late Archbishop Fulton Sheen say on a television program that the church needed a saint who knew what it was to sit in the bleachers of a ball park and eat a hotdog and drink a Coke. Archbishop Sheen was making a rhetorical point, but it contained a grain of truth. While we have now canonized some American saints (Elizabeth Seton, etc.), they hardly reflect the peculiar texture of modernity.

The Catholic tradition has encountered a plurality of cultures and social conditions. It has shaped those cultures and been shaped by them. The culture of the developed countries of the West (I have in mind preeminently the countries of North America) is not *per se* inimical to religion as was the culture of imperial Rome. Indeed, some have argued that this culture nurtures Catholicism by giving it the room to breathe, expand, and compete for the allegiance of the modern mind. The culture of modern times does carry with it the corrosive forces of modern secularism and material well-being for the many wherein, by turns, the Christian life can be sidetracked, blunted, or rendered irrelevant. Material well-being can bring with it contrary tides: self-satisfaction and self-loathing or guilt. It has been well said that Christianity has taught people to endure poverty, but has not known how to teach people to live well with affluence.

To put the matter another way: What does the Christian vision, as it is mediated through the Catholic reality, look like when it is seen against the background of apartment houses, video games, health spas, automobiles, fast foods, money markets, and all of the other *impedimenta* of middle class life? As we have seen, Tertullian once asked rhetorically: "What does Athens have to do with Jerusalem?" The modern version of that query might be: What does Disney World have to do with Christ? It is easy to see the ways in which a Christian might live in a *barrio* of a Latin American city; models of privation are part and parcel of the Catholic tradition. It is more difficult to visualize what the models might be for a Chrstian living in the suburbs of New York or Atlanta or Toronto. It may well be that heroic sanctity, peculiar to our culture, is already now aborning.

American Spirituality: Problems and Prospects

Our tradition honors saints of every age, sex, social class, and culture. There are housewives, queens, ex-prostitutes, reformed alcoholics, eccentrics, monks, bishops, soldiers, the very old and the very young. There are many who attract us through their saintly generosity and some who repel us by their single-mindedness. There are very few saints, however, who come from North America and those that do seem distant from us in both time and circumstance. The American church honors some persons informally—one thinks immediately of Thomas Merton or Dorothy Day—as if they were saints. They inspire us and help us to imagine sanctity since they know our language, habits, foibles, demons, and the character of both our greatness and our sinfulness.

In the previous section we alluded to the need for more models who could help us to understand the character of sanctity for our time and culture. Those models should be powerful enough to (a) demonstrate that deeply committed Christian living and life in a postindustrial society are not mutually exclusive and (b) sketch out the challenges which our time and place throw up before us and paradigmatic responses to those challenges.

It would be helpful to know what the particular challenges/responses are for our age and time. To outline them seems a gigantic task deserving a volume in its own right. It is a task where the temptation to generalize seems unavoidable. For that reason we need to emphasize that we can only *outline* while recognizing that not every nuance can be noted or every contingency accounted for. We can note, at best, the major preoccupations of our most able commentators. Nor can we even propose adequate responses to the challenges we do recognize. Those responses are precisely what we look for in those who can still grasp the Gospel "in these times" and respond to it without fleeing the demands of history or culture. The best we can manage is to recognize the "signs of the times" with the faith that the Spirit can be heard and in that hearing we will find a way. To the list we propose others will undoubtedly make other additions or feel free to ignore what we have said as being alien to their own experience.

1. Living in an Age of Ecclesial Turmoil

Were one to read in tandem *The Wanderer* and *The National Catholic Reporter*, both American Catholic newspapers published in the Midwest, it would be tempting to think that they were writing about quite different denominations. The former emphasizes papal authority, the traditional teaching authority of the church, an absolutist sexual morality, and a firm conviction about the nature, dignity, and character of the Roman Catholic church. The latter, by contrast, opens its pages to revisionist discussions about the papacy, the teaching authority of the bishops, and is positive about the possibility of a married clergy, recent thinking about sexual ethics, and the ecumenical character of the church. The former is staunchly anti-Marxist while the latter is tolerant of the ideas of the left.

The difference in both tone and substance between *The Wanderer* and *The National Catholic Reporter* is a microcosm of the tensions existing in the larger church. Protestant scholars like Langdon Gilkey and Catholics like Andrew Greeley have argued that an old form of religious consciousness is fast disappearing in the Roman Catholic Church and a new religious consciousness is now aborning, with its character not yet clear.[8]

That the old Catholic consciousness is dying seems clear. Greeley flatly argues in a number of works that the old apologetic immigrant Catholicism collapsed in America almost over night. Gilkey's book argues that post-Vatican II Catholics are passing through in one generation what Protestants went through for over a century, namely, the fires of modern culture and the rise of historical consciousness. The plain fact is that Catholicism is radically different by any measure than it was less than a generation ago.

The "old church" served Americans well. It provided identity, protection, meaning, and community to a people who entered a culture which was both insular and openly anti-Catholic. That immigrant church is now in its death throes. The only remnant of the older siege Catholicism still extant is in Eastern Europe (note the many discussions about the traditional character of Polish Catholicism) and it is maintained there only as a counterbalance to the repressive nature of the official culture. Pessimists view the demise of the traditional culture of Catholicism with more than alarm; they consider it an unmitigated disaster. Such persons see in Pope John Paul II the last hope of providing enough disciplines to stem the tide of religious chaos. Optimists see all of the same symptoms (decline of vocations to the religious life, falling off of converts, etc.) as the painful, if inevitable, pangs attendant on the new birth of a church which will replace the old monarchical church of the past.

The challenge inherent in the present situation is, of course, how to live with the ambiguity of being between the times. Most of us have neither the intellectual rigor nor the prophetic insight to see the direction of change. The only thing that is clear is that there is confusion, the old sureties are eroded, everything is in flux, and the future seems unclear. In that turmoil we seek examples from those who can teach us fidelity, not to factions, but to Christ as Christ is discerned in the church.

The temptation, of course, is to "vote with one's feet" and opt out of a confused and confusing institution. Many have exercised that option in our time and many have done so in good faith. However, if the Catholic tradition is a community in time and space seeking to be faithful to the Gospel, we also need to remember that the church has passed through crises before. Perhaps the best we can do is to try to emulate the example of that paradigmatic modern Simone Weil who described her spiritual strategy as being that of "waiting in patience." Waiting in community is an act of faith in a community which has nourished the believer just as surely as the believer has created the community.

2. The Catholic Tradition and World Culture

To speak of world culture in a few pages seems doomed to failure of precision. It is important, then, to attempt some measure of precision. Very briefly what is meant here by world culture is the bond that links us together as a world in a manner which would have been unthinkable fifty years ago by advanced techniques of communication and access to information. One small example: When the World Cup Finals in soccer are played, nearly a quarter of the world's population either sees or hears the game as it is played. Through technology one out of four persons on earth is focused on a single event. The implications of such a fact are staggering.

The point of all this is that we can now know what is happening in the far reaches of the world in a vivid and direct manner. That expansion of our experience has obvious religious and ethical ramifications. It was once natural for people to live in a particular community or city or nation without any larger reference to judge their lives. We cannot do that today. Poverty is a fact of human history and always has been. What is new is that poverty, misery, famine, distress, and disaster intrude on our dinner hour through the simple agency of television. That intrusion brings with it a question: Can we as *Christians* ignore the reality of endemic world poverty? And if not—as is obvious—how do we relate to the series of facts that come our way so effortlessly? Obviously not everyone will respond as missionaries, activists, or others who work exclusively with the problems of the world. On the other hand, a check in the collection plate or a pledge to a relief agency does not seem to exhaust the responsibilities of being a Christian. Raised consciousness does not seem to mitigate responsibility; it enhances it.

World hunger is only one serious global issue among others. Current debates about disarmament, world economy, ecology, population growth, the depletion of resources, the distribution of wealth, and other issues present both challenges and responsibilities to every Christian. If we take seriously the teachings of the Second Vatican Council[9] about the role of the church in the development of human culture and human well being, we must seek ways of living out the biblical notion (expressed so clearly in the opening chapters of the Book of Genesis) that creation and humanity alike are a gift of God and a reflection of the divine giver.

The appreciation for this heightened sense of world consciousness has been aided immensely by the thought of Teilhard de Chardin (cf. Chapter 5) who, more than any other Catholic thinker in this century, has perceived the world (as opposed to this or that country or person) as the arena of Christ's salvific work. His visionary notion of the world is deeply grounded in the theological virtue of hopeful love: God not only creates the world, but sustains it and is its *telos*. That vision sees the world in terms of our responsibility for its movement toward its *telos* by being co-creators, stewards, and workers for the future. Teilhard's vision might seem grandiose when seen in all its sweep, but in its peculiar emphasis and through its particularities it provides insights for all who wish to live in a way which builds up the Body of Christ that is both the church and the world: "Our own behavior must provide an example of what can be effected in man by his passion for the world when it has been transformed by the love of Jesus Christ."[10]

Global consciousness is also linked to the emergence of a world spirituality. The positive attitude of the Second Vatican Council toward the religions of the world has spurred scholars, spiritual writers, and other seekers of spiritual perfection to search the religions of the world for insights that would deepen the Christian experience. Indeed, many writers seek a greater convergence in the search for God. Commentators like the late Thomas Merton, William Johnston, Raimundo Panikkar, Thomas Berry, Ewert Cousins, Paul Knitter, David Steindl-Rast—to name only a few—have written widely on the ways in which the spiritual experiences of the world's religions may enhance the depth of our own spiritual life.[11] These writers would agree with the assessment that "Western theology of the next century will address itself primarily to dialogue with the great religions of the East . . . this dialogue will be a miserable affair if the western religions do not rethink their theology in the light of mystical experience."[12] It should be clear that concern for world spirituality is not simply an elitist preoccupation. Not everyone has either the inclination or the leisure to sit *zazen* under a Zen master. All concerned Christians, nonetheless, can learn from other traditions if they are open to such learning. Who would deny that we can profit from the Eastern emphasis on silence as a positive force in religious growth? Who cannot see that a consumer society might benefit from an acquaintance with the Taoist orientation toward harmony with the natural world in which we live? Global awareness of these values comes easily enough; the absorption of them is more difficult. It is a sad fact that every guru with the price of an Air India ticket to these shores can find a ready coterie of believers. It is a sad fact because many will "turn East," totally ignorant of the religious richness of their own tradition. How much more satisfactory it would be if we were able to explore the roots of our own faith expanded by the valuable experiences of other traditions. Is that not what Father Dunne has in mind when he speaks of "crossing over" to other traditions in order to return "home" enriched and strengthened?

3. Catholics and the Contemporary Study of the Bible

In the last hundred years we have become increasingly conscious, as a religious people, that our perception of Christian doctrine is very much dependent on the culture in which we live. The crisis of Modernism at the beginning of the century was very much an attempt, however flawed, to come to grips with that insight. What I think we do understand very clearly today is that doctrines do not float out in space as so many naked propositions to which we give the assent of "I believe." Modern historical consciousness has forced us to believe, assimilate, and express what it is when we say in our lives that Jesus is Lord—which, after all, is the basic act of faith for every believer.

That growth in faith is clearly seen in the pages of the New Testament itself. We understand that the Gospels do not report Jesus in the same way that the *New York Times* reports current events, namely, with every effort to set out the facts as they are immediately perceived. The New Testament announces its aim of giving witness to the great things which God has done in Jesus who is the Christ and what those great things should mean for us. St. John tells us that he wrote about Jesus so that we might believe that he "is the Christ, the Son of God, and that believing we may have life through his name" (John 20:31).

There is no portrait of Jesus in the New Testament. What there is can best be described as a complex anthology of whom early followers of Christ sensed him to be. We have the crucified one of the passion narratives, the cosmic Christ of Colossians, the mystical Christ of the Johannine corpus, the apocalyptic healer and Suffering Servant of the Synoptics, the secret of the universe of the Apocalypse, and so on. No single description does full justice and a synoptic view of the whole never plumbs the depth of the mystery of Christ.

This complexity in the New Testament helps us to see how the saints of the past modelled their lives on rich, but necessarily incomplete, pictures of Christ. The Christ of St. Francis of Assisi is not the Christ of the desert Fathers and Mothers just as the cosmic Christ of Teilhard de Chardin is a far cry from the revolutionary prophet or the suffering servant of the liberation theologians.

Who then is Christ to be for today? How does the tradition preach (and people model) the Christ who is to be the center of our contemporary experience? Theologians have provided us with many ideas, but, in the final analysis, believers must experience Christ after their own "searching out of the scriptures." They must confront the question once asked by Jesus: "Who do people say the Son of Man is?" We can specify that question for our time by setting the question into two contexts:

Who is the Son of Man who best walks the neighborhoods of our towns and cities in postindustrial America? How does that Son of Man relate to the common tradition of those who in history have attempted faithfulness to Christ? Another way of saying it is: We need a Christ who resonates with what David Tracy has called "common experience," and we need a Christ who is faithful to the witness of the tradition.

A greater grasp of history has removed from our reach some of the more sentimental consolations of the Gospel. It was once very easy—as both medieval and Renaissance art so vividly illustrates—to view the world of Jesus as a fantasy land of bright stars, angels, and singing choirs or conversely as darkened skies, rent curtains, and gaping tombs. The naïveté of this narrative setting has given way to a starker Jesus who struggles with his culture, has "bad" companions, wrestles with the real demonic forces, overcomes death, and conquers it in new life. The charge has been made that modern scripture studies have whittled away Jesus, leaving only a shadowy figure. Quite the contrary is true: We now see Jesus as one who cannot be so sentimentalized. Jesus now demands to be either ignored or grasped in such a way that changes. To borrow from contemporary criticism: In the New Testament *we* do not read about Jesus; the *New Testament* reads us. That is what is meant by the dynamite of the Gospel: Evil does not have the last word; we have good reasons to expect life both as individuals and as a community.

4. The Catholic Tradition Tomorrow

If we live in an age of great problems, as we most surely do, clear recognition of those problems is the first step toward their solution. The great task of the Catholic tradition in every age is to reappropriate and proclaim anew the tradition's faithfulness to Christ. This is always done in the particularity of a given culture. Our age is no different; what makes it unique is only that its problems are peculiarly its own. But what are these particularities? Let me suggest, not specific ones, but several areas which press in on us with some force.

(1) How do we live in the pluralist culture of present-day Catholicism? The monarchical character of post-Reformation

Catholicism is gone forever. Diversity and plurality are the very character of the present-day church. Local churches exist more and more in tension with the universal church. That has always been the case to a certain degree, but today the tension is more open and more articulated. The tension itself is not all that bad. A dialectical clash between the needs of the local church and the universal one is a healthy state of affairs. Total local autonomy can easily slide into sectarianism, just as total uniformity "from the top" can become—as we have seen in the past—a source of rigid conformity. Creative tension between the two not only does not create chaos, but nourishes the deepest sense of catholicity if some kind of balance can be maintained.

The balance we seek will recognize a diversity in culture while insisting on the irreducible bonds which tie the particular charisms of a local church to the universal expression of catholicity. Many of the current struggles within the church over vexatious ecclesiastical questions—struggles which are not always edifying—derive from a desire to set out a new calculus of equilibrium. The desire for women's ordination or a married clergy, for example, is essentially a struggle between new perceptions of the way we live today and the old perception about the practice of a historical church.

New calculi of equilibrium are always to be sought. They must include both the particular needs of the local church and the self-understanding of the universal church. The tension between local and universal has many analogues in current discussions: conscience versus authority (e.g., the question of contraception); freedom and fidelity (e.g., the autonomy of theologians and the demands of the *magisterium*); choice and obligation (e.g., the character of ministerial roles). In the search for these new foci of equilibrium we look for leaders who can reconcile and serve and theologians who can instruct and clarify. Most of all we need models who can indicate how the demands of particularity can be made manifest in their appreciation of catholicity. How is one to be American and Catholic; liberationist and Roman; African and Christian; etc.

(2) The local/universal dialectic reaches deeply into the arena of social ethics. If we take seriously the notion that the church

is the body of Christ, we must reflect again on the observation of St. Paul about how that body must function: "If one part is hurt, all parts are hurt with it. If one part is given special honor, all parts enjoy it" (1 Cor. 12:26).

With our sense of global consciousness (discussed above) we need to articulate a vision and a practical program to reach beyond our immediate lives, both individual and communal, to the needs of the larger world community. This is both a civil and a religious imperative. The issue has been cogently stated by Charles Curran:

> Distributive justice as a mediating concept properly emphasizes the biblical concept that the goods of creation exist for all human beings. Too often, especially in the context of the United States, a rugged individualism and a poor concept of freedom have characterized the understanding of the ownership of goods. Distributive justice avoids the pitfalls of a narrowly individualistic concept of justice and rightly emphasizes the Christian belief that the God of creation destined the goods of creation for all human beings. . . . It seems to me that it serves quite well as a mediating concept between the Gospel demands and the realities of the present situation. [13]

Father Curran links the basic notion of justice with the biblical concept of the gift of creation as being the patrimony of all of humanity. He also notes the practical need to propose workable schemes of implementation. Wisely sidestepping ideological solutions, Curran nonetheless makes a rigorous case for action based both on political ethics (justice) and on the call of faith (the biblical imperative).

We know so much about the myriad human problems of today that indifference to them seems at bottom callous. Our need to work at problems—no matter how limited we perceive our chances of success to be—needs specificity. Peter Maurin used to counsel people to step outside and begin to do good in the name of Christ. We need some similar action even if we are not getting to the structural problems of poverty or destitution. We can at this moment feed a hungry person or clothe a naked one even if we cannot propose adequate means for eliminating hunger or want. What a fine first step it would be if every Catholic community (parish, school, etc.) in the industrialized West would pair with a similar center in the less developed parts of the world in order to share our bounty and— if moved—our substance both as a matter of simple justice and as a response in charity. That direct activity might then lead us to reflect on the structural causes of the situations we attempt to succor. In that case praxis would lead to analysis and then to action once again.

(3) Finally, we petition in every age with the words of the apostles: Lord, teach us to pray. In the final analysis Christian faith is not assent to doctrines but communion with God in Christ. Our generation has seen both an upheaval in the life of prayer (witness the disarray of our liturgical life as we attempt to sort out the local/universal tensions) and unprecedented new forms of devotional and liturgical prayer which encompass the ecstatic worship of the charismatic, the devotion to new forms of contemplative prayer, the diverse forms of liturgy and para-liturgy, and changed forms of devotionalism in which the old sacramentals have given way to newer biblical styles of devotionalism. Some of these trends and experiments may be evanescent, but their very presence denotes an intense hunger for prayerful communion with God. Whatever be the disarray of the institutional church, this upsurge in the life of prayer must be seen as one of the more hopeful signs of the times. The very catholicity of the Catholic tradition has stood us in good stead in this search. Catholicism has a vast repository of spiritual forms ready to be renewed and reused according to the needs and exigencies of the moment.

It is in this arena that the example of the saint is most pertinent. Saints are, above all, people of prayer. Whatever heroism they exemplify in their lives is essentially tied to their great sense of communion with God. One of the great hopes of our age is that the paradigmatic figures whom we admire have taught us how to sense God in the context of this world's needs. The late Pope John XXIII combined simple piety with a passion for a renewed church. Thomas Merton, in his monastic fastness, reached out to those who made peace and eschewed racism. Dorothy Day raised her voice with the psalms as she lived amid the squalor of the Lower East Side in New York. Mother Teresa reminds us of the horrors of the life of the urban destitute in the midst of an intense life of direct and uncomplicated piety. The late Archbishop Oscar Romero of San Salvador may have summed up the quality of sanctity for our time: He was gunned down execution style while saying Mass. His crime was an outspoken championing of the poor. He is the most conspicuous of many who have ended their days in a similar fashion.

What we recognize today is that prayer cannot be detached from human concern. Even the pure prayer of the contemplative reaches out in compassion to the world. It was a genuine insight when the church made St. Teresa of Liseux, a cloistered Carmelite, the patroness of missionaries. It was not that her prayer was the energy for others who did not pray but a sign of intense solidarity with those who must act in the world. She lived out an observation that her fellow Carmelite, St. Teresa of Avila, had made centuries before. At the end of a treatise on the graces of mystical prayer St. Teresa insisted that the penetration of the interior castle was, in the final analysis, a reconciliation of the apparent dichotomy between action and contemplation. St. Teresa wrote:

> ... we should desire and engage in prayer, not for our enjoyment, but for the sake of acquiring this strength which fits us for service . . . . Let us not even consider such a thing: believe me Martha and Mary must work together when they offer the Lord lodging, and must have Him ever with them, and they must not entertain Him badly and give Him nothing to eat. And how can Mary give Him everything, seated as she is at His feet, unless her sister helps her?[14]

Speak to me not of Christianity, a militant once said to a French worker priest, but show me some Christians. The only ones we can show him without shame are the saints. To do less is to wound the body of Christ.

Notes

1. Lawrence S. Cunningham, *The Meaning of Saints* (San Francisco, 1980).

2. Karl Rahner, "The Church of the Saints," *Theological Investigations*, vol. 3 (Baltimore, 1967), p. 100.

3. *Dogmatic Constitution on the Church*, art. 9, in *Documents of Vatican II*, ed. Walter M. Abbott, p. 26.

4. See the instructive pages on this topic in Hans Küng, *The Church* (New York, 1967), pp. 296–313.

5. The only full-length study of this genre that I know of is Karl Josef Kuschel's *Stellvertreter Christi? Der Papst in der zeitgenössischen Literatur* (Zurich and Cologne, 1980). Kuschel also studies the underside of the fictional portrayal of the papacy reflected in such works as the controversial play *The Deputy* by Rolf Hochhuth and the painting of Francis Bacon.

6. Hans Küng, *On Being a Christian* (Garden City, N.Y., 1976), p. 497.

7. Ibid. George Tavard's "The Papacy and Christian Symbolism," *Journal of Ecumenical Studies*, Summer 1976, pp. 345–58, has some very sophisticated observations about the symbolic role of the papacy in relationship to its office as traditionally understood. It is a brief but helpful corrective of Küng.

8. Langdon Gilkey, *Catholicism Confronts Modernity* (New York, 1976). See also Andrew Greeley, *The New Agenda* (New York, 1973).

9. *The Pastoral Constitution on the Church in the Modern World* (in *Documents*, pp. 199–308) is particularly pertinent in this regard.

10. Pierre Teilhard de Chardin, *The Heart of Matter* (New York, 1978), p. 217.

11. The special issue of *Cross Currents*, Summer/Fall 1974, under the title "Word out of Silence," is an extended report of such religious dialogue.

12. William Johnston, *The Inner Eye of Love: Mysticism and Religion* (San Francisco, 1978), p. 11.

13. Charles Curran, "Social Ethics: Agenda for the Future," in *Toward Vatican III*, ed. David Tracy et al. (New York, 1978), p. 150.

14. The *Interior Castle of Teresa of Avila*, trans. E. Allison Peers (Garden City, N.Y., 1961), p. 231.

Readings and Trajectories

There is a heightened interest in the saints. Besides the older books like Hippolyte Delehaye's *The Legends of the Saints* (Fordham, N.Y., 1962) we now have some very recent research: Peter Brown, *The Cult of the Saints* (Chicago, 1981); Lawrence S. Cunningham, *The Meaning of Saints* (San Francisco, 1980); Benedicta Ward, *Miracles and the Medieval Mind* (Philadelphia, 1982); Patrick Geary, *Furta Sacra: Theft of Relics in the Middle Ages* (Princeton, 1978); Donald Weinstein and Rudolph Bell, *Saints and Society* (Chicago, 1982).

The relationship between scripture and contemporary culture has been addressed with great learning and clarity in a series of studies by Raymond Brown. Besides his magisterial scriptural commentaries one should consult: *Biblical Reflections on Crises Facing the Church* (Paramus, N.J., 1975) and *Critical Meaning of the Bible* (Ramsey, N.J., 1982).

Catholicism and the American experience has been the subject of much reflection by authors like Andrew Greeley, David O'Brien, etc. Some recent works include sociologist John A. Coleman's *An American Strategic Theology* (Ramsey, N.J., 1982); and James Hennessy, *American Catholics: A History of the Roman Catholic Community in the United States* (New York and Oxford, 1982); the collected essays *America in Theological Perspective*, edited by Thomas MacFadden (New York, 1976).

Some of the shrewdest comments on the relationship of the church and American society have been made by American novelists like the late Flannery O'Connor, Walker Percy, Wilfred Sheed, Mary Gordon, and a number of younger writers who reflect on their experience of being American and Catholic.

Charles Curran's *American Catholic Social Ethics: Twentieth Century Approaches* (Notre Dame, Ind., 1982) is an important discussion of social issues from a distinctively American perspective.

Index